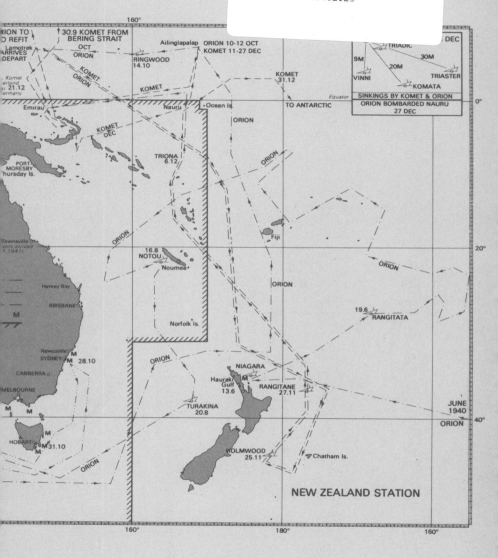

160°

RION TO
O REFIT

30.9 KOMET FROM
BERING STRAIT

Ailinglapalap   ORION 10-12 OCT
KOMET 11-27 DEC

DEC

TRIADIC

OCT
Lamotrek
ARRIVES
DEPART

9M

30M

ORION

RINGWOOD
14.10

20M

VINNI

TRIASTER

ORION

KOMET
31.12

KOMATA

Komet
erland
u 21.12
ermany

KOMET

ORION

KOMET

Equator

TO ANTARCTIC

SINKINGS BY KOMET & ORION

ORION BOMBARDED NAURU
27 DEC

0°

Emirau

Nauru   Ocean Is.

KOMET
DEC

ORION

PORT
MORESBY
hursday Is.

TRIONA
6.12

ORION

ORION

Fiji

Townsville
vors arrived
1.1941)

20°

ORION

16.8
NOTOU

Noumea

ORION

Hervey Bay

BRISBANE

ORION

M

19.6
RANGITATA

Norfolk Is.

SYDNEY   M   28.10
Newcastle   M

NIAGARA

CANBERRA

Hauraki
Gulf
13.6

ORION

MELBOURNE

RANGITANE
27.11

M   M

TURAKINA
20.8

JUNE
1940

M

ORION

HOBART   M 31.10
M

HOLMWOOD
25.11

Chatham Is.

ORION

NEW ZEALAND STATION

160°   180°   160°

MERMAIDS
DO EXIST

To the memory of

Terry and Paul

and for

Fayne, Nicholas, Hedda
Stuart, Diana, James, Michael, Philippa
Lynne, Patrick, Joseph, Louise, Gabrielle, Monique

MERMAIDS DO EXIST

The autobiography of
Vice-Admiral Sir Henry Burrell

Royal Australian Navy (Retired)

M

First published 1986 by
THE MACMILLAN COMPANY OF AUSTRALIA PTY LTD
107 Moray Street, South Melbourne 3205
6 Clarke Street, Crows Nest 2065

Associated companies and representatives
throughout the world

National Library of Australia
cataloguing in publication data

Burrell, Sir Henry, 1904–
    Mermaids do exist.

    Bibliography.
    Includes index.
    ISBN 0 333 41540 X.

    1. Burrell, Sir Henry, 1904–   . 2. Admirals —
    Australia — Biography. I. Title.

359'.0092'4

Set in Bembo by Graphicraft Typesetters Ltd., Hong Kong
Printed in Hong Kong

Contents

Foreword by Admiral Sir Anthony Synnot   vii
Author's Preface   ix

1   Sub-Lieutenant 1904–26   1
2   'Salt-Horse' 1926–29   25
3   Navigator 1930–38   41
4   Director Operations and Plans 1939–40   70
5   Washington Interlude 1941   92
6   HMAS *Norman* 1941–42   111
7   HMAS *Norman* 1942–43   135
8   Final Stages of World War II 1944–46   154
9   Gaining Experience Ashore and Afloat
    1947–54   183
10   Years of High Responsibility 1955–58   217
11   Chief of Naval Staff 1959–62   237
12   Epilogue   275

Appendix I Joint UK–USA Staff Conversations —
    Telegraphic Reports by Australian Naval
    Attaché   284
Appendix II Letter from Author to Parliamentary
    Sub-committee on Defence Matters — Joint
    Committee on Foreign Affairs and Defence,
    1982   301
Notes   307
Bibliography   311
Index   313

Foreword

The period covered by Vice-Admiral Sir Henry Burrell's career was one of great changes for the Navy. Australia's strategic policy shifted from the reliance on Britain as the leader of our Commonwealth defence to a similar relationship with the United States when that country joined the Allies in 1941, and then, during Sir Henry's time as Chief of Staff, moved towards our present more independent stance. Military technology made enormous advances. On joining his first ship, Midshipman Burrell would have found a gun-ship Navy still in the early years of steam-turbine propulsion; submarine and anti-submarine warfare were in their infancy; the importance of air power at sea was not properly understood. When he retired, missiles were quite common, aircraft carriers were the capital ships of large navies, radar was in general use and gas turbines were about to replace steam.

As an historical document Sir Henry's book is therefore of considerable interest. It provides a valuable contribution to our store of Australian military information. Military autobiographies are of particular importance for it is only by having the personal views of people who were involved closely with defence policy that our historians will have adequate material to research. Those with a story to tell should do so; as time passes it becomes even more important that such autobiographies are written before memories fade or before participants take their story with them.

Sir Henry's book has the added virtue of being not merely a professional account of matters of historical interest but also a vivid story of the life of a naval officer whose service spanned both peace and a world war; it covers all ranks from cadet-midshipman to vice-admiral, both in Australian waters and overseas. While the autobiography of a naval officer might suggest a heavy and technical story, the author has explained sea terms which might be unfamiliar and liberally seasoned the text with evidence of a puckish sense of humour, thus providing a readable narrative which both laymen and sailors will enjoy.

We should therefore particularly welcome this auto-biography as a very readable account of a naval career during an interesting period and also as a contribution to our military history. Australia is an island continent dependent for its wealth on trade; as such the sea is of abiding importance to us all. It is good to be reminded of this.

Admiral Sir Anthony Synnot,
KBE, AO, RAN (Retired)

Author's Preface

A few years ago my inquisitive son wanted to know something of my naval career. He was only fourteen years old when I retired, so I put pen to paper. After a couple of years and some urging from academic quarters, and encouragement from my late wife and late son-in-law, I found I had written over 250,000 words. Obviously this required editing to a publishable size. I was fortunate that Mr Brett Lodge (contributor to *The Commanders* by Major David Horner and author of biographies of Generals Sir John Lavarack and Gordon Bennett) agreed to take on that chore. I thank him for that and much valuable advice throughout the entire process.

I wish to thank, for help in diverse ways, Admiral Sir Anthony Synnot, Dr John Cashman, Dr Hugh Smith, Captain Sam Bateman, Captain Alan McIntosh, Ms Elizabeth Nathan and Mrs Ginian Redmand (Australian Archives, Canberra), Dr H. J. W. Stokes, Mr Somerell, Mr Grieve and Mr McKenzie (Defence, Canberra), Commodore Ian Richards (Australian Naval Advisor, London), Mr M. R. Williams (Naval Historical Branch, Ministry of Defence, London), Mr James Cook (mapping), the Australian War Memorial library staff, the Australian Archives, Melbourne, the Antarctic Division (Department of Science and Technology), Mr J. W. Crompton and Mr Alan Stone (Defence Research, Salisbury), the Director-General of the Australian Archives for arranging access to classified documents and Ms Margaret Bacon for typing the original manuscript.

As a cadet-midshipman I joined the Royal Australian Naval College in January 1918 at the age of thirteen. My naval life covered a large part of the twentieth century, from the coal-burning and oil eras to the nuclear age.

Throughout my long career I have met and worked with many people. However, I have referred by name only to a few shipmates and close associates. This has meant neglecting a host of naval officers and ratings whom I hold in the highest regard. In particular, my wartime accounts are not fair in this regard to the unnamed rank and file who served with me. If there is any credit they share it.

Except as a midshipman, when I was required to keep a journal, I have not kept a diary. In fact, at sea in wartime, it was a punishable offence to do so. The exceptions were the monthly 'Reports of Proceedings' by captains. Searches at the London Public Records Office and the National Archives in Melbourne revealed that the greater part of my Reports, when in command of HMAS *Norman* (Chapters 6 and 7), have been lost. My Confidential Report by the Commodore of my flotilla suffered the same fate. The unkind would say 'Just as well!'

Photos (unless otherwise stated) come from many Department of Defence (Navy) authorities, the National War Memorial, the US Navy and from my personal collection.

All maps and the fair chart of the Helford River initially were drawn by me.

In the front endpaper map, the tracks of the German raiders were taken from *The War at Sea*, Volume I, by Captain S. W. Roskill, p. 278. In the Battle of Ceylon map, the tracks of ships of the Eastern Fleet and the Japanese First Carrier Striking Force were taken from *Royal Australian Navy 1942–45* by G. Hermon Gill, p. 17. My additions are diagrammatic. In the back endpaper map, the tracks of the Japanese First Carrier Striking Force were taken from *History of the United States Naval Operations in World War II*, Volume III: *Rising Sun in the Pacific*, by S. E. Morison, p. 385. The enemy tracks mentioned above were, obviously, reconstructed from German and Japanese records.

1
Sub-Lieutenant
1904–26

There is a tincture of salt water in my veins. My great-grandfather, Henry Burrell, was born at Illogan in Cornwall in 1783, and in 1800 entered the Royal Navy where he held a number of appointments including yeoman of the powder room in HMS *Phoenix*. My grandfather, Thomas Burrell (born in 1829), also served in the Royal Navy. After almost thirty-one years he retired as a quartermaster and became a coast-guard at Lyme Regis in Dorset, where my father, Thomas Henry Burrell, was born in 1860. He began his career at Maidstone in Kent as a pupil teacher, but soon after he and his brother migrated, as 'free settlers', to Australia, where my father opened a school at Kenthurst. It was there that he met and married my mother. He was a patriot to his bootstraps and although a frustrated sailor, he contented himself with the army on a part-time basis. While at Kenthurst he trained with the Parramatta Lancers, a militia cavalry unit, and it was only with difficulty that my mother prevented him from volunteering for the war against the Boers in South Africa.

It was at about this time, the turn of the century, that my father was transferred to Wentworth Falls, where his enthusiasm for civic and church affairs made him prominent in the community. As well as being the school teacher he was the secretary of the school of arts, president of the rifle club, a member of the Church of England synod, a church warden and a non-sermonizing lay reader. He was also the standby organist and sang in the choir as well. All in all he seemed at that time to run Wentworth Falls. In his spare time he would carry on with the design of his yacht and add to the lists of spare gear and provisions he would need, knowing he would never be able to afford it.

My mother, however, was fully occupied in rearing five children, of which I was the third, and the only boy, and was sometimes frustrated in her attempts to make ends meet by my father giving to the poor before consultation with the household's chancellor of the exchequer. She was the second eldest of nine children of good Mackay stock — a Scottish father and an English mother — and was a great supporter of the clan. Her early childhood years were spent in the Ballarat district of Victoria and later near the Bogan River at Coolabah, north of Nyngan in New South Wales, where my grandfather made a reasonable living from merino sheep. While still a teenager she began the school in Coolabah, taking as the first pupils her younger brothers and sisters, before marrying my father and later moving to Wentworth Falls.

I was born there on Black Friday, 13 August 1904. It was said that Mrs Burrell gave birth to a broad grin with an ear at each end.

I cannot remember well the time we spent at Wentworth Falls. My earliest recollections were seeing the crown placed upon the altar at church on the coronation of King George V and being woken one night in 1910 to see Halley's Comet.[1] For centuries the arrival of Halley's Comet has been taken as a sign of forthcoming calamity; of course, I did not know in 1910 that I would live through such an astounding, if not calamitous, era and that I would be able to show the comet to one of my grandsons on its return in 1985–86.

Later, when my father was moved to Prospect on the Main Western Road five miles from Parramatta, west of Sydney, we built a cottage at Wentworth Falls so that we could return there for Christmas each year. Seven Hills, two and a half miles away, was the nearest railway station to Prospect, and although we acquired a horse and sulky, there were nevertheless many walks to catch the train, passing on our way the hotel which declared in bold letters that it could provide 'Good accommodation for man and beast'.

My father was the organist at St Bartholomew's Church and I was the slave operating the bellows. I pumped, using a long wooden handle, and a plumb-bob showed the amount of air in the reservoir. I would pause from time to time to watch the indicator approach the 'empty' mark, but one Sunday I cut things too fine and the Christian soldiers marching onwards fell flat on their faces with exhaustion. Pa was not amused and, later, neither was I.

While we were at Prospect, and a week or two before my tenth birthday, the Great War began. Bands were playing, Kitchener's finger was pointing from posters and the Australian Imperial Force was being formed for overseas service in aid of the Empire. The Battle of Jutland remains in my mind for no other reason than the statement I heard that Jellicoe was the only man who could have lost the war in twenty-four hours. However, my most vivid recollection is of an earlier battle — the Battle of the Falkland Islands. There was something romantic for a young lad to hear of a signalman keeping watch on Sapper Hill above Port Stanley, where Admiral Sturdee's battle cruisers, *Invincible* and *Inflexible*, and several cruisers were coaling ship feverishly. By a strange twist of fate, another Battle of the Falklands almost seventy years later saw another HMS *Invincible* take a leading part.

My mother wished she had let my father go to the Boer War, for, although he was fifty-five years old, he presented himself for service. Despite his age, the recruiting officer was impressed by his credentials and asked him to state his age as forty-five, which he refused to do but was enlisted just the same. At first he was based at Liverpool Camp but was later sent to Egypt. At home this meant that there were some new problems to overcome, not the least of which was money. A sergeant's pay did not go far towards keeping five children, so my mother decided to take over teaching at the school while my father was away.

By 1916 my two elder sisters had enrolled at the high school at Parramatta and, at the instigation of my mother who felt that I should be in a larger class, I was attending Parramatta Primary School. This meant a change in my daily routine. First thing in the morning I would ride my bicycle to collect a bucketful of milk from Mr Hicks' dairy and then catch a lift to Parramatta on the milk cart. Since my sisters had to walk to Seven Hills station to catch the train, I would take their books with me on the cart.

When school finished there was time for homework before walking the half-mile to Parramatta station to catch the train, followed finally by the two-and-a-half-mile walk home from Seven Hills station. We thought nothing of it then as it was the only way we could learn, and I think the increased competition at Parramatta was beneficial because it allowed me to pass into high school with a bursary.

The year 1917 was notable because it was the beginning of my association with the Navy. About the middle of the year I noticed an advertisement in the paper calling for recruits to enter the Royal Australian Naval College. I showed the advertisement to my mother but since she was not too pleased at that time with either men or war, I think she deliberately pushed the matter from her mind. However, I persisted until she finally sent for the application forms feeling, I am sure, that my chances were slim. The papers duly arrived and I set about collecting a doctor's certificate and a testimonial from the parson to the effect that I was a fit and proper person for naval service. The next step was an appearance before a selection and medical board at Garden Island in Sydney, at which what now seem predictable questions were given dull answers. There was, however, one bright spot when I was asked the meaning of 'SOS'. I replied 'senior orderly sergeant', which at least was an answer.

The rest of the year was spent at school and in speculation of which other professions I might pursue: architecture, surveying, or perhaps something to do with mathematics. Nothing was settled until one Saturday morning when my name appeared with thirty-five others in the newspaper. I arrived home from the grocer's shop on my bicycle waving the paper, and my mother guessed, what was for her, the worst. The die was cast, I would join the Navy.

My motivation for choosing the Navy as a career is difficult to determine. Of course, my father's interest in the sea pervaded our home, and the sight of ships passing out to sea during our holidays at Manly and Coogee brought to my mind thoughts of Columbus, Vasco de Gama, Magellan, Cook, and even the *Tom Thumb*. Also, Herbert Barling, the son of the station master at Wentworth Falls, had joined the Naval College in 1915 and perhaps the sight of his uniform caught my interest. It is likely that the overwhelming female presence surrounding the only son and a natural desire to compete played their parts as well. However, of this I can be sure: when I signed the forms I had no idea of the type of life to which I was committing myself.

Cadet–Midshipman

In early January 1918 my mother saw me on to a train at Sydney's Central Station, bound for Bomaderry on the south coast of New South Wales. Upon arrival there, we thirty-six young gentlemen were ushered into a dilapidated bus for the journey to the Royal Australian Naval College at Jervis Bay, twenty-five miles away, over a narrow road with culverts instead of bridges crossing the many streams on the way. I was all of thirteen years and five months, and short for my age as well. However, I faced the unfamiliarity of the Navy with a friend from my year at Parramatta High School, Neil Sherlock, and with the firm conviction that mermaids did not exist.

We arrived several days before the senior terms returned to the college from Christmas leave, which gave us time to be kitted up and settle in. Our first issue consisted of a pair of trousers, a black shirt with lanyard, a cap and badge, and one pair of boots. We were then measured for our other uniforms and given a little time to learn the geography and rules of our new home. The prominent and vast playing ground, for example, was the quarter-deck, which had to be saluted on entering — a lesson I learned well, and for many years afterward I tended to salute any plot of grass. As we had to run around the quarter-deck between rising at 7 o'clock and breakfast an hour later, it was also that hallowed ground which established my position as equal slowest runner in my term.

After our arrival there was not much time to take in

5

the beauty surrounding the college, which is situated on Captain's Point in the south-west corner of Jervis Bay. However, I remember the boat harbour with the steam yacht HMAS *Franklin* moored inside the breakwater, and the bay beyond. The cliffs on the north side of the entrance made a neat silhouette, especially at moonrise, with an imposing lighthouse perched atop Point Perpendicular. To the south was Bowen Island, a fine place for picnics and to stalk wallabies. How they came to be there no one knew. Between these extremities were spread some of the whitest beaches in the world, and beyond was the Pacific, its horizon, when a heavy swell was running, breaking up to look like great migrating whales.

It was not long before the other three terms, comprising about eighty cadets, arrived from leave and set the college in full cry. The term senior to us had the task of administering a harmless initiation, the worst part of which was to run the gauntlet up a flight of twenty steps while being belaboured with sandshoes by the seniors lining the stairs. One senior cadet (later an admiral), David Harries, seemed to take a particular interest in my welfare, but I was determined to obey every order until I had discovered the form. His favourite ploy was to come up to me and say 'Sing, Burrell, sing!' I would then break into song with 'Many brave hearts are asleep in the deep ...', my excuse being that it was the only song I knew. Naturally, this riled Master David and earned me a few rebukes on my stern, but he soon became bored and left me in peace.

Each term at the college was assigned an officer whose duties were similar to those of a school housemaster. With the assistance of a petty officer and a signal rating, he also taught us elementary seamanship, such as knots and splices, boat-sailing, semaphore and morse, the rule of the road, anchors and cables, and sea-boat drill. My term officer was Lieutenant-Commander Cotton-Stapleton, RANR, who had quarters in our dormitory as well as married quarters beyond the bounds.

Daily at 8.45 am inspection at divisions took place in the gymnasium with the commander in charge. At the conclusion the Roman Catholics were fallen out to pray, implore and praise with their padre, while the remainder prayed for deliverance and better food with a Protestant padre. The commander would then conclude with a few announcements and threats before we were marched to the classrooms to improve our minds.

The three instructional periods before luncheon were broken at mid forenoon when buns and milk were laid out in the mess room; but we always seemed to be some distance away when dismissed, which meant that I, as an habitual late arrival, invariably enjoyed but half a bun and a splash of milk.

In the afternoon there were two periods of instruction followed by sport. After this came showers in preparation for the evening meal at 7 pm. The shower cubicles were lined in metal with narrow corrugations and so provided irresistible opportunities for the contraltos, bassos, and particularly the *basso profundos*, amongst us to exhibit their musical prowess. This cultural event was followed by an unexciting meal in the messroom. It was to be many years before the messing allowance reflected the fact that growing boys have big appetites.

After dinner we removed ourselves to the study blocks for an hour's silent prep on a specific subject, after which those whose turn it was would make use of the only two baths. This luxury was enjoyed only once every nine days, its poor substitute during the intervening period being a shower in the morning. By 9 o'clock the day was over and an officer would carry out night rounds, checking that the clothes laid out on each chest were in accordance with a master diagram, but I am sure we were none the tidier for it. After lights out the lighthouse on Point Perpendicular would send a flash across the dormitory three times every twenty seconds, but it never kept me awake: it seems the tired human frame can adjust to almost any extraneous light or noise.

The academic curriculum was in many respects similar to that of a normal high school, with just a pinch of nautical spice where approporiate. Our French vocabulary had a distinct list towards naval ranks, types of warship and seamanship terms. History concentrated on naval actions, with Geoffrey Callender's fine volumes of

Sea Kings of Britain as the backbone of the course. Unfortunately, the history of our own country was neglected — Australia seemed to be too young to justify spending much time studying its nineteenth-century progress.

I also studied spherical trigonometry and integral calculus, and could even draw the wiring of an electric motor. Long periods were devoted to engineering and, looking back, it now appears that too much effort was spent on the practical aspects: I learned to use both wood and metal lathes, to make screw threads of any dimensions, and to braze, weld and shape metal; but the benefits of such knowledge did not justify the time spent acquiring it. However, the theoretical side of engineering was excellent value. It allowed me later to understand the problems that beset a ship, or a fleet, without wasting time in prolonged instruction from the ship or fleet engineer officer. The basics of navigation, pilotage and geography were also very helpful, but the result of having so many subjects to study which had some practical advantage for young seamen was that English came a poor last in the curriculum. Little time was given to introducing cadets to the joys of poetry and literature. In fact, the whole course seemed designed to eliminate spare time in which to read. Consequently, there seemed every likelihood that the finished product would be an illiterate engineer who could enjoy to the full sailing and stargazing during weekends in a French condominium. There were notable exceptions, however, such as the erudite and poetic A. W. R. McNicoll who was a product of the 1922 term.

We passed through the 'facts of life' stage without instruction. Not even having had the advantage of living on a farm I was surprised when the facts inevitably became apparent, the final proof coming from observing the silhouette of the captain's wife on her way to early morning service. Growing up in the RANC environment produced no problems of which I was aware. I had queries about life, but was given no time to brood upon them. Smut was at a low level, and four-letter words did not enter our sheltered lives. The stories one heard later about the happenings behind the gymnasium at great colleges in England read like fiction to me. However, I was to receive a few shocks when I first went to sea, and a few personal lectures before leaving the college would have been beneficial.

On the whole, life at Jervis Bay was interesting and enjoyable. On Sundays we were free to roam the countryside, filled with native wildflowers and wallabies, and to pick blackberries. These we took to a nearby boarding house to be made into pies, for which we paid with the postage stamps our parents sent us. We must have been hungry at times, for on occasion we would lower a window in the mess rooms and procure a handful of ship's biscuits. They were made of solid stuff indeed and took a long time to soften, but we accepted the risk of sucking them in prep after dinner. Today, ship's biscuits are usually kept in a sealed tin in a seaboat as emergency rations, but in earlier days these were likely to house 'weevils'. These were long, thin, red worms named after an RN victualling yard. The experienced seaman, before eating his biscuit, would tap it on the table to encourage the bigger weevils to find alternative accommodation. Being the blind member of the three wise monkeys would have been an advantage at feeding time.

Sport played a large part in our lives and fortunately, I thoroughly enjoyed every type of ball game except soccer, for which I think my skull was too thin for painless heading of the ball. My regret is that I was never quite good enough to get into the cricket first eleven. As a result I received no coaching, which leads me to the conclusion that the 'college must win' attitude was overdone at times, to the detriment of students.

Each year the cadets were expected to put on some form of entertainment and I became involved in the production of an expurgated version of *Twelfth Night*. Perhaps it was my alliterate, slightly twisted, wit which had me cast as Sir Andrew Aguecheek, a thoroughly stupid fellow. I well remember the fun we had in staging the play and the lesson it taught me — that something seemingly impossible, if worked at steadily, can be mastered, and, more personally, that if someone else can do it, then so can I.

Towards the end of the third term of my first year the Great War ended. I had served in the Navy for eleven months, eleven days and eleven hours when we hurried out to ring the bells, cheering and singing. It had been a long war, one from which my father returned to take over the school at Prospect until his retirement.

My second year at the college coincided with the visit to Jervis Bay of the battle cruiser HMS *New Zealand*, the visit being made the more memorable as she was the flagship of Admiral of the Fleet Viscount Jellicoe.

The following year, 1920, we were presented with an even greater spectacle of ships in Jervis Bay. The swift and graceful battle cruiser HMS *Renown* arrived flying the Royal Standard of HRH the Prince of Wales and was accompanied by HMAS *Brisbane* with the Naval Board embarked. It was a glamorous occasion and we were honoured to shake the left hand of the heir to the throne, as his right hand had been reduced to pulp by the hearty handshakes of enthusiastic Australians. Of course I did not then know that one of the entourage, an equerry, Commander Dudley North, would be my captain in a few years' time.

By 1920 our theoretical seamanship and engineering knowledge had advanced sufficiently to be tested from time to time in the 350-ton *Franklin*. These were unhappy times for me since, like Nelson, I was not a good sailor. Consequently I did not wish *Franklin* well, a wish which came true when she sank in heavy seas during the Second World War while employed as the examination vessel at Port Kembla.

By 1921 I was sure that I could make the grade, but then there came the news that the Washington Conference on disarmament had set strict limits on the number of ships each country could maintain. My final year was spent under the cloud of reductions in the Navy, which would mean fewer officers. Naturally, I hoped that I would be amongst those to stay on and so be able to pursue a growing ambition to specialize in navigation.

I did not know much about the duties and responsibilities of a navigating officer, but I enjoyed the mathematics: working on charts using parallel rulers and dividers, and handling a sextant. The charting of great lengths of the Australian coastline by Matthew Flinders from a sailing ship without accurate timepieces seemed to me incredible. To be able to navigate a ship from Fremantle to Aden and to know from sun and star observations that the light on Cape Guardafui would come into sight at a particular time and on a particular compass bearing had a faint air of magic about it. I was to find better reasons in the years ahead for the (N) specialization, but in the meantime my immediate aim was to remain in the service. In the words of Mr F. B. Eldridge, my history master, in his *History of the Royal Australian Naval College*:

> The Washington Conference and an agreement on the subject of naval disarmament ... was very much to affect the Australian Fleet — viewed as it was by the outside world as part and parcel of the British Navy, and to be reduced accordingly. It is, of course, always easy to be wise after the event, and therefore it is easy for us now to see that Britain's preparedness to reduce her naval power was merely taken as a sign of weakness and provided an opportunity for those who saw in it an opportunity which might be turned to their own advantage. It is significant that the whole emphasis of disarmament fell upon the Navy and no mutual agreement was arrived at concerning a reduction of armies.[2]

Australia honoured her signature on the Washington Treaty by sinking her only big ship, the battle cruiser *Australia*, in 150 fathoms off Sydney on 12 April 1924.

The end of my fourth year was marked by the Governor-General's parade, the speeches and the prize-giving. It was a proud occasion, but unfortunately none of the speeches made that day left an impression that I could carry with me into the years ahead. I did not receive a prize, but I graduated tenth in order of merit, and was hopeful that that might be enough to keep me in the service. When the reductions were announced my term had been reduced from the original thirty-six to fourteen, including me, for which I was thankful.

Midshipman

I joined HMAS *Sydney* in mid-January 1922 in the city after which she was named. The naval berthing area comprised destroyer head and stern mooring buoys in Farm Cove and two cruiser buoys and berths alongside Garden Island. The destroyer berths, with Government House, the Botanical Gardens and Mrs Macquarie's Chair on three sides, were possibly the finest in the world.

I left Circular Quay by ferry and came aboard *Sydney* as a midshipman (known in the Navy as a 'snotty'), a rank I was to hold for the next two and a half years while I completed my sea training. I was given a hammock and a slinging berth in a passageway alongside a groaning refrigerator to which I soon became so accustomed that I would wake if it stopped making its terrible racket.

My interest in navigation was enormously encouraged on my second day aboard *Sydney*. A collier secured alongside and all hands were required to load the coal and then transfer it to the bunker openings on deck. A hoist of ten bags of coal would be dumped on deck, each bag then being manhandled on to a barrow and trundled to the bunker opening, where it would disappear into the bowels of the ship in a great cloud of dust. There was always a 'coal ship record' to be broken and so we were driven hard, with only regulation breaks for coal-impregnated sandwiches. I soon learned to put Vaseline around my eyes to prevent penetration of the dust and thus avoid that painful, debauched look which would linger for several days. The only people excused this onerous task were the telegraphists (because it supposedly affected their hearing) and the navigator. Obviously the lesson was to become a navigator, which I determined to do as quickly as possible — but not swiftly enough because by the time I had achieved my goal the days of fuel-oil had arrived.

The task of a midshipman is to learn the trade on the job and as such he is not a responsible officer who can be called to task for any misdemeanour, a happy state which continues until he has passed all the requirements for promotion to lieutenant. Of course, he can be verbally blasted to high heaven. There is a story of a midshipman who, while nominally in control of a picket boat, rammed and smashed the flagship's starboard ladder, upon which the flag captain sent a signal to the midshipman's captain: 'Your midshipman lost his head and smashed my ladder.' The reply was despatched: 'Am sending shipwright to repair your ladder. Please return my snotty's head.'

Three-quarters of our time at sea was spent familiarizing ourselves with the seamanship aspect of the profession, the remaining time being devoted to engineering. There was always a midshipman of the watch whose task it was to write up the deck log, watch how the rule of the road was applied, and fulfil the role of general messenger. It was also one of his jobs to prepare what was known as 'ki' for the personnel on the bridge. The method was to take a big jug and a large cake of cocoa and sugar combined, scrape the cake into the jug, fill it with cold water and insert the steam pipe into the mixture. An abundance of froth and bubbles resulted and when boiling point had been reached, the steam would be turned off, the cockroaches brushed from the top and the brew transported to the bridge.

Compared with later years, life at sea at this time was relaxed. There were few night exercises and little training in steaming without lights, but with a war not far astern the tempo was probably bound to be slow. My first voyage in the *Sydney* was to Hobart where the regatta held every February on the Derwent River had a number of attractions for the Navy. If the number of Navy wives who once lived at Sandy Bay is any indication, then the reverse applied as well. The visit to Tasmania was combined with an exercise period, at the end of which the squadron, decked out with bunting, anchored off the Domain and we proceeded ashore to join in the festivities.

My next voyage was to the tropical north to Noumea, Tanna and its active volcano (which we climbed, receiving a large dose of sulphur for our efforts), and the New Hebrides. In November I was given a month's experience in HMAS *Stalwart*, and thoroughly relished my first taste of destroyers.

However, whatever my personal enjoyments may have been, the times were not all pleasant for the Navy as a whole. As already mentioned, the British Commonwealth, the United States, Japan, France and Italy had signed the Washington Naval Treaty. This agreement established the ratios of capital ships and aircraft carriers between the principals. The main effect for the Australian Navy was that cruisers were not to exceed 10,000 tons displacement or mount guns of a calibre larger than 8 inches. The results of agreements such as these and the establishment of the League of Nations was a widespread and misplaced dependence on the proposition that peace was assured, and for Australia in particular, the limiting of the RAN's active fleet to three light cruisers, three destroyers and one sloop. That we were naive in this matter would not become apparent for a decade.

At that time the most senior graduates of the RANC were only lieutenants. With the exception of Rear-Admiral Sir Francis Hyde, it would be another twenty-two years before an RAN officer commanded the fleet, and twenty-six years before we provided the first Australian Chief of Naval Staff. In the meantime, the Navy was being built by RN officers on loan and some permanent service RAN officers with various backgrounds, including state naval forces, Royal Navy, Royal Naval Reserves, and RAN Auxiliary Forces. The latter were enthusiastic in developing the new service, but their experience, with notable exceptions, was limited.

The prospects in our Navy must have appeared to be at a low ebb compared to those in the United Kingdom for we did not attract officers of a high calibre and later I realized that my training had suffered because of this. It was patently clear to me that the social life of many of my seniors took precedence over the service, despite the explanation that although they may have been bon vivants, they were, nevertheless, good seamen. In the years which followed, when it became clear that our Navy would survive, the calibre of RN officers improved vastly and some outstanding officers rendered us great service.

During my time on board *Sydney* there were two English gentlemen who were brothers and both lieutenant-commanders. Known as the 'brothers make and mend' (a title derived from the afternoon holiday given to make and mend clothes), one could not expect to see either on board in the afternoon. One day we were standing open-mouthed as one of the brothers, the cable officer, was making an unholy mess of mooring ship.[3] In a moment of weakness the captain shouted from the bridge, 'Stop that, you bloody fool!' The cable officer stood to attention, turned towards the bridge, saluted and replied, 'Aye aye, sir. Before you said that only you and I knew it. Now the entire ship's company knows, sir!'

A wise Naval Board and a generous Admiralty agreed that Australian midshipmen should have RN experience, so in April 1923 a number of us set off by Orient Line to England. The sport on board appealed to us but our low finances precluded much social activity at the bar, a problem we found quite embarrassing for many years, until the Treasury faced the facts of service pay. Thus the victims of a largely uneventful voyage approached Plymouth Sound where we were to take on a Channel pilot: the start of a great experience for Midshipmen Sherlock, Oom and Burrell. We were disembarked in the pilot boat with our gear and spent the night at Devonport Barracks, three wide-eyed young men of nineteen years. The following day we took train to Weymouth and transferred to a one-carriage affair to cross the isthmus to the Royal Naval base at Portland where we were to join the light cruiser HMS *Caledon*. We were met at the station by a subaltern of the Royal Marines who told us there was a boat waiting at the nearby steps.

As I made for the boat I soon realized that I was alone: Neil and Karl had taken off in the opposite direction. I was senior by a couple of weeks, but they made it perfectly clear that nothing would prevent them having a hearty meal of steak and eggs before joining the Royal Navy. What could I do but have lunch?

When we finally arrived on board we were arraigned before the captain, who happened to be none other than the Prince of Wales' equerry, Captain Dudley North. We had kept the great man from his golf, and he made his displeasure obvious, especially as we had not joined in our No. 1 Round Jackets with dirks. For the next three weeks the motor boats were to be hoisted by day and the Australians did all trips by sailing whaler or cutter. However, it was an enjoyable stunt and we learned a lot.

We lived in the gun room where our messmates were a sub-lieutenant and two RN snotties. The room was incredibly small and I worked, ate and slept on a bench behind the mess table. It soon dawned on us that we were oddities, particularly in regard to dress and journals. Our uniforms were badly cut, with buttons pulling in all directions, and the standard of our journals, particularly the sketches, was deplorable. For a drawing we would simply cut a page from a cheap drawing book, use blue-black ink and get it over with in twenty minutes. The RN standard required proper drawing paper, Indian ink, drawing pens, neat printing, detailed soundings, neat borders, and in some cases a wash of indian ink and water could be used to good effect; two hours was the minimum time spent on the work. Over the next year I redrew the offending sketches in my journal, for it was a highly competitive world and later valuable marks were allocated to the journal.

After some normal fleet exercises, *Caledon* was despatched in June 1923 to show the flag in the Baltic, as an expression of British interest in the region. To observe foreigners and their ways of life in unfamiliar places was the beginning of a new perspective for we 'young gentlemen'. Any knowledge of night life, however, was excluded. Midshipmen were a protected species and normally had to return on board by 7 pm. Copenhagen lived up to its tourist reputation, with the mermaid on her rock and hordes of cyclists pedalling furiously along their special roads. Unfortunately we sailed before the laundry arrived, and so perhaps there are still in Copenhagen two dozen of my stiff white collars waiting to be collected.

Our diplomatic visit to the Baltic involved visiting Memel (Lithuania), Riga (Latvia), Reval (Estonia), Hango, a quiet seaside resort in Finland, and Stockholm. On the return trip, we were required to be Britain's representative at her Trade Fair at Gothenburg.

During our time in *Caledon* some Home Fleet exercises brought us to Invergordon in Cromarty Firth, a well-protected harbour on the east coast of Scotland, north of Inverness. Proceeding to a berth off the village, we passed the conspicuous wreck of the battleship *Natal* which some years before, and without warning, exploded, capsized and rested on the bottom with her bilge keel showing; sabotage was suspected. As it was considered an ideal exercise area there were many squadron and fleet exercises in the Moray Firth. Accommodation ashore was non-existent, so the wives, fiancées, and fleet followers (politely dubbed 'the fishing fleet') with all their magnetism could not distract the fleet in its warlike training. The next move for the squadron was to proceed to Loch Ewe on the west coast, passing through the treacherous Pentland Firth where, on one occasion, a heavy Atlantic swell opposed by strong tidal streams actually swept overboard the bridge of a cruiser.

The 'C' class cruiser's outfit of boats had small carrying capacity, so in the United Kingdom waters a converted drifter was attached for landing liberty-men. Our drifter was required on the west coast so commonsense suggested using the Caledonian Canal, the more sheltered route.

Lieutenant-Commander Nelles, a future Chief of Naval Staff of the Canadian Navy, was put in command, assisted by Midshipmen Bourne, Oom and Burrell. A pilot was embarked at Inverness for the journey through Loch Ness and Loch Lochy. As the North Sea level differed from the Atlantic, we had to pass through the locks at Inverness and Fort Augustus which regulated the levels of water. To work the lock gates we all provided the chain-gang type workforce — round and round the capstan with a great tree-trunk clasped to one's bosom. Night was beginning to fall as we lowered through the final locks. We intended to anchor off Fort William for the night and sent for the pilot, but we had overlooked the propensity of a

Scottish pilot for a wee dram. He had found the locker and was in no state to guide us through the dark to the Fort. Nor was the chart much help to this multinational combination. We took soundings and eventually felt our way to an anchorage, where Lieutenant-Commander Nelles told me to see if I could 'fix' the ship. The best I could do was to report that we were anchored in the middle of the school yard. There was nothing for it but to send the pilot ashore in a dinghy and turn in.

At dawn we continued: down Loch Linnhe, up the Sound of Mull and past Tobermony, where a diving party was salvaging remnants of the Spanish Armada. So with the Isles of Rhum, Eigg and Muck on the port hand, we entered the Sound of Sleat, before passing through the narrows, known as the Kyle of Loch Alsh, a beautiful sound in any dialect. Thence we proceeded to Loch Ewe to rejoin the squadron.

Early in November 1923 the fleet began assembling in Spithead for a review in honour of the Dominion premiers. The Royal Navy and Spithead are synonymous, for Spithead is the approach to Portsmouth harbour, the most famous of the naval bases. It is also the approach to Southampton Water, the embarkation port for the great Atlantic ocean liners. To the west is the harbour of Cowes, the home of the Royal Yacht Squadron and famed throughout the yachting fraternity. Westward, in the Black Forest, grew the timber which made the wooden walls of England and caused us to sing 'Hearts of oak are our ships'. I found Portsmouth dockyard full of history — near the old *Victory* was the large piece of coral, from the Great Barrier Reef, which had remained stuck in the hull of Captain Cook's *Endeavour* when she grounded off what was to be known as Queensland. The Dominion Prime Ministers came, we cheered them on their way and our days in the quiet of the gun room of HMS *Caledon* were at an end.

Experience of large ships was to be our lot and we were appointed to HMS *Malaya*, a battleship with eight 15-inch guns. She was attached to the Atlantic Fleet and was under the command of Captain Roger Backhouse. Too young to judge the prospects of senior captains, we were unable to forecast that he would become the First Sea Lord, but obviously we were in good hands. We were but three from a self-governing Dominion among thirty-three RN midshipmen, a mixture of thirteen- and eighteen-year-old entries, and we knew we would be tested at every opportunity. We were fortunate to have time to gain detailed knowledge of our ship while enjoying a cruise in the Mediterranean, where we were to exercise with the Mediterranean Fleet based on Malta.

Gibraltar was the first excitement. Berthing there is always dramatic and an Admiralty book on ship-handling makes special reference to berthing at the South Mole. After reading it you feel there is only one conclusion possible: you will ram the South Mole bows first! Next came the magnificent Grand Harbour of Malta, which, with its deep water, steep-to, and numerous inlets, is able to shelter many large ships. Sliema, on the opposite side of Valetta, the capital, was reserved for destroyers and submarines. To us, Malta was the isle of bells and smells. The rocky outcrop had little soil, and some had even been shipped from Italy. As a consequence the people were poor and conditions squalid. We were more fortunate: tennis at the Marsa Club, cricket at the Corrodino and indoor bowls at the Junior Officers' Club gave a lot of pleasure and exercise. Polo was popular, but although inexpensive was far beyond a gun room officer's purse. During each of my subsequent visits to Malta I became more convinced that non-polo players were at a distinct disadvantage in the Mediterranean promotion stakes.

The Home and Mediterranean Fleets sailed for combined exercises. At the conclusion of the exercises the annual regatta would be held in a quiet anchorage at Pollensa Bay in Majorca.

On our way back to England we again visited Gibraltar, where, invariably, there was a death in the fleet. It seemed that I had assumed the role of professional mourner because somehow my name kept coming out of the hat when drawing for a place in the funeral party.

We were learning everything we could about the

ship, including the drill for a 15-inch turret, which was quite complicated, particularly in checking out all the safety devices. As our knowledge was increasing, so too was the Navy's, for in England at this time the use of the aeroplane was gaining prominence in fleet affairs. The battle squadron was attacked from the air by torpedo-carrying aircraft, and in a 15-inch concentration firing by two battleships the fall of shot was reported by air. These were major advances since the First World War.

Malaya then visited Scapa Flow where we inspected the scuttled German High Sea Fleet, most of which had sunk on an even keel with bridges, masts and funnels above water. Soon the Atlantic Fleet ships were assembled at Spithead for a Royal Review on 26 July. Two unusual ships in the review were the aircraft-carriers HMS *Hermes* and HMS *Argus*. The latter was a strange sight for the bridge structure was on a lift and descended clear of the flight deck when operating aircraft. The funnel gases were carried in trunks at either side of the ship and exhausted at the stern. We also noticed the King's racing yacht *Britannia*.

About this time we were cheered by a government decision to start a five-year development plan which provided some hope for the RAN of the future: two 10,000-ton cruisers and two submarines were to be built in the United Kingdom. For us, however, other matters loomed larger for 2 August 1924 was seamanship exam day, the culmination of many years' training and effort. The naval officers comprising the board were not the ogres we had expected, and although battleship details were included in the questioning, general seamanship predominated. In the rule of the road a 100 per cent result was not difficult. I made the grade.

With the examination over I reflected upon the previous two years and seven months, crowded with invaluable sea experience in various fleets, ships and naval stations, which had provided such a sound basis for a naval career. It is a great pity ,to say the least, that this sea period for junior officers has, over the years, been reduced; the best naval university is the sea itself.

Leave was available until the end of the year when we

were all due to appear at the Royal Naval College, Greenwich, as acting sub-lieutenants. I took a fortnight's break but with no family in England and no money, I retired to the Royal Naval Barracks in Portsmouth where a job was created for me to lecture to new entry stokers on naval history.

Seniority as a lieutenant was decided by success (or otherwise) at RANC, where one could gain a few months; in the seamanship examination for the rank of lieutenant at the end of one's time as midshipman; in courses at the Royal Naval College, Greenwich, in non-nautical subjects; and at specialist courses — torpedo, gunnery and navigation — at Portsmouth.

A first-class pass in seamanship had given me some confidence, but there were keen contests to come. The Royal Naval College at Greenwich was a pleasant break from the sea. On the Thames, it was handy to London and all its attractions, and with Nelson on his column, the Royal Standard fluttering bravely in the wind at Buckingham Palace, all was well with the world, except that a sub-lieutenant's pay did not permit much freedom of movement. To my delight the cut-off for a first-class pass was 75 per cent. Two down and three to go, and off to Portsmouth and Whale Island, known throughout the world as the home of the gunnery school (gas and gaiters).

The course there covered guns and gun controls in all their forms, and ceremonial from royal guards to funerals. Alacrity, smartness and efficiency abounded. Over the centuries Whale Island had built up a great tradition and the gunnery staff were all dedicated men. No army sergeant-major was more efficient and noisy than the gunner's mates of HMS *Excellent*. It was all overdone but one had to admire the enthusiasm and the results it achieved. Where else but at Whale Island would you find the after-dinner port being passed in a pair of silver gun-carriages? The signature tune at these dinners was, 'Braganza', which was that of the Queen's Regiment of Foot which, years ago, had embarked in HMS *Excellent* and had bequeathed the tune to the ship. The guest night words to 'Braganza' were inevitably bawdy:

Here they come, fife and drum,
Bloody great soldiers everyone,
Earning half a crown a day
For putting the girls in the family way.

Thanks to the high standard of staff and their enthusiasm, which must have been catching, I scored a first-class pass. Three down and two to go.

Next was the navigation school, HMS *Dryad*, which was known as the 'Wrecker's Rest' and was in the Portsmouth dockyard alongside the house of the Commander-in-Chief, Admiral Sir Edmund Fremantle, whose son was on my course. On guest nights when exuberant sub-lieutenants would go over the wall and pinch the admiral's grapes, it was convenient to have a friend at court.

I had made up my mind to become a navigating officer. Navigation fascinated me and still does: to be able to trust an Admiralty chart strikes a chord within me. A host of skills is employed in hydrography, cartography and celestial navigation (with its solving of spherical triangles). I was determined to master the art. The navigator is the chief adviser to his captain on the handling of his ship while entering harbour and berthing, which, in difficult wind and tidal conditions, is a big challenge. Officers of other specializations only came into their own for short periods of time at sea. When a gunnery firing was over, the gunnery officer would retire from the scene and analyse the fall of shot at his leisure. Similarly, after firing torpedoes, 'Torps' would retire to his cabin and take even longer to find out why two torpedoes missed. But a navigator would be getting the ship in the right position for both the gunnery and torpedo firings and would then carry on with the navigation job after the firings were completed. It was a 24-hour-a-day job, but I wanted to be a good ship-handler as well, and this seemed the best way to achieve it.

To stand a real chance of obtaining selection to join the band of navigators it made good sense to obtain a high pass in this sub-lieutenant's course. Some 'examsmanship' worked like a charm and I proceeded to the

The 'second' age of man—Henry Burrell   Cadet-midshipman

AN College, Jervis Bay—study blocks and gymnasium with eminent clock tower

HMAS *Australia* and two 'Town' class cruisers secured to buoys between Man of War Steps and Garden Island *(Australian War Memorial)*

HMAS *Sydney (Australian War Memorial)*

HMAS *Tasmania*—similar to the *Tattoo (Australian War Memorial)*

next course, which was torpedo and mining at HMS *Vernon*. This course was our final one and a bit of an anti-climax. Torpedomen are such nice quiet fellows that the noise at Whale Island would madden them. They love playing with electricity and batteries and an electric train set under the house was the normal home entertainment for father and son. The mechanics of a torpedo I could understand but when it came to electrics I found difficulty in understanding the principles involved.

Oral exam day arrived, and with it disaster: the examiner had the wiring drawing of an engine-room telephone exchange and invited me to trace the flow of power. I had never seen this before and I floundered at too many hurdles and never looked like 'getting back to negative'. Consequently I missed the bus. Four firsts and a second do not impress.

The courses at Portsmouth were not all work. In the winter months I played rugger for the United Services team, varying between the first and second teams; I was an average hooker but a better goal converter. Our opponents were spread around Hampshire and London and included the Honourable Artillery Company whose ground was in the City of London, within sight of the Old Lady of Threadneedle Street, and worth many fortunes. Their hot bath was the size of a small swimming pool. In the summer I played cricket with a businessmen's team, the Hampshire Wanderers. We were scroungers in a way for we could not have home games since we did not possess a ground. Nevertheless, it was enjoyable and I quickly learned some important lessons, such as never ask to borrow a bat, bring your own cricket bag, and if you possess some old cricket caps, trot them out occasionally.

Portsmouth was considered a good proving ground for London plays and there were many firsts tried out there. It was a chance to check judgements with the London critics. I was to return to Portsmouth many times, where the decrepit cross-harbour ferry is still known as the 'Gosport Liner'. Gosport leads on to the village of Alverstoke overlooking Spithead and the Isle of Wight. Most of the inhabitants there are retired naval officers who love the naval atmosphere. In those days a captain, on retiring, would be promoted to rear-admiral on the retired list, which led to an absurd situation in Alverstoke. If you were to walk along the lanes and say 'Good morning, admiral' to all and sundry, particularly the gentlemen gardeners, you would be right almost every time. In the United States Navy, such gentlemen are impolitely called 'tombstone admirals'.

So ended my courses for the rank of lieutenant. At this stage in my career it was clear to me that I had been a slow developer, both mentally and physically. But the accumulation of knowledge had brought with it confidence and I looked forward to the hurdles ahead despite an innate shyness. It only remained to go to sea as a sub-lieutenant and obtain a watchkeeping certificate to become a lieutenant and an officer responsible for his every action. If a midshipman in a picket boat rams the admiral's barge, all is forgiven for he is just a snotty. An acting sub-lieutenant who joins the 'reciprocal club' (a 180 degree error) in a report to the captain on the course of a tanker, receives only a blast. For me those days were now all but over.

2
'Salt-Horse'
1926–29

A 'salt-horse' is an executive officer without specialization knowledge. He is regarded simply as a seaman. The
next step in my career was to obtain a watchkeeping
certificate when my captain considered I had sufficient
knowledge and was trustworthy enough to be officer of
the watch alone on the bridge at sea. In the absence of
the captain, the officer of the watch is in complete
operational charge of the ship, subject to standing
orders issued by the captain which lay down the circumstances in which he wishes to be informed (there is a
direct voice-pipe from the bridge to his cabin) so that he
can decide whether or not to come to the bridge. If
immediate action is required, such as man falling overboard, the officer of the watch would take the appropriate action and then inform the captain.

Before I was due to return to Australia I was sent to
the battleship *Valiant*, then part of the Mediterranean
Fleet, to obtain my watchkeeping certificate. In June
1926, the fleet anchored in a long, quiet bay at Argostoli,
in the Greek Ionian Islands, for the annual regatta.
HMAS *Melbourne* was present and I was appointed to
her to return to Australia and also to gain further
watchkeeping experience at sea.

When I returned to Australia I took my foreign
service leave. The Australian squadron, under the command of Commodore George Francis Hyde, consisted
of the cruisers *Sydney*, *Melbourne* and *Adelaide*; the
destroyers *Swordsman*, *Tasmania* and *Success*; the depot
and squadron repair ship *Platypus*; and two surveying
ships *Moresby* and *Geranium*.

Commodore Hyde's name ranks high in the history
of the Royal Australian Navy. After flying his flag in the
Royal Navy, a high honour, he served in Victoria

Barracks in Melbourne as First Naval Member for six years until he was relieved on his retirement in 1937 by Admiral Sir Ragnar Colvin.

After some months at sea I must have convinced Captain Patterson that I could be trusted as officer of the watch at sea and 'was in all respects able to carry out the duties of a lieutenant'. My seniority was backdated to 15 July 1926. If I behaved myself, I would be a lieutenant-commander in eight years, but after that the next step on the ladder (to commander) would be by selection, otherwise I would soldier on to the ripe old age of forty-five and be retired. Weighing up my chances, I deemed it advisable to allow an AMP representative, hovering around Garden Island, to earn a commission on a policy payable in 1949. I would collect a small amount of 'deferred pay' at that time but thought some additional money would sustain me while I gained knowledge to enter the workforce. Maths, sharp pencils and parallel rulers attracted me, but the competition about 1940 would be keen. In the meantime I had good shipmates and plenty to do.

Nevertheless, as the most junior lieutenant on *Melbourne*, opportunities to take responsibility and gain experience were very limited and so I was pleased to receive an appointment to HMAS *Tasmania*, which with *Swordsman* and *Success* formed the destroyer flotilla.

I joined *Tasmania* before Christmas 1926 and found myself of low caste in this destroyer. I was the correspondence officer, appointed without staff, and the confidential book officer. As the former I had to see that the routine reports were prepared on time and be able to unscramble the draft letters of the captain, Harry Howden, a lieutenant-in-command, and one who would make a name for himself and his command during the Second World War. As confidential book officer I was required to muster and sign for any valuable books, signal publications, ciphers and other publications.

My arrival, and that of another officer soon after, meant that the ship was run by six lieutenants. I had a hammock and chest of drawers in the cabin flat, which was also my office; the typewriter sat on a chest which functioned as my desk. In harbour there was only battery secondary lighting, which was poor, and I required two candles in order to do my nocturnal typing.

My captain was a most unusual man; in *Tasmania* I soon came to expect the unexpected from him. He signed his official correspondence using a broad-nibbed pen, but not before he had jabbed it a few times into a block of wood. On his desk he kept a plaque which carried one of Nelson's standing instructions: 'The order of cruising will be the order of battle'.

Harry Howden's foibles sometimes involved the whole crew. One night we were returning from the north to Jervis Bay, of which the northern headland is Point Perpendicular, whose flashing light was mentioned earlier when describing my time as a cadet. We all knew that the coastline there was steep-to, but Harry decided to steam close to the cliffs, regardless. There was a long swell running and it was crashing against the rock wall. We were so close to the cliffs and the lighthouse that the light above us was lost to sight. The gunner on the back of the bridge was heard to remark: 'I expect the lighthouse keeper is lowering his fenders'. Only a failure of the main engines could have got us into trouble, but, like Queen Victoria, I was not amused. The sailors knew that Harry was slightly eccentric, although he was sound in dealing with matters of importance. There was just room for Harry in a small navy.

Soon we were back in Sydney. After a refit over Christmas, the Anniversary Regatta in Sydney and the presentation of the King's Colour to the squadron by the Governor-General, the squadron sailed for Hobart in late January 1926. In Bass Strait, *Tasmania* was detached to show the flag at Devonport and act as flagship for the Mersey Regatta over the weekend. This was followed by the usual regatta festivities and annual musketry course at Hobart. The rifle range at Sandy Bay (now the site of the University of Tasmania) was adjacent to the cemetery — an ominous arrangement with trigger-happy sailors around. Although we were sometimes called upon to send parties to help deal with bushfires surrounding the city and suburbs, as a rule we were spoiled in Hobart with dances attended by the especially attractive local lasses, whose boyfriends, we understood, gave in gracefully and left Hobart temporarily for the trout streams. It was not until mid-March that the squadron returned to Sydney.

The three months after our return were devoted to activities concerning the visit in the battle cruiser *Renown* of Their Royal Highnesses the Duke and Duchess of York, which was to culminate in the opening of Federal Parliament in Canberra. The squadron met *Renown* in the approaches to Port Jackson and escorted her to the official landing in Farm Cove where the royal guard was under the command of Lieutenant R. R. Dowling (later to become Vice-Admiral Sir Roy). The Navy was given special recognition that afternoon when the Duke visited both HMA ships *Sydney* and *Adelaide* and inspected their ships' companies. We were kept busy escorting *Renown* as it visited various Australian ports. 21 April brought a nice touch:

Their Royal Highnesses wish to thank the Australian Squadron for the salute fired yesterday on Princess Elizabeth's birthday. They feel it a special honour that this customary ceremony should be done on the first anniversary by ships of the Royal Australian Navy.

Australians seemed to have a warmer appreciation of their Navy than the federal government, and officers and ratings were entertained generously during this tour. In Adelaide the Citizens Entertainments Committee even provided taxis to convey officers to and from official functions — a kindly act as service pay was not one of its great attractions.

The big moment in the royal tour was the opening of the new Parliament House in May 1927 in Canberra on its transfer from makeshift quarters in Melbourne. The building was meant to be a temporary affair, but it was more than fifty years later that the design of the permanent Parliament House in Capital Hill was resolved. The Navy was required to play a part in the royal ceremony by providing one of the three service royal guards and an escort of naval ratings. Ten ratings from *Tasmania* and I were detailed to form part of the guard. We camped opposite the Prime Minister's Lodge in a bare field which is today occupied by the Swedish and Philippine embassies. The White Ensign and a quarter-deck, marked by white stones, created some sort of nautical flavour around the bell tents. On the great day itself, inevitably, the participants saw little of the action, although I did catch a glimpse of the panorama of power in full regalia on the top steps of Parliament House. For me it was an historic occasion for three reasons. I saw the future King, whom I was to serve in the Second World War; I saw the future Queen Mother who, throughout my lifetime, grew to be the most gracious and gentle octogenarian to be found in any country, in any walk of life; and I also heard Dame Nellie Melba sing the national anthem unaccompanied.

After the royal visit, as we settled back into the routine of peacetime sailoring, *Tasmania*'s officer complement began to change, and our labyrinth of lieutenants disintegrated. George Stewart was relieved by a Royal Navy officer; David Harries moved on, leaving me to inherit a decent job, that of 'unqualified' navigating officer, and we got on with training for war. In those days a destroyer's offensive capabilities rested on guns and torpedoes but the fire control arrangements were primitive. Although we practised periodically with slow-moving targets, experience was limited owing to a shortage of ammunition, which was strictly rationed.

A flotilla torpedo attack, or threat of one, was still a potent factor in naval warfare, but for it to be effective torpedoes had to be released on the bow of the enemy at fairly close range. By night, before the days of radar, the sighting would be at close range, but by day the problem was to get to the firing position in the shortest time, with the ships of the flotilla on a line of bearing roughly at right angles to the probable course of the torpedoes. Therein lay the skill of destroyer captains. Having sighted the enemy and estimated course and speed, the problem can be resolved by a relative triangle. However, an immediate and reasonably accurate course for the flotilla or ship to steer is needed and this requires what is called a 'relative eye'. First get going in the right direction at high speed and then make minor adjustments, after the Battenburg (the solver of relative triangles) has produced the accurate answer. Some seamen officers are born with a 'relative eye', some develop it by careful study and others just do not have a clue. Fortunately for me, I was in the first category and had plenty of opportunity to improve with practice and it has stood me in good stead all my nautical life. A 'relative eye' comes into play in most movements of fleet units. It is required by all civilians in cars or bikes when crossing unmarked intersections.

In October the unpredictable and courageous Harry was relieved by an RN lieutenant-commander, an admirable fellow in every way except that he just did not know how to handle a destroyer, particularly berthing and unberthing at a jetty. It was an experience that was to stand me in good stead in the future, for if, in the opinion of the navigator, the captain was handling his ship in a dangerous manner, it was the navigator's duty to inform him. Obviously, the utmost tact would be required since captains, like most motor car drivers, think they are the best handlers of their craft in the world. Since I was not yet a qualified navigator I wondered if the rules of the game applied to me in my 'unqualified' state. It made little difference — when the ship or the jetty was about to suffer severely, I could not keep quiet. When leaving a jetty, somehow we always seemed to have a strong wind bearing us on to it, but to employ a tug to haul off the stern was unthinkable in the destroyer fraternity. The correct drill is to go ahead on a spring, kick the stern out and then go astern with high revolutions and get clear before the wind can take effect. In my captain's first effort, he went astern much too early. The break of the forecastle caught a pile on the jetty and slowly wrenched it free. These piles were held in place by very long bolts with large nuts, which were pulled out through the adjacent support, making the most piercing noise which suggested that the ship was being torn in twain. The damage was probably only £100 but we had to start all over again. I suggested that the ship in the prevailing wind should be pointed out at least thirty degrees before casting off and being given the gun. As I was not told to keep my views to myself I had a lot to say on many future occasions and hope that I saved his reputation as a ship-handler.

On leaving a ship, one's captain is required to write a confidential report which goes to Navy Office, where, over the years, one's reputation and abilities are recorded. An officer's file is the only information made available to the Naval Board when promotions are being considered and this practice is accepted as being fair. The captain is required to supply the departing officer with a 'flimsy' (the paper is very thin) which is supposed to give a brief but true reflection of the confidential report. It reads: 'This is to certify that W has served as X in HMAS Y from ... to ... during which time he has conducted himself ... Z', followed by the captain's general view of the victim, to include defects as well as assets. Z is highly significant — 'to my entire satisfaction' is normal; 'to my satisfaction' suggests reading up notes on farming; 'entirely to his own satisfaction' suggests committing harakiri as an appropriate reaction or at least packing the suitcase. For a few years my flimsies included the phrase 'a promising young officer' but this disappeared in later years and I began to wonder if I had lost my promise.

The flimsy from *Tasmania* worried me. If the serving time was under three months the captain could refrain from expressing his views. When I left in January 1928 I had served a week short of that period, but we had had a lot of close contact and he knew me well. To my surprise my report read 'under three months'.

When I left *Tasmania* to join *Sydney*, under Captain G. L. Massey, she was about to pay-off (and eventually was sold as scrap). The three months in my old ship was really a stopgap. *Sydney* carried out the usual routine of visiting, training and refitting. During this period I took the opportunity to call on Paymaster Captain 'Charlie' Parker at Navy Office in Melbourne who (under the second naval member) was in charge of officers' appointments. A delightful man, friendly and charming, he was one of the many characters in the RAN between the wars. His forecasts of one's future appointments were seldom accurate yet somehow the visits always seemed worthwhile. I remained keen to specialize in navigation (which needed a five-month course at HMS *Dryad* within the walls of Portsmouth naval dockyard).

In the normal course, I would have hoped to secure the nomination for 1929. However, the navigators in the Royal Navy had been seriously shocked when the first lieutenant of the Navigation School (a lieutenant-commander) had been passed over for promotion to commander and it seemed that navigators, the so-called 'salt of the earth', were falling from grace. The reason was that although the navigators were excellent at their job, they took little part in the actual running of the ship (man-management) and were content to navigate at sea and correct their charts in harbour. This brought home to me that, as yet, I was too inexperienced in the handling of men and needed more time at sea before specializing, lest I suffer the same fate.

In the Seaman Branch, senior lieutenants could volunteer to sub-specialize in gunnery, torpedo, signals, submarines and navigation or remain 'salt-horse' (seaman specialists). After promotion to commander, the specialist qualification was dropped, except in a few cases — the fleet gunnery officer could be a commander (G). Only about half could expect to be promoted to commander, so choosing one's specialization needed careful thought. For example, a gunnery lieutenant-commander had to handle a large proportion of the ship's company and such an officer would make a good second-in-command of a big ship. Conversely, a navigator had only one rating to look after, so his man-management would be suspect but his shiphandling in a sea command would be money for old rope. I told Captain Parker of my concern and that I would be prepared to delay doing a specialist course to gain more sea experience and to accept the risk of missing out in later years. In due course I found that I had been appointed to commission HMAS *Canberra* in the United Kingdom and wondered if I had forfeited my chance of becoming a navigator.

In 1924 the United Kingdom Labour Party came to power and delayed work on the new Singapore naval base. To offset this setback our government then instituted a five-year programme to construct, or acquire, two 'Kent' class cruisers, two submarines and a seaplane carrier. I understood the government had a surplus of £4 million at that stage and could afford two cruisers at £2 million apiece. *Australia* (built by John Brown's at Clydebank in the Firth of Clyde) was the first cruiser to be completed and was commissioned on 24 April 1928. *Canberra* was the second, in the hands of the same famous builder, and was due to be ready for service in mid-1928.

It was decided to charter RMS *Beltana* to take to the United Kingdom those of *Canberra*'s crew not already there. After an uneventful passage, at Clydebank *Beltana* secured alongside a brand new cruiser — a ship with a number, but without a name.

The next day, 9 July 1928, the ship was commissioned as HMAS *Canberra* with the Australian flag on the jackstaff, the White Ensign at the ensign staff, and the commissioning pendant at the masthead. It was marvellous to commission a brand new ship of great fire power (eight 8-inch guns in four turrets). The mess decks were vast, the cabins comfortable, and the upper deck high above the water level. It would be easy to blame the Royal Corps of Naval Constructors for a design which wasted a lot of space (and there was much criticism) but the construction conditions laid down in the Washington convention embodied formulae with tonnage and gunpower limitations. Consequently, to produce a 10,000-ton cruiser with eight 8-inch guns, high speed and long endurance required a ship 630 feet long with a high freeboard which had the grave disadvantage of making her more readily detectable at night. In the Battle of Savo Island in 1942, *Canberra*'s conspicuous silhouette could well have been responsible for the Japanese sighting and opening fire before they themselves were detected.

I was about to experience the life of a 'salt-horse', or non-specialist lieutenant, as a divisional officer, a turret officer and a watchkeeper, in harbour and at sea. My division was a quarter of the ship's seamen complement and the men comprising it looked to me for help, advice and support, particularly in arranging classes for their advancement. Difficult social worker cases I diverted to the clergy. I expected the sailors to behave themselves, to keep their mess deck clean and to keep their kit up to date. To know each by name was an early requirement, but I tended to keep aloof from their private lives and left it to them to tell me of events such as fatherhood.

The first thrill was the maker's sea trials. We proceeded down the Firth of Clyde to the more open water off the Isle of Aran — the velvet green of Scotland being ever in evidence. I was not used to a ship under way being silent and vibration free, at least until we were doing more than twenty knots. With four screws the ship was designed to generate 80,000 h.p. and produce a speed of more than thirty-one knots. The power and turning trials met Admiralty specifications and so the captain signed a receipt for the ship on a simple piece of paper.

Having been accepted, *Canberra* steamed down the west coast through the Irish Sea on passage to Portsmouth, there to prepare for a royal visitor. Equipment trials would come later. I was on familiar ground passing through Spithead and entering Portsmouth harbour where the following day, 17 July, we were to be honoured by a visit from His Majesty King George V. All ships in Portsmouth, including *Victory* which was permanently in dry dock, *Nelson* and *Warspite* were dressed overall. The King was received on board *Canberra* with the usual honours and stood aft on the quarter deck while the entire ship's company marched past in single file.

After this great honour we sailed for Portland to 'work-up', a way of describing the conversion of a lump of steel into an efficient fighting unit. Every department had much to learn but my particular interest centred on 'X' turret, manned by men of my division. All I knew about an 8-inch turret was that after firing the guns had to be brought to an elevation of 10 degrees, the fixed angle for loading and reloading. Fortunately my ordnance and electrical artificers had preceded us to the

United Kingdom and were conversant with the working of the turret — the O.A. with the hydraulic power and the E.A. with the electrics and fire control arrangements. The latter enabled all turrets to be controlled from a main gunnery control position high on the bridge superstructure. If this should be put out of action, each turret could be controlled and fired by the turret officer in local control. I knew 15-inch and 6-inch gun drill, but this 8-inch was quite new. The gunner's mate normally would teach gun drill, but as he had no opportunity to learn, I decided to do the teaching. The drill instruction made some progress but we were constantly hampered by mechanical teething troubles. The power to operate the turret came from an electric motor generating hydraulic power, but the pump gave endless trouble and oil leaks in the piping were almost continuous. We were to have this problem for a long time, but eventually the day came for our first full calibre firing at a battle practice target.

It was a day to forget. Our first round went off, only to be followed by a deathly silence of some seconds. I thought the pressure pump had gone off the board (I had failed to read in the drill book that the recoil of the gun builds up pressure in the system hence the reduced noise as the pump eases). I was then expecting the 'gun-ready' lamp to light up to show that the next round was ready for firing. It did not. It transpired that the operator had thought that the cordite charge had not entered the bore, so he had re-rammed. This created a real pot mess, consisting of broken sticks of cordite with signs of black powder from the base of the charge. A spark from a short circuit in these circumstances could have been disastrous. About this time we learned of an explosion in 'X' turret in a sister ship HMS *Devonshire*, which gave one plenty to ruminate upon.

Tests and trials continued and we reached a reasonable state of efficiency when, in mid-October, we proceeded to Invergordon, the fleet exercise base on the Moray Firth. Our first 8-inch full calibre shoot firing broadsides (all eight guns together) was against the old battleship *Centurion* which was being controlled by wireless. The captain ordered 'Open Fire' and the gun control officer, Lieutenant Sherlock, instructed 'Shoot'. There was then a slight pause until the roll of the ship brought the gyro-controlled contacts together, when eight 8-inch projectiles were despatched with a roar. The new ship could not stand up to the blast — the electric power went off the board so firing could not continue, and the bridge structure was in a mess. It transpired that the plating was too light for the job. *Centurion* had had one bollard on the quarter-deck removed, and we were credited with a one broadside, one straddle.

While at Portsmouth, we were honoured by a visit from Princess Mary, who had launched our ship on 31 May 1927. It was my turn to be the Officer of the Royal Guard, a little tough for a hopeful navigator.

In the first week of December 1928 we set sail for Sydney via the Cape. It was the beginning of a pleasant voyage and our first port of call was Gibraltar where we secured alongside the South Mole. Always interested in ship-handling, I noted that we left harbour stern first. It sounds unseamanlike but in the circumstances prevailing (a strong westerly) it was the safest way out. With slight stern way when turning, the ship's stern will move into the wind, a point which I was to remember.

We looked in at Las Palmas in the Canary Islands, had a game of cricket at Freetown (Sierra Leone), and on to the artificial harbour which had just been completed at Takoradi on the Gold Coast. There all I saw was a dockside filled with cocoa-beans. We then moved east into the Gulf of Guinea to Lagos, where the locals challenged us to a game of hockey. Noel Coward had something to say about people who went out in the tropic sun and twenty minutes each way proved to me he was right.

Down the west coast of Africa we had to cross a deep ravine in the seabed gouged out many miles to seaward by the Congo River. We sounded our way across and so fixed the ship's latitude and longitude. By New Year's Day 1929 we were in Cape Town, which always reminds me of the First AIF diggers who, after breathing some Cape brandy, led three horses into the GPO and asked for stamps to post them back to Australia.

Little did I think then that in the years ahead, Cape Town, Simonstown and Durban, and the sea routes around South Africa, were to become well known to me. We had an appointment at Simonstown so we steamed round the peninsula where Table Mountain is situated and, in the wake of Vasco de Gama, the Cape of Good Hope. Simonstown was one of the many dockyards set up by the Royal Navy in strategic positions throughout the world. From there we sailed to Durban.

Being a harbour watchkeeper as well, I saw little of Durban except beautiful surfing beaches and an abundance of wattle. We were soon in the Roaring Forties bound for Fremantle. With a fleet at sea at night, there is never a dull moment on the bridge, but on this occasion there was little to do. The chances of sighting another ship in 39 degrees S latitude were extremely remote and there were no navigational hazards except St Pauls Island. The main concern was to see that the quartermaster steered a mean course. With the following wind and swell, the ship was yawing continuously, making the steering of a steady course impracticable. Still, it was a chance to get to know the midshipmen of the watch, the leading signalmen and bridge personnel.

After an uneventful voyage we proved that Rottnest Island was charted correctly and berthed in Fremantle harbour. On arrival our gunnery officer and captain of the ship's rugby team, Joey Burnett, who had played rugby for the Royal Navy, a rare feat, issued a challenge to Western Australia. The game was new to the land of gold and Swan beer, and so not surprisingly their team was not very good and we managed to defeat them.

We were now part of the Australian Fleet, under Rear-Admiral Hyde. Our sister ship *Australia* had arrived in Sydney from the United Kingdom (via the east coast of Canada) in November 1928 and immediately became the flagship. Admiral Hyde ordered us to visit Bunbury, Albany, Adelaide and Melbourne, and arrive in Sydney for leave on 16 February 1929. Thus the public were given a chance to see if their taxes were being well spent and I trust they considered the Navy a good investment for an island continent.

Leave and docking immobilized the ship until early

April when we steamed down to Jervis Bay to become efficient again after the rest from drill and the unavoidable drafting changes. We then travelled north to Hervey Bay (off Bundaberg, Queensland) to increase efficiency so that we could take our place in the fleet.

After a visit to Brisbane and Bowen, *Canberra* returned to the Hervey Bay area to join the flagship *Australia*, with *Albatross*, *Anzac*, *Success* and the New Zealand cruisers *Diomede* and *Dunedin* in fleet exercises. One make and mend day during an exercise the admiral decided to have a seaplane race using the Seagull aircraft carried by each of the large cruisers on a catapult amidships. A triangular course, all in sight of the fleet, was marked by buoys around which an unorthodox but morale-boosting race was flown.

In late June the fleet returned to Sydney. After some leave, *Australia*, *Canberra* and *Anzac* visited Brisbane for show week, a visit which was becoming an annual affair, and the locals gave the fleet a rousing welcome. Unaccountably, there seemed a preponderance of females in the crowd to wave good-bye. A circumnavigation of Australia had been ordered for *Canberra* and so, after further exercises in Hervey Bay, we parted company with the flag and set off to emulate Matthew Flinders. The passage inside the Barrier Reef today is well marked and, with the aid of radar is safe for the careful mariner, despite the strong and variable tidal streams. However, as radar had yet to be invented, we anchored each night. Navigating the long stretch of the Barrier Reef under sail and uncharted was a remarkable feat and must have been a nightmare. To have grounded only once showed great seamanship by Captain Cook, when safety depended on the skill of a masthead lookout in detecting submerged reefs and the skill of the captain and crew in taking appropriate action. After a quick trip across the top of the Gulf of Carpentaria, we arrived in Darwin and berthed at slack water.

A ship is full of 'characters' and we were a happy crew, at least so far. Mess rules played a part in producing harmony: alcohol was regulated by a financial limit for each month, the wine book being inspected by the captain. It was as well to have 'birthday' noted

The naval camp opposite the Prime Minister's Lodge *(above)*, and the naval contingent of
the services parade ready for review *(below)*, on the occasion of the opening of Parliament
House by the Duke of York on 10 May 1927.

Point Perpendicular lighthouse, marking the northern headland at the entrance to Jervis Bay. (The light went out!)

HMAS *Canberra*, dressed and manned ship alongside Portsmouth Dockyard, in the presence of HM King George V

against a conspicuous amount. Bridge was discouraged as it formed cliques and winners found it difficult to refuse an invitation to play when they should be doing other things. The use of hard cash was not allowed — the results of a gambling game were written up in a card book. At dinner, discussion of religion, politics or the mentioning of women's names were penalized and payment had to be made in terms of a round of port.

Sailing from Darwin on 17 September en route for Broome we were required to report on the suitability of Browse Islet for use by flying-boats but the reef was found to be without a suitable lagoon and to be dry at low water. We arrived at Broome at high water and anchored exactly in the selected position. I went ashore and climbed out of the motor cutter on to the jetty but by the time I returned, I was surprised to find the jetty high and dry — I had a long walk in the mud to get to the ship's boat. The following day, when the time came to weigh, the harbour had contracted to a small basin surrounded on three sides by mud flats. After weighing, the ship had to turn 180 degrees at rest before moving ahead down the channel. This was done and the ship started moving but we had not gone far before slowly coming to a stop — we were aground. Fortunately the tide rose very smartly, so we were able to return to the anchorage to see if any damage had been done. Alas, the ship's double bottoms had suffered severely, hundreds of rivet heads having been sheared off, but there were sufficient oil fuel tanks unharmed to permit us to continue our programme. It was a sad ship that sailed from Broome. Naturally, grounding is taken very seriously by the powers that be. On the other side of the coin, my Lord Commissioners and the Naval Board are not always aware of near misses, which, if known, would attract the sternest censure.

The pleasure at circumnavigating Australia had lost much of its bloom by the time we had visited Fremantle, Albany, Port Adelaide and Port Melbourne. However, there was a bright spot — it was our turn to represent the Navy in Melbourne at Cup time. Finally secured alongside in Sydney, it was time for Christmas leave. By this time my father had retired and settled in

Wentworth Falls where my astute mother had had a cottage built alongside our original homestead and which we had used as a holiday home.

I soon learned that my gamble at risking my specialist course in navigation to gain 'salt-horse' experience had paid off. I was to leave the ship in January 1930 and proceed to Portsmouth. My commission in *Canberra*, sadly now at an end, had stood me in good stead and I hoped that in the future I would not be described as 'just a good navigator'. I had learned a lot about handling men.

3
Navigator
1930–38

I left Sydney in January 1930 for Portsmouth, where the 'Long (N)' course would begin at the end of the first week in April. A term of young midshipmen was also required to further their experience in the Royal Navy and I was directed by the Naval Board to be 'snotties' nurse' during their passage to the United Kingdom aboard an Orient liner. I was required to see that they had some experience in using a sextant to fix the ship occasionally by sun and stars and I presumed that I was also to be responsible for their spiritual, moral and physical welfare.

I had some six weeks to fill in before my course started so I was appointed to HMS *Winchester* (a 'W' class destroyer) which operated daily from Portsmouth and carried out gunnery firings for training classes from Whale Island, the famous HMS *Excellent*. I came to know well the channel entrance to Portsmouth harbour, Spithead and its east and west approaches.

The (N) course was to last five months. Success would enable one to be a qualified navigator, that is, qualified to navigate small ships. A shorter course later would enable one to be navigator of big ships such as battleships and aircraft-carriers. It was a highly intensive course with only eleven lieutenants as students.

The crash course was to delve deeply into the theory of astro-navigation, magnetic and gyro compasses, tides and tidal streams and the like. However, I had been away from school for a long time and the pace was too hot for my grey matter for about three weeks, after which the oil had seeped into the bearings and the machine started to spin smoothly. It was a relief to find the brain was still there.

There were two sea-going tenders attached to the

school to enable us to gain practical experience, including pilotage. Each student was given a different problem and mine was to navigate into St Helier, Jersey, using only the ship's magnetic compass. The tidal streams are strong around the Channel Islands but I was doing quite well until I noticed the compass becoming erratic. I had to con by eye and indulge in some rapid chart reading. It transpired that the instructor had put a magnet in his pocket and moved close to the compass — an unkind act, but a good test in the handling of the unexpected. There was of course no real danger as he knew the harbour approaches quite well.

Although both navies had a surveying service, specialists in navigation would have a lot of knowledge which could be put to use in that field, so it was appropriate that we should spend a week at their game. We were given the task of surveying from scratch the entrance to the Helford River which I understand was the setting for the pirate hideout in Daphne du Maurier's book *Frenchman's Creek*. Finally, back at the school, we each had seventy-two hours to make a fair chart. The foray into the hydrographic field was most enjoyable and later on was to pay dividends for me. For some time my masterpiece graced the back of the toilet door, but has now taken up a more genteel residence in the Naval College Museum.

Two weeks before the end of the course we were told of our next appointments, which suggested we had all made the grade. Against my name was *Hindustan*. No one had heard of such a ship. Apparently the shipbuilders, Swan Hunter and Wigham Richardson, at Newcastle upon Tyne were building a sloop for the Royal Indian Marine and as part of the contract the ship had to be delivered to Bombay. It was a case of an RAN officer being loaned to the RN for duty for the RIM. I wonder who arranged my pay?

I duly arrived in Newcastle, County Northumberland, and found diggings in Jesmond Dene. The ship was fitting out at Wallsend. Navigators buy their sextants and Zeiss binoculars from Mr Lee on The Hard at Portsmouth. Super binoculars are essential and I still have mine. It is a matter of gamesmanship. The idea is to be first to sight land, lighthouse, ship's masts hull down, submarine periscope, in fact anything of interest.

After storing ship in Portsmouth we set off for Bombay with the thought passing through my mind that it was a strange quirk to entrust the safety of a brand-new ship to a brand-new navigator. One morning, off the Portuguese coast, my captain borrowed my sextant and deck watch and took a sun sight and disappeared to the chart house to work it out. Not a word was said but thereafter his trust in me was never in doubt.

After fuelling at Gibraltar, we proceeded to Malta and berthed in Valetta harbour. The city of Malta is situated on a huge soft sandstone structure like a three-sided pyramid, sheer on the north side, with hundreds of steps leading up to the city plateau from the east and west. The north side faces Sicily. The east side provided deep-water berths for main fleet units, and the west side the famous destroyer and submarine haven.

In the Navy, it is almost obligatory to 'acquire' things for one's ship. Our gunner (T) spotted a 44-gallon drum of anti-fouling paint some hundred yards from the ship. He considered it would be good for use on the scuppers or come in handy for something, so he proceeded to roll it along the dock; he was doing well until a policeman appeared alongside. Quick as a flash the gunner said, 'Give us a hand, will you?' and the arm of the law obliged.

There was nothing unusual in the passage through the Suez Canal and the Red Sea and on to Bombay where we handed over the ship unblemished. The officers were to stay at the Taj Mahal Hotel.

The city was quiet, a *hartal* (a day when everything shuts down) having been declared, and we had to dwell a pause too while we waited for the army troop transport which was to return us to England. When we boarded the ship we found it filled with officers, other ranks, and their wives and families; it was a cruise to forget. It was obvious that the womenfolk survived the privations of life in India much better than the men who seemed very tired and uninterested in life. Even after casting their pith helmets in unison into the Suez Canal, they showed little sign of enthusiasm at returning to their homeland.

On reporting to Australia House, I was directed to Portland to take up an appointment to HMS *Pangbourne* as the navigating officer of the First Minesweeping Flotilla. This sounded like the kiss of death to me but I knew the rudiments of minesweeping.

I took a train to Weymouth and transferred to the local track to Portland, which three innocent snotties had traversed back in 1923. On 4 February 1931 I found the flotilla berthed at the loading jetty, three ships on either side, and I reported to my captain, one James Powell. My predecessor turned over the job in smart time and departed, leaving me as the duty officer over the weekend for the three ships on *Pangbourne*'s side of the jetty. I did not think it a kindly gesture but there was worse to come. I noted that the following week's programme was 'Annual rifle range practice for all ships — officer-in-charge H.M.B.'. Each minesweeper officer complement consisted of a lieutenant-commander in command, a first lieutenant, a sub-lieutenant and engineer officer, plus one or two reserve officers under training. Unfortunately I was the only lieutenant and I was soon to discover that the flotilla was a backwater; the captains were men without hope of promotion and the first lieutenants did not think much of their chances either. This was a challenge but I had to learn my own job first.

I was beginning to learn how to handle the rather cold RN officer approach which in some ways was understandable. The RAN was growing up under RN tutelage and showing signs of being competitors in general naval knowledge and efficiency. The RN approach seemed to be, 'Let's take them down a peg', but I found one solution which worked in this case, and in two other RN ships in which I was navigating officer. The answer was to hide your light under a bushel — don't speak at breakfast, don't suggest a game of tennis, but rather do nothing and wait to be asked, and even then don't appear enthusiastic. After a few weeks one was accepted fully.

Portland harbour was selected as the minesweeping

base, because water, clear of the shipping lanes, was available to the west of Portland Bill, off the Chesil Beach, where we could exercise undisturbed. The flotilla would sail each weekday at 8 am and after three weeks at exercises we would remain in harbour for a week to self-refit, boiler clean and get the paperwork up to date.

The flotilla trained many reserve officers and ratings in minesweeping and after some time the work became so tedious that each spring the flotilla was allowed to stow away its sweeping gear and embark on a spring cruise. Captain Powell wanted to visit King's Lynn in the Wash, Stavanger and Bergen in Norway and I talked him into adding Odda in the Sor Fiord, a place I am sure had never before been visited by one of His Majesty's ships. So we set off up the Channel and passed through the Straits of Dover — to navigate a line of six ships through that congested area was like an Australian driving a car with five trailers around the Arc de Triomphe. Canute was not available when we entered the Wash to give us tidal information but we managed to negotiate the River Ouse and find berths at King's Lynn. Norfolk is very low lying and would be the first to flood if the Arctic ice started to melt. It would be logical for the King's Lynn Yacht Club to be called the 'Ouse Booze', as indeed it was. We then crossed the North Sea to Stavanger where we were well received.

The entrance to the Sor Fiord is only about forty miles north of Stavanger. As the crow flies Odda is quite close to the entrance but to get there we had to steam about seventy-five miles in a north-easterly direction and then turn south for twenty-five miles. It was an impressive one hundred miles of fiord, steep-to on both sides, with very deep water and completely free of navigational hazards. The weather was very pleasant and I felt that no man could ask for more. Odda was only a village but one junior officer obtained permission to remain behind for forty-eight hours and rejoin by ferry at Bergen — a question of *cherchez la femme* in the most unlikely places.

The approach to Bergen was good tourist fare with the land steep-to. However, there were almost too many eyes on the crowd of onlookers while berthing to notice that the gantry of one of the dockside cranes was rapidly closing our topmast. 'Full astern both' saved us more than embarrassment by the smallest of margins. An unusual township, Bergen was quite isolated from the rest of Norway except by sea. Although there was plenty of motor transport about, it had all come by ship. Once ashore, three of us planned to have a mixed party at the local theatre. Rodney Spencer (first lieutenant), when telling the messman not to come back without six tickets must have threatened dire punishment if he failed; we were given tickets for a box. On our entry, the entire theatre audience rose to its feet. An explanation was not forthcoming, although we suspected we had been given the royal box. Our respite from minesweeping had been very enjoyable and an uneventful return to Portland was the prelude to summer leave.

In those days, naval officers, in the early part of their careers, were expected to present themselves before their sovereign at a levee. I made application through the normal service channels and was duly summoned to St James's Palace to be received by the Prince of Wales, standing in for a sick father. Full dress was the order of the day: full dress coat, cocked hat, epaulettes and ceremonial sword belt. Mr Gieves, almost my life-long creditor, loaned the outfit and had the photographer handy.

Our first duty after the levee break was to proceed to Spithead and to be present on the occasion of the float plane race conducted by the Royal Aero Club for the Schneider Cup Trophy on 12 September 1931. The course was triangular around Spithead with only about thirty miles in each lap. Britain won the trophy with a supermarine Napier 55 seaplane with an average speed of 281 miles per hour. Great was the rejoicing but it was no thanks to the government of the day. We all owe Lady Houston a great debt as she financed the design and construction of the winner, the forefather of the Spitfire, which would be one of our main assets in the Battle of Britain.

Soon the first lieutenant and I found ourselves discussing improvements in minesweeping. Our ideas coincided and one which was to bear fruit was the possibility of sweeping at night. This would be tiring, but in war, with increased personnel, would also be a great advantage and to our delight Captain Powell encouraged the idea. At the end of each sweeping lap, the minesweepers were required to turn in formation through 180 degrees and make the next sweep so that there was no gap in the swept water. By day this was achieved using special dan buoys, but by night the buoys would have to be lit. The range of a light on a dark night, when the light of a match can be seen many miles, then became the vital factor. We laid down 800 yards visibility as our aim and in Portland harbour we tried out many types of lights and colours and settled on battery-operated red lights. However, our initial efforts with the flotilla were not very successful.

On 17 October 1931 Captain Powell, appointed to my old ship, *Caledon*, was relieved by Captain G. J. A. Miles, who would command the mighty *Rodney* during the battle with the *Bismarck*. He, like Captain Powell, had also been a navigator by trade and so we all spoke the same language on the compass platform. He too showed enthusiasm about the night-sweeping project. I told him the Admiralty Minesweeping Manual was well out of date and required rewriting rather than amending, and that I had already made some progress. The idea appealed to him and we talked Rodney Spencer into rewriting the 'sweeping deck' part of the process. He played his part well. This chore kept me on board much of the time and since the captain had not brought his wife down from the country, he too put in some night work. The task took about six months but was accepted by Admiralty and remained the standard textbook until the advent of magnetic, pressure and acoustic mines in the Second World War. As German raiders laid contact mines in Australian waters during the war, my special knowledge was to be an advantage.

In March 1932 we were required to put our flotilla to an unusual sweeping need. A merchant ship, to the westward of Portland Bill, reported that a submarine in trouble had been seen in Lyme Bay, off Chesil Beach. Apparently the stern had been high in the air before it disappeared. The Admiralty had been experimenting with submarine designs to add to their underwater attributes. Submarine *M2* was built with a turret to house a 12-inch gun, but in October 1931 this was removed and the turret converted into a seaplane hangar with rails, catapult and crane added. It was this submarine which had been exercising off Chesil Beach, possibly in the vicinity of Abbotsford. She had not reported for some hours.

Although an official explanation was not offered, we supposed that the hangar doors had been opened a fraction too early on surfacing and so flooded the submarine. Our job was to try to locate it and we worked continuously for days, single ships retiring from time to time to refuel. About the eighth day, for reasons I cannot understand, the sweep brought up a signalman's cap and a pair of hand flags and we marked the position. Divers confirmed that we had found *M2* but the chance of any survivors had been ruled out days before. It was all a great blow to the Navy and particularly to the submariners.

Training reserves in day sweeping, exercising night sweeping and drafting a textbook kept me busy but I could still find time for tennis and hockey. Once again the time arrived to work out a summer cruise programme. I suggested that we concentrate on places where RN ships of deeper draft could not go. The captain's slim gold pencil approved the Channel Islands, Amsterdam, through Kiel Canal to Horsens and Aarhus in Denmark, and Frederikstad in Norway.

I had been to the Channel Islands before but this time I could enjoy the quiet, unusual charm they offered. In St Helier was berthed the latest of Sir Thomas Lipton's *Shamrock*s of the America's Cup fame. The members of the Royal Yacht Squadron for generations have been permitted to fly the white ensign in their yachts. Sir Thomas Lipton was denied the honour. It seemed that a tea merchant was not a fit and proper person to have that honour.

Our mile-long flotilla successfully traversed the Straits of Dover yet again and arrived at Ymuiden, the entrance to the Grand Canal leading to Amsterdam. Professionally, I was a bit concerned about my ability to work out the times of high and low water there since the mathematical formula has sixteen variables, one of which was Ymuiden's geographical position. I had to have the right answer so wrote to the harbour master and asked him to send me a copy of the local tide tables — so much for time spent at school. We embarked a pilot and set off down the canal. A few miles before arrival, the pilot uttered the Dutch equivalent of 'Golly gosh, the railway bridge across the canal is about to close! We must aground run'. There was a beam wind blowing and, not having met the problem before, I had not thought out the answer. Captain Miles signalled: 'Stop engines', followed by: 'Turn ninety degrees to starboard together'. He then ordered that ships maintain position by slow movement on one engine. It was odd to be navigator of a flotilla with all ships on the mud and not to have ruined one's promotion chances. We looked down full of curiosity upon acres of tulips in full bloom, through which a man with a scythe made his way down the rows removing the blooms to improve their value at auction. (At a Dutch auction the auctioneer starts at a high figure and keeps reducing it until some brave man puts up his hand.) The railway bridge opened, the flotilla floated, and we were on our way.

A death in the Royal Family meant that there would be no ceremonial and so we had more time to tour Amsterdam. I visited the Rijksmuseum and gazed on Rembrandt's magnificent *The Night Watch*, or, to give it its full title, *Corporaalschap van kapitein Frans Banning Cocq, genaamd De Nachtwacht*. *The Merry Toper* by Frans Hals added a seventeenth-century 'guest night' touch but I cannot remember where I saw my favourite oil, the *View of Delft* by Johannes Vermeer van Delft. That people are prepared to pay huge sums for so-called 'modern art' is beyond my understanding.

Soon we were back into the North Sea, with trawlers and drifters everywhere. Drifters lie at the lee end of their nets and the rule is to keep well clear to avoid a false claim for damages. Diverting slightly to inspect Heligoland we set off to pass through the Kiel Canal. The entrance to the canal is at Brunsbuttelkoog, near the mouth of the Elbe, and it enters the Baltic at Hultenau, close to the harbour of Kiel. We embarked a German pilot who remained strictly dull and neutral. I would have liked to have tried him out with a joke, in German, before he left us.

I then had the pleasure of a lifetime, to navigate through the Little Belt until arrival off Horsens. As the chart was insufficient as a guide into the harbour, we embarked yet another pilot. We were the first ships of the Royal Navy to visit Horsens since Nelson turned a blind eye at the Battle of Copenhagen.

Aarhus was but a few hours' steaming and we received a kind welcome. Denmark gave the appearance of one great dairy farm. Steaming north through the Kattegat, we passed close to Gothenburg, reviving memories of a sailing indiscretion as a snotty. And so to Frederikstad, a sizeable township at the eastern entrance to the Oslo Fiord. I was sorry I could not make the short trip to Oslo.

On arrival alongside I was handed a scrubby piece of paper on which was typed:

To the officer in charge of provision in HM Brittish Man of War.
Sir,
I've got a deep and eager wish that you from me would buy your fish. While you are staying in Frederikstad you'll make a beggar proud and glad. The fish I sell are new and frish and to be sure of prudent price in the marked place the second stand you'll find this writer S. O. Strand.

I told our messman to pass around the word — fried 'frish' fish sounded fine and fit for a flotilla. The sailors behaved themselves throughout the cruise, possibly because the alcoholic content of the local lager was lower than in Great Britain.

Back in Portland summer leave was due once more. The Royal Navy and Royal Marines each year were permitted to hold their lawn tennis championships on the hallowed courts of Wimbledon, with the exceptions of the centre and number one courts, and so the first lieutenant and I put our names down for singles and doubles. The standard was too high for us, but for those knocked out in the first round of the doubles there was a plate competition in which Rodney and I managed to make the finals. We, the losers, each received an engraved silver napkin ring which allows me to say quite truthfully that I won silver at Wimbledon.

I was to return to Australia toward the end of the summer. By that time the rewritten minesweeping manual was ready to be sent to the Admiralty and we had made good progress with night sweeping. With experienced personnel, particularly the captains, we had shown sweeping at night to be quite feasible. I like to think that the *Pangbourne* team made a real contribution to the minesweeping world and that perhaps we raised the status of the flotilla so that no longer was it a dead-end appointment.

I arrived back in Australia to find that the Depression had forced the 'active' fleet to be reduced to *Australia*, *Canberra*, *Albatross* (seaplane carrier) and the destroyer *Tattoo*, and was to be further reduced in March the following year by the paying off of *Albatross*. I wondered where I could fit in and on 5 December 1932 I discovered the answer when I joined *Tattoo* as first lieutenant and navigator. The popular feeling was that both functions could not be combined but there seemed no good reason why this should not be. When the second in command was busy navigating, the third in command had a chance to show his ability. We were a small but happy team with Lieutenant-Commander John Miller at the helm.

Tattoo was not taken in hand for her refit until late January 1933, thus we missed the annual jolly in south Tasmanian waters. We rejoined the squadron under the command of Rear-Admiral R.C. Dalglish at Port Melbourne in early March and soon after, as predicted, *Albatross* left us to pay off and be taken over by the Royal Navy.

I was kept busy for my six months as first lieutenant with the usual exercises, including torpedo and gunnery firings. The sole destroyer was given odd jobs, such as showing the flag at Launceston, taking cadet-midshipmen to sea for experience, and carrying out firings for trainees from Flinders Naval Depot. My time in the ship was short-lived but I enjoyed proving that one man could perform the tasks of both first lieutenant and navigator.

At this time negotiations were under way with the Admiralty to borrow four elderly 'V' and 'W' class destroyers and a flotilla leader. The selection comprised the flotilla leader, *Stuart*, and the destroyers *Vampire*, *Vendetta*, *Voyager* and *Waterhen*. These destroyers were completed in the latter part of the First World War, so the flush of youth had long faded. Stuart, a larger vessel, was of the same vintage and specially designed to lead flotillas. Good fortune favoured me again and I was appointed flotilla navigator in *Stuart*. My presence was required in Chatham dockyard by early September, so it was back to England by sea and yet another passage through the Suez Canal.

There was much work in bringing an old ship from reserve back to operational status and the RN loaned us Captain A. G. Lilley as captain (D). Finally we sailed with *Vendetta* on 17 October 1933 and were joined at Portsmouth and Devonport by *Vampire*, *Voyager* and *Waterhen*. The long voyage via Suez was before us.

We tried out many screening diagrams and, when away from traffic, would steam without lights in the cooler latitudes. There were daily navigation tests half an hour after apparent noon when all ships would be required to hoist their noon positions. Mine would be held back so that they could not copy me. So close to noon, the latitude could not be far out but longitude depended on a sunsight about 8 or 9 o'clock in the morning and a correct estimate of the distance covered over the ground between that time and the noon sight. I had to be on my mettle lest my reputation suffered.

We passed through Gibraltar and Port Said, and made our way to Colombo where I was able to enjoy lawn tennis at the Garden Club. There could not be a more pleasant tropical club in the world and over the years I was to have many enjoyable afternoons there. Soon, however, we were in Singapore which in those days was sleazy with few attractions and we were not sorry when we left for the last leg of our voyage home. We arrived in Sydney on 21 December 1933.

The years 1933 and 1934 showed an awakening of that section of the government's defence conscience pertaining to the Navy. Our destroyer flotilla filled a big gap and by May 1934 Cockatoo Island had laid down a new sloop (*Yarra*). The survey ship *Moresby*, out of commission since 1929, was brought back into service and money was allocated for oil and fuel tanks in Darwin and additional tanks for Sydney. It seemed we were on the move at last.

I was to stay in *Stuart* for a further sixteen months; during that time the composition of the flotilla was varied to enable ships to be refitted. That work, carried out up to 1939, made it possible for those aged ships to be reliable units in the early years of the war. With able officers and men the flotilla made a big contribution to the war effort in the eastern Mediterranean and earned the proud name of the 'Scrap Iron Flotilla'.

However, that was yet to come, and in the meantime the flotilla filled in the year 1934 profitably by exercising. We made the most of the oil-fuel allowance and gave intensive training to officers and men who sensed that it could be put into practice in the not too distant future.

In April 1934 Admiral Dalglish was relieved by Rear-Admiral W. T. R. Ford. He was a very live wire and smartened things up considerably. Not moving in such circles, many of us were led to believe that he stated his views strongly to the Naval Board and if thwarted would threaten to be returned to the Royal Navy. I believe he was responsible for obtaining (as in the Royal Navy) the privilege of ships at sea receiving duty-free cigarettes, tobacco and alcohol. After two years he left us to become Flag Officer-in-Charge Malta where he endured the terrible bombing onslaught in June 1940 when Italy entered the war and earned a great reputation, particularly with the Maltese.

During a visit to Port Kembla I was given the job of a minor survey around Tom Thumb Island. It was a matter of running lines of soundings from the ship, fixing the ship frequently from shore objects. However, it was in the spring that my surveying knowledge was put to use. *Stuart* was to visit Port Lincoln, Wallaroo and Port Augusta in Spencer Gulf, South Australia. At

Port Lincoln we were to give a concert party in aid of the new maternity wing of the local hospital. However, after being informed by the harbour master that the chart was inaccurate, it was necessary for me to do a rush survey of the southern third of the harbour, assisted by all available hands, including the doctor who took turns with the chief at reading a tide pole.

After our Gulf visits we steamed back to Melbourne for the Cup. We then had a date to join the squadron as part of the royal escort for the Duke of Gloucester, who arrived in Sydney with the cruiser *Dunedin* on 22 November. The Duke of Gloucester was in Australia for Victoria's centenary celebrations and returned home in our cruiser *Australia* which proceeded to England on exchange service early in 1935.

I had been promoted to lieutenant-commander in July 1934. A lowering of the pay scales had been made during the Depression, and had been taken well by service personnel who appreciated the plight of the country. I did not receive, therefore, an increase in pay with the higher rank. I married during the Christmas leave period in 1934.

The flotilla's main activity in March 1935 was a combined exercise with the New Zealand squadron in Hauraki Gulf and it trained many officers and men both from permanent and citizen forces. En route, after rounding North Cape, nature then decided to trim me down to size. I was never a very good sailor and off the Bay of Islands we were soon heading into a southerly gale with a mounting sea and swell. It was quite an ordeal; I had never been so seasick before nor have I since. We were doing revolutions varying from seven to nine knots just to keep steerage way and I dared not leave the bridge. If the ship should get the wind more than about forty degrees on either bow there was every prospect that she would broach to, when the roll of the ship, combined with the gale-force wind, could cause her to capsize. I held on to the compass for support for twenty-four hours until the front passed and we started making headway.

The Naval Board had some problems to solve in 1935. The second HMAS *Sydney* was under construc-

54

tion at Wallsend-on-Tyne and would be ready for commissioning in September. Mounting eight 6-inch guns, eight 21-inch torpedo tubes and able to make thirty-two knots, she was to be a valuable addition to the RAN. The old four-funnelled coal burner *Brisbane* had been out of commission for six years. Laid down at Cockatoo Island dockyard in 1913, her useful days had been spent. With the exception of *Platypus* and *Adelaide* (50 per cent coal) she was the last of the coal burners and now her disposal was the problem. The Naval Board decided that she would be commissioned to transport the five hundred officers and ratings for *Sydney* to the United Kingdom and then be sold for scrap. I would go with them as I too had a date to keep there, although in that matter there was, if you will excuse the pun, some latitude. Before a navigator becomes eligible to navigate big ships, as mentioned earlier, he is required to return to the navigation school for some more intensive schooling. After completing that course I was to be lent to the Royal Navy.

This time I was to work my passage, so once again I collected the impedimenta of my calling, with charts to cover the Fremantle-Singapore-Suez Canal route. The ship was to be commanded by Captain Charles Farquhar-Smith, a gentle man who did not know how to raise his voice. He was known as Sampan Charlie, presumably because of an incident at Hong Kong.

Approaching Socotra on 12 June, the Admiralty ordered us to proceed with all despatch to Aden and Shab Kutb, as a sloop, HMS *Hastings*, had grounded. Apparently *Hastings*, approaching Port Sudan on the west side of the Red Sea, ran into a prolonged dust storm, but continued on since the ship's dead reckoning placed her well clear of the many reefs at Shab Kutb. There is an unwatched light on the western side turning to red over the dangerous sector, but this had been obscured by dust, and *Hastings*, well out of her reckoning, grounded on a reef.

On the 13th, *Brisbane* filled all coal bunkers at Aden, in five hours, and sped northwards, with seamen assisting the stokers. It was not possible to make plans until the situation on the reef was known, but we knew the approach would be tricky since the reefs were not charted accurately. The next evening, Friday the 14th, we sighted the lighthouse and the sloop. My problem then was to satisfy myself that we could approach her safely, and with lookouts aloft we approached to within half a mile of the edge of the reef. The water here was too deep for anchoring, so we stopped while the commander went over to discuss the position with the captain of *Hastings*. The ship appeared to be within one hundred feet of the edge of the reef, and, to the eye, there seemed no reason why we should not succeed in towing her off. After conferring it was decided that we would attempt to tow the next day, Saturday. While *Hastings'* inner bottom was shored down and the ship lightened during the night, *Brisbane* manoeuvred in the vicinity of the reef. It was a worrying night for me. The tow-line was to be 150 fathoms (900 feet) of 5.5-inch wire and two shackles (150 feet) of 2.5-inch anchor chain.

At 5 o'clock the next morning we prepared for the first towing attempt. *Brisbane*'s stern had to be held as close to the reef as we dared. Unless we were very close to the *Hastings* the weight of the 5.5-inch towing wire would be too great for it to be manhandled over the reef. Finally the heavy wire was secured, the tow streamed and *Brisbane* could begin the salvage. We had to be careful to ensure that the tow-line did not clear the water and become bar taut, as it would then part. Under ideal conditions we slowly increased horsepower until we were making revolutions for sixteen knots on both engines, which was an extremely powerful haul. Then the towing line parted in the fairlead on board *Hastings*. This was, to say the least, a bitter disappointment and in poor humour we set about recovering the tow. This was a difficult task requiring every hand to haul the cable and then the wire back on to the quarter-deck.

After a second failure, we entered the God-forsaken harbour, Port Sudan. We returned to the reef for a third attempt. This failed so we were released and sailed for Suez. We learned later that a pinnacle of rock had pierced *Hasting*'s hull and held her fast. Our efforts could not have succeeded, and it was not until six

months later that she was refloated at the next high
water (there is one high water and one low water in the
Red Sea each year). My hair was no longer black after
spending days and nights in uncharted waters.

Every man in *Brisbane* had worked with a will to help
a sister ship in trouble, and that included heavy manual
labour at abnormal hours. The sight of a ship in such
distress was not a happy one. It seemed to me then, and
still does, that the brightest light should mark danger,
such as the reef on which *Hastings* grounded. The
brightest lights are white and they should be used
instead of red ones, which could then be reserved for
harbours and Kings Cross.

After a quiet run northward, we finally entered the
main traffic stream and anchored in the Bay of Suez. A
Suez Canal company official came on board to establish
the ship's tonnage under the special Suez Canal scale,
which determined the cost of the passage through the
Canal. A French pilot saw us safely through the Canal
and we set course for Malta and on to Gibraltar.
Taking stock of the passage, the training we had given
to *Sydney*'s new crew had shown good results, but on
the technical side our obsolete equipment bore little
resemblance to that in a modern cruiser.

We had been aware that the King would be inspecting
his fleet at the Silver Jubilee Review in Spithead on 16
July 1935, about a week after we were due to arrive.
However, owing to the Red Sea delay, we were now to
arrive the day before the review when all ships would be
moored with great precision in their appointed berths.
As we would have to pass through this armada, we
anchored inside the Solent for a few hours to wash
funnels and the ship's side. We then passed through D
and E lines making as little smoke as possible. Perhaps it
was a fitting final parade for *Brisbane* after such a long
life. We were given a 'paying off' berth close to Whale
Island, but *Australia* (then attached to the Mediterranean
Fleet) thoughtfully gave an open invitation to visit and
to view the proceedings. Unfortunately, I could not
accept but did not miss the famous BBC broadcast that
evening, in which the announcer reported that 'the
fleet's lit up'.

I had to return all navigational gear to the appropriate stores at Portsmouth dockyard and report to HMS *Dryad*. *Brisbane*'s ship's company, after destoring, commissioned the powerful HMAS *Sydney*, of which Commander John Collins was to be executive officer.

I was soon back to HMS *Dryad*, the 'Wrecker's Rest', for the eight weeks' first-class ship or 'dagger' course, after which a navigator changes his rank suffix from (N) to (N⋆). It was really a rescrub of the qualifying course, laying emphasis more on the latest thinking on tactical and strategic matters than on theoretical navigation. There were only four in the course, so it was almost a tutorial. The motto of the school oozes self-praise: 'Nobis Tutissimus Ibis' ('With us, thou wilt go safely').

The final part of the course was at the Air Ministry in London, behind Australia House. In those days the navigator was also the meteorological officer, and the Air Ministry ran meteorological courses for all three services. In 1935, a Scandinavian propounded a new theory by which temperature changes predominated over barometric pressure as the main guide to weather. It really was the birth of 'warm fronts', 'cold fronts' and 'occlusions', and for a while 'isotherms' took precedence over 'isobars' but it soon became apparent that the combined use of the factors gave the best picture on which to make a forecast.

With the course behind me, my loan service was to start on 16 November 1935 with an appointment to HMS *Coventry*, the same class as HMS *Caledon* in which I had served in 1923. After attending the Silver Jubilee Review in July, *Coventry* was sent to Chatham to be converted into an anti-aircraft cruiser, the first of its type, and so once more I joined a ship in a distressing mess in Chatham dockyard. The new armament was to consist of ten 4-inch anti-aircraft guns with two directors.

My captain was J. W. Rivett-Carnac, DSC, with Lieutenant-Commander Fuller as the first lieutenant. I suppose the important man in the ship was the gunnery officer — Lieutenant-Commander A. F. Campbell. He had to try to produce satisfactory results with a new type of fire control system without the assistance of the designers. While we converted, it became increasingly clear that Mussolini intended to acquire Abyssinia by force and our thoughts drifted to the prospect of war. By early September the Mediterranean Fleet was despatched to Alexandria and units from other stations, spread over the globe, were converging on the Mediterranean.

The Mediterranean fleet originally consisted of four battleships, four 'County' class cruisers, four 'D' class cruisers, one aircraft-carrier and twenty-seven destroyers. Admiral A. B. Cunningham wrote:

> ... The Mediterranean was being steadily reinforced from all over the world — the aircraft carrier *Courageous*, the Second and Fifth Destroyer Flotillas, the Second Submarine Flotilla and two minesweeping flotillas from the United Kingdom: the *Berwick* and mine-laying cruiser *Adventure* from China. The Battlecruiser Squadron, a squadron of cruisers, and a destroyer flotilla from home were sent to Gibraltar, while the East Indies Squadron, destroyers from China and the cruiser *Diomede* from New Zealand concentrated at Aden. The Second Destroyer Flotilla, from the Home Fleet presently went on to the Red Sea ... [4]

Two cruisers plus the return of *Sussex* from exchange duty were Australia's contributions. HMAS *Australia*, on exchange service, returned to the Mediterranean after the Jubilee Review and was present in the First Cruiser Squadron at Alexandria. Meanwhile, the new *Sydney* had commissioned and, at the end of October, joined the Second Cruiser Squadron guarding the western end of the Mediterranean at Gibraltar.

On 2 October Italian troops invaded Abyssinia. Although victory could take time, without outside interference it was inevitable. The League of Nations met five days later and agreed to sanctions being applied, but many countries showed little enthusiasm for carrying them out. A late date was fixed for the embargoes to be implemented which gave the Italians plenty of time for stocks to be accumulated. The chance of war had been reduced but Mussolini's treatment by Britain and France can be said to have driven him towards the Hitler camp.

Coventry's conversion completed, we passed into the lock which allowed entry and exit to and from the tidal Medway and, as ever, the last bunch of dockyard maties completed their job as the lock gates were opened for our departure. We went to Portland to work up, particularly with our new anti-aircraft control system. There was no great excitement over the results; nevertheless, in the hope that we would be a valuable addition to the great force at Alexandria, we were ordered there to help cope with the Regia Aeronautica if need be.

On 20 December King George V died. A great sadness fell over the Empire and particularly those who had served him in his naval forces. We always thought he showed a particular attachment to those who go down to the sea in ships. Edward VIII was proclaimed King two days later.

Our voyage to Alexandra was uneventful. Entering and leaving harbour, I did have trouble with my captain's lack of experience in handling a readily manoeuvrable light cruiser. I should point out that at that time there was not even a short course to teach shiphandling to prospective captains of any rank. The answer, which applies to all seaman officers, is to take every opportunity, when within earshot of the bridge, to listen to the manoeuvring orders and watch the results. Gain experience before the responsibility descends, is a good rule.

On arrival, we were given little rest. We took part in fleet exercises but our main preoccupation was to bring our new armament to a reasonable state of efficiency. That required many trials and showed up many errors. Late in February we were part of a unit privileged to try our anti-aircraft skills against a radio-controlled 'Queen Bee' target, catapulted by *Australia*. After the exercises, the Queen Bee was still intact but refused to obey orders. At other times drogues, towed at a safe distance from the aeroplane, were used for anti-aircraft practice. The story goes that the shell bursts from one ship were creeping towards the towing aircraft; then one burst ahead of it. This was too much for the pilot, who shouted over the radio, 'Cease fire! Cease fire! I'm towing the bloody thing, not pushing it'.

Our gunnery officer spent long hours in harbour trying to work out how his gunnery could be improved. We would be pleased when bursts were in line with the target although they could be far away in reality (for we were dealing in three dimensions). The burst position depended on setting the fuse correctly for the time of travel involved. Unfortunately, our new high-angle director was incapable of achieving success except by fluke, and it was to be some time before the advent of the proximity fuse (a device to detonate the projectile when it passes close to an object).

At Alexandria Sporting Club I managed some tennis, but I found the night life ashore sordid, and in any case it was better to avoid local food because of the discomfort which seemed always to follow it.

Meanwhile the Italian troops were making good progress in Abyssinia and the general air of tension was easing. Finally on 5 May 1937, Addis Ababa was captured, although Emperor Haile Selassie had escaped, and the war was over. Sanctions were not lifted until early July. Then, by degrees, fleet units were returned to their stations. However, Mussolini, his chest bursting with pride, was about to suffer some self-inflicted headaches. A right-wing revolutionary movement attracted him like a magnet, so when General Franco, who had staged a military revolt against the Republican government of Spain, asked for aircraft, Mussolini was pleased to send them. A prolonged civil war seemed certain. Little did I think I would have a small part to play in this bloody war.

In August *Coventry* returned to the United Kingdom, where I found an appointment waiting for me to join *Devonshire* on 3 November. I was not disappointed at leaving *Coventry* for I was returning to a 10,000-ton cruiser, a sister ship to our *Canberra*. The refit in Devonport almost over, we were preparing for the ship to return to the Mediterranean Fleet, under the command of Captain G. C. Muirhead-Gould, DSC, who had recently returned from a tour of duty as the United

Kingdom's naval attaché in Berlin. During the war he was to be the Commodore Commanding East Australia Area.

Before we sailed, there was a ceremony in the Plymouth Guild Hall where the Lord Mayor presented the ship with a replica of Drake's drum. However, murmurs concerning it were being reported from the lower deck and the master-at-arms discovered that there was superstition on board about the presence of the drum. It was supposed to be the harbinger of bad luck, but just how a replica could be such is hard to imagine. Nevertheless, the glass trophy case was short of one drum next morning.

We then set off to join the fleet in Malta. By then I was becoming accustomed to the Malta scene, with its ever-optimistic 'fishing fleet', its promotion-conscious polo players, its bells and smells. One sensed the eyes of admirals' wives, in their flats overlooking the Grand Harbour, searching for 'holidays' (or gaps) in ships' clotheslines. Each day, after morning divisions, the company carried out physical exercises. The normal order was 'off caps and jumpers' but our commander was reputed to be a nudist, and was said to have met his delightful blonde wife in a nudist camp in Germany. He was the first to order 'off singlets' as well. This shocked many, including some users of binoculars on the upper *barracas*. They were prudish days.

We carried out the usual tactical, gunnery and torpedo exercises and were detailed to try out the efficiency of our turrets. We were to fire fifty-two rounds per gun in broadsides at a battle practice target; we were being permitted to expend 416 8-inch shells at great cost to the taxpayer. Throughout the trial we were doing twenty-five knots and had seven guns firing in the fifty-second broadside, which would be rated as a first-class pass.

Returning to harbour, we found a strong southerly had got up and that we were allocated a berth at the southern end of the harbour. Valetta was at that time full of ships, thus narrowing the channel. If we entered in the normal way, we would have to turn 180 degrees in the berth, using tugs. However, it would only require one tow-line to part and we would be in real trouble. I explained to the captain that the only seaman-like way to handle the problem was to enter harbour stern first and although his eyebrows wobbled, this plan eventually was agreed upon. Going astern into a wind the ship will remain very steady and some slight juggling with rudder and main engines will enable minor alterations of course to be made. We told the quarter-deck that, when the stern approached the stern buoy, if they were snappy, we could dispense with the tug which would be standing by. All went like a charm: guards were saluting, the band was playing, and the stern wire went out smartly. Our only worry was the admiral's barge secured to the flagship's lower boom. From the bridge it looked extremely close, to the faint-hearted, but there was no real risk. Whether a stern board became the regular approach to that berth in blustery southerly weather I never discovered.

On *Devonshire* we carried a catapult to fire Queen Bee target aircraft, which resulted in our being sent to Alexandria to become the Queen Bee firing ship. Alexandria had not changed since my last visit except for the almost complete absence of ships. Queen Bees had been operated off Alexandria before but the local captain of the port, Admiral Wells Pasha, had expressed his concern that the aircraft might get out of control and crash into his oil-fuel tank farm. However, the captain reassured him that we had firm control. The drill with the Queen Bees was to catapult one off and then control it by wireless transmitter using a two-number telephone dial type transmitter; for example, to turn right one would dial forty-seven and to turn left seventy-four. For landing, a line with a lead weight was attached to the joy stick. When the craft was put into a slow descent, the lead eventually touched the water and acted as a drogue, pulling back on the joy stick for a perfect landing. This was really a very accurate method, but of course the inevitable day dawned when our Bee refused to obey dialled orders and was last seen heading for Alexandria. It was just as well that we landed Drake's drum for the plane smacked into the Lower Mex lighthouse. Admiral Wells was not amused and the locals still cannot understand what happened to the pilot. However, good things seem never to last very long — the Spanish War was about to claim our attention.

Parliament (the Cortes) controlled Spain until 1936, by which time the schisms in the country had made a civil war inevitable. Hitler and Mussolini were keen to assist Franco's Nationalists if only to have an opportunity to test new weapons and battle tactics. On the other hand, the communist Republicans had a natural ally in Russia and received more than sympathy from France.

As the war progressed, Germany assisted Franco greatly. Hitler shipped, mostly through Portugal, a complete fighting unit — the Condor Force of 6,500 men, four bomber squadrons, a fighter group, anti-aircraft and anti-tank units. The Germans operated in four columns helped by their friends within the enemy gates (the original 'fifth column'). Italy also sent many thousands of Black Shirts. Russia helped the Republicans with aircraft and army vehicles, while communists organized the International Brigades. France helped with pilots, aircraft and war material. Somewhat surprisingly considerable numbers of volunteers were arriving from many countries.

It soon became obvious that if a European war was to be avoided, some form of pact was required by which non-belligerents would agree not to interfere, to stop sending men and war material. The idea of 'non-intervention' was accepted, with tongue-in-cheek, in August 1936. The result was the establishment of a Non-Intervention Committee to attempt to police the agreement, which is where *Devonshire* came in. Responsibilities for particular ports, frontiers and sections of coast line were laid down and finally agreed upon in March 1937 and observers were placed at these ports to supervise the unloading of cargoes. It was all a mockery as Italy and Germany were bringing in arms without pause and now had to police themselves.

We on *Devonshire* really had no authority. Of course, a ship could be ordered to stop but if she refused we had no authority to use force. When released from our unsatisfactory employment, we spent much time exercising from Malta and, on one cruise, showed the flag at Algiers and Tangier.

My time in the ship was running out for I was to attend the 1938 Staff Course at the Royal Naval College, Greenwich. A new rule regarding officers' confidential reports had just appeared. If there was anything of an adverse nature in a report, the captain was to inform the officer personally. I was much surprised to be called to the captain's cabin and told that in my report he had underlined in red that I was 'too familiar with the sailors', to which I could only mumble 'Aye aye, sir', and walk out. Perhaps I should have mended my ways, but I had no intention of doing that. In my view, the ship would have been more efficient if officers and ratings had been in closer touch. My relief was to be none other than my good friend 'Gats', Lieutenant-Commander Galfrey Gatacre, RAN. I left the ship in a small pocket in Valetta harbour and the next day stood near the Naval Signal Station to see how *Devonshire* would extricate herself. She squeezed her way out without the slightest trouble. I was almost depressed; it seemed that no one was indispensable.

After my staff course I expected to be employed in a staff appointment and so was aware that my departure from *Devonshire* could mean the end of my days as a navigator. No doubt I had been spoiled by a pleasing variety of appointments, but it was time to search for fresh pastures. A navigator at sea needs to rise early in order to take star sights half an hour before sunrise and by then I had seen enough sunrises to last me for a long time. It was almost four years before I was to see another sunrise at sea. Since 1922 I had enjoyed enviable experience at sea and the privilege of serving under many captains, both RN and RAN, who were to distinguish themselves during the Second World War.

January 1938 saw me back at the Royal Naval College at Greenwich, after an absence of thirteen years. The old palace had retained its charm but the cabins were still austere and the messroom still underground. It was to be many years before the famous Painted Hall was restored, so the cherubims and the seraphims on the ceilings had to wait a while before the blowing of their west winds could be revealed.

After the successful completion of the staff course for

lieutenant-commanders and commanders, one was entitled to place the letters 'psc' after one's name. The course was meant to be instructive, but was at the same time designed to show prospective staff officers the thinking and preparation behind staff papers. Instruction was by two lectures before lunch followed in the afternoon by a set problem or some compulsory reading. Also, outside lecturers were brought in to help broaden our horizons. Initially we studied the principles of war and how to 'appreciate' a situation.

The principles of war can be tested in any encounter that had taken place years before they were enunciated and so we each had to put Lord Nelson to the test. Before the Battle of Trafalgar he gave thought to a method of defeating the enemy. In order to keep signalling to a minimum in the approach and in the battle, he distributed to each ship of the fleet a secret memorandum laying down the tactics to be employed. Historians conclude that Nelson had the right 'object' — 'the destruction of the enemy' — and stuck to it.

Appreciations of various situations seemed to me to be a most valuable part of the course. They varied from the 'Staff Officer' types, where time is no object, to a 'Captain of a Ship' situation where rapid decisions are required. In the first instance the problem was sorted into facts and probabilities; then followed the possible courses of action. The advantages and liabilities of each are then considered, which would lead logically to a recommended course. This could take five or six pages, but a senior officer has not the time to wade through it. He will look at the possible courses and the recommendation. Should he be in doubt, he will consider again the pros and cons, and even send for the staff officer and argue out the problem.

When dealing with strategic and tactical problems, the 'Principles' become applicable, of which the selection of the aim is of prime concern. Take, for example, 'the safe and timely arrival of the convoy' and 'the destruction of the enemy', both laudable aims. However, if you are senior officer of the escort of a troop convoy, with only a few ships in the escort, what do you do when a troop ship is torpedoed and sinking? Do you send one destroyer to pick up survivors or not? There was a striking lesson in the First World War when three cruisers, *Cressy*, *Aboukir* and *Hogue*, were steaming along and one was torpedoed; the second stopped to pick up survivors and was torpedoed; the third did the same and suffered the same fate. Objectively, one can easily argue that the wrong 'object' — to save lives — was chosen.

The quick appreciations took the form of complex situations for which half an hour was given for the solution until finally a tricky problem, which could arise on the bridge, would require an almost immediate answer. Staff solutions would be given in all cases. It made an excellent training ground for efficient and quick-thinking staff officers which, of course, was the aim of the course.

There were some navigational type problems for which the course was divided into syndicates of two or three. Anyone with sense would snap up a navigator, particularly when night work would be needed. One such was Commander Robert St Vincent Sherbrooke who had a couple of evening engagements in London which he was loath to cancel. The problem did not require any research on my part. He was quite prepared to put his initials on my paper. He was none other than the future Captain Sherbrooke, VC, DSO. As captain of the destroyer HMS *Onslow* he was senior officer destroyers escorting a convoy to Russia in midwinter on the last day of 1942. Short daylight and low cloud produced a murk of varying visibility; conditions to which heavy seas added no joy. Out of the half-light appeared two large ships and some destroyers. Immediately, *Onslow* led his destroyers towards the enemy, all the while firing 4.7-inch guns and making a bold threat to attack with torpedoes. At close range, with a short running time for a torpedo, the chances of hits were high. The enemy therefore retreated from the approaching menace but soon returned to try to find the convoy. Sherbrooke was on hand to repeat the threat, noting that the enemy heavy ships were a pocket battleship and a heavy cruiser. The enemy retreated again but not before a shell burst near *Onslow*'s bridge,

Sherbrooke receiving a hit in one eye and some minor wounds which forced him to go below.

He had set the pattern of offensive action and this was repeated twice before the Germans sensed that help for the destroyers was at hand and disappeared into the fading light to safety. The losses in convoy and escort were but one destroyer. The Staff College would be pleased to cite Sherbrooke as an example of how to choose the right 'aim' — the safety of the convoy — and how he maintained it in such brilliant fashion. He was rewarded with the Victoria Cross but sadly lost the sight in one eye. His actions had incredible repercussions: it is now history that when Hitler received word that his pocket battleship *Hipper* had been damaged by destroyer gunfire, one of his destroyers had been sunk, and that the convoy was unscathed, he lost interest in his navy and allowed it to wither.

After a summer break, we joined the Army and Air Staff College in a combined session at Aldershot where we formed syndicates and played out some war games. One Friday, back at Greenwich, the course was asked for two substitutes to play cricket for the MCC Third Eleven against a team at Woolwich. I had played a lot of cricket, with indifferent success, so I volunteered. However, luck was on my side in the batting section and although too many balls were sent to 'cow shot' corner, I managed to make a half century. I can now add to my list of superficially impressive achievements that of making a half century for the MCC.

In September Hitler shocked but hardly surprised the world by breaking the Munich Agreement and so the order for naval mobilization was given. All the staff college students received immediate appointments, of which mine was navigating officer in the large cruiser HMS *Emerald*, preparing to commission in Chatham dockyard. So it was back to the Medway. After a month the crisis was supposed to have passed. Chamberlain returned from his visit to Hilter, waving the worthless piece of paper and predicting 'peace in our time'. This gave us only a short breathing space. *Emerald* was then paid off and after I had returned my special stores I went back to Greenwich. The course continued but it took some time for those sent abroad to wend their way back.

At the end of the course, before Christmas, I returned to Australia by sea. The time spent at the staff college had filled a gap in my experience, as the last piece completes a jigsaw. I was out of touch, however, with the RAN perspective. I was to return home fully convinced that war was inevitable. I could not believe that Chamberlain was so naive in his evaluation of Hitler, but his attitude to rearmament seemed to confirm that he did not foresee major difficulties. As a junior officer I listened to the lone voice of Winston Churchill repeatedly exhorting the country to wake up. His rhetoric may have been exaggerated, but there was no doubting his sincerity. Nevertheless, the legacy of the placid era of the learned, pipe–smoking Stanley Baldwin was difficult to shake off.

4
Director Operations and Plans
1939–40

Having spent money training me in staff matters, the Naval Board lost no time in attempting to draw a dividend. I was to report on 8 March 1939 to the 'stone frigate', otherwise known as Victoria Barracks, situated in St Kilda Road, Melbourne. In those days the official appointment read: 'you fail to do so at your own peril'.

This was to be my first shore job, apart from courses, since going to sea in 1922, and for me the Second World War started as soon as I began. My job was designated Staff Officer 2 (in effect Director of Operations and Plans) and I was to be inside the 'Yogi House', the domain of the omnipotent and dreaded Naval Board.

In those days the Board comprised the First and Second Naval Members and the Civil and Finance Members, who were, respectively, Admiral Sir Ragnar Colvin, RN, Commodore M. W. S. Boucher, RN, and Mr A. R. Nankervis. The First Naval Member was the adviser to the government on naval matters and in the absence of the Minister for the Navy he was Chairman of the Naval Board. The Second Naval Member was responsible for personnel and logistics, the Finance Member looked after finance and civil personnel and the Secretary to the Board was the highly experienced and knowledgeable Mr G. L. Macandie.

The First Naval Member was also Chief of Naval Staff (CNS). Obviously he had to be a highly experienced naval officer and seaman, as indeed Colvin was. He was responsible for all matters relating to operations in peace and war, for major questions of naval policy, for strategy and the conduct of sea warfare, and for the security of Australia's sea communications. The Naval Staff who did the spade work for CNS was headed by the Assistant CNS (ACNS), Captain J. A. Collins, who acted as CNS deputy. However, in the absence of CNS, the Second Naval Member (a seaman officer) would assume the responsibility.

The other members of the Naval Staff were the SO 2, the SO 3 and the Director of Naval Intelligence. Lieutenant-Commander George Oldham (the SO 3) and I did the workload of operations and plans. The operational side dealt with defence of trade, troop convoys and their protection, warship movements, defended ports, naval control of merchant ships and the examination service. Planning covered war plans, training policy and the use of weapons, local defence policy, minelaying, booms, and liaison with army and air force. George Oldham, having had air experience, dealt with aviation matters and I dealt with specialist navigation problems.

It should be pointed out that although the Naval Board was the superior operational authority, experience had shown that this should be delegated to the senior officer on the spot, that is, to Rear-Admiral Commanding Australian Squadron (RACAS) when ships of his squadron were involved, or to a local Naval Officer-in-Charge if an incident occurred in his area. The classic example of misplaced interference is said to have occurred in the closing stages of the Battle of Jutland when Admiralty ordered the Grand Fleet to steer a certain course. War with Germany seemed inevitable within a matter of months. The Singapore naval base was completed in early 1939, but at the official opening no mention was made of heavy ships being based there. Our naval defence was founded on the ability of Great Britain to base a capital ship force there but it was becoming obvious that, in a war against Germany and Italy, sufficient forces could not be spared to constitute an effective deterrent to Japanese ambitions. Secret discussions took place in May 1939 between RN and USN staffs on the disposition of naval forces in a combined war, with specific reference to western Pacific problems, but the possibility of the United States going to war unless attacked was extremely remote. The popular catchcry in that country was: 'Our sons must never again come home in wooden boxes'.

With war imminent, it was essential to ensure that two 'bibles' of the Navy were up to date. The first, the War Book, was a secret publication which laid down the actions and responsibilities of all government departments in the event of war. The Naval Staff was interested in the fleet, the reserve fleet, the mobilization of reserves, bringing defended ports to a state of readiness, setting up naval control of shipping service and an examination service, guarding oil fuel tanks, ammunition supplies and so on, seemingly without end. The Naval Stores and Victualling Branches, the Inspectorate of Ordnance Torpedoes and Mines, and the Directorate of Naval Works all had to be geared for great activity to ensure that the logistics and construction matched requirements. The second 'bible' was a book containing 'Special Telegrams', which was simply a collection of code words. When received by signal each word would give authority for the actions defined against it in the book. The words and their meanings enabled the full state of war readiness to be achieved step by step in a logical manner by each authority ashore and afloat. I was surprised to find that work on the naval section of the War Book and the 'Special Telegrams' was far from up to date. A sense of urgency seemed to have been lacking. Seldom have I worked harder than during my first four months as SO 2, one of the main tasks being to define the actions required by the recipients of certain 'Special Telegrams'. In addition, many interservice meetings took place to coordinate the country's war effort. To my surprise I found that neither Navy Office nor ships had detailed knowledge of the Army's coastal defences, such as the positions of guns and their arcs of fire.

The Admiralty informed us in June that they would be giving advanced summer leave to their fleets and calling up reserves in the same manner as in the First World War. The commissioning of ships in reserve would then follow. By this time our books of 'Special Telegrams' had been completed with, as it turned out, very little time to spare. With government approval our war machine was being started up in accordance with the War Book. The Naval Special Telegrams were despatched in orderly sequence throughout July and August and squadron movements were altered so that ships would be near their war stations. The signing of the Russo-German non-aggression pact in August made Hitler's intentions quite clear. It was time for the Navy Office war organization to be set up. We needed three watchkeepers to man our operations room around the clock. Signal traffic would soon become heavy, and although Oldham and I would have to carry the weight we also needed three reliable individuals who would see that one of us was back in the office in emergency. These were Commanders V. C. Eddy, C. R. Price and A. V. Knight, who rightly called me many times during the night, when a taxi would be sent to my home and a cup of coffee would welcome me on arrival in the office. We should have organized their appointments much earlier, which would have permitted us more time to train them. Two of the three were lieutenants RN who had been promoted on the Retired List.

Meanwhile, the various Naval Officers-in-Charge in the capital cities were busy carrying out orders. Among a host of activities, reservists were being summoned and the reserve fleet was being manned. The Examination Service in each port was being made ready to check the credentials of all ships wishing to enter and mariners were being informed of the rules for the control of shipping, such as the procedure for entering and leaving a defended port.

The Admiralty enquired if our 6-inch cruiser, *Perth*, returning to Australia from the United Kingdom via the West Indies, could be retained on that station. This required a submission to the government which we prepared giving the pros and cons. The pros won and the Admiralty was informed. We were to prepare many similar papers during the following year.

On 25 August we received an Admiralty 'Special Telegram' requiring us to requisition four passenger liners on its account and convert three of them to armed merchant cruisers and the other to a victualling stores issuing ship. It had been arranged previously that the RAN would provide the ships' companies. We were informed that *Australia*, commissioned on 28 August under the command of Captain R. R. Stewart, RN, after her modernization, would not be 'worked-up' and ready to rejoin the squadron until 29 September.

Intelligence made it clear that a German attack on Poland was imminent. The Defence Committee, particularly the CNS, considered that it would be a wise move to have Australia enter the war within minutes of Britain's declaration of war. Such a move could pre-empt any surprise naval activity by German forces, such as submarines and armed raiders, in our waters. Mr Menzies gave his approval to this proposal.

The German attack eventuated and Britain issued her ultimatum. We knew of its refusal by the receipt of the Admiralty 'War Telegram' at 9.15 pm Australian time on 3 September. Our 'War Telegram', already signed by the Second Naval Member (in the absence of Admiral Colvin who was in the United Kingdom), was lying on the staff table. Captain Collins nodded and our world war started. We sat back with the curious feeling that we had played our part, that our work was finished for the time being and that it was up to the fighting men to get on with the job. In fact our work had just begun. Ships of our squadron were at their war stations and all German merchant ships had left Australian ports days before. The Naval Control Service and the Examination Service were in operation.

The RAN built up its war readiness smoothly. On 9 September *Stuart*, on anti-submarine patrol, reported attacking a submarine north of Port Jackson. The contact had all the characteristics of the real thing and the depth charge attacks appeared successful. However, the contact was a combination of rocks and current; the southerly current, perhaps stronger than usual, passing over the rocks on the sea-bed gave an impression that the contact was moving. It soon became apparent that the German submarine effort was concentrated in the North Atlantic. Anti-submarine patrols were discontinued to permit ships to carry on with 'working up' exercises in earnest. Approval was given to construct two further 'Tribal' class destroyers.

In mid-September the Admiralty asked if we could spare a second cruiser and some destroyers. As Japan's entry into the conflict was deemed unlikely for some time, the government accepted our argument that the Australia Station was over-insured and agreed to the request with the usual proviso that the ships would be returned if trouble should arise in the Far East. Accordingly, on 14 October, *Hobart* and the 10th Destroyer Flotilla sailed for Singapore. To make up for the absence of *Perth* and *Hobart*, the government approved the taking up of two coastal passenger liners, *Manoora* and *Westralia*, and converting them to armed merchant cruisers.

My major concern was the possibility of enemy raiders attacking shipping in our area and it was necessary to keep an eye on events far afield to ensure that we received adequate warning of such an eventuality. HMNZS *Achilles* had left New Zealand on 29 August to patrol off the west coast of South America. The next day we learned that the merchant ship *Clement* had been sunk in the Atlantic by a pocket battleship and it was soon established that a second was on the prowl. *Deutschland* was in the North Atlantic and *Graf Spee* off north Brazil. On 22 October SS *Trevanion* was sunk in the South Atlantic and then all was quiet for a month. The next move came on 15 November when *Graf Spee* appeared in the Mozambique Channel. Obviously we did not know where she would strike next and so our problem was to decide where best to station *Canberra* and *Australia* — off Gabo Island, or off Cape Leeuwin. Our greatest concentration of shipping was in south-eastern Australia and as there was no certainty that the Pacific was free of danger, our two cruisers were positioned to protect that shipping. By 23 November the Admiralty had some evidence that two supply ships for the raiders *Graf Spee* and *Deutschland* had arrived in Montevideo. The Naval Staff, concerned that the *Graf Spee* might move towards our south-west area, instructed *Canberra* and *Australia* to be there by 28 November, the earliest time by which the raider could have crossed the Indian Ocean. *Sydney*, with Captain Collins now in command, was already in the area. However, two ships on the Australian trade run, *Doric Star* and *Tairoa*, were sunk on 2 December in the South

Atlantic by a pocket battleship, but both managed to get off their enemy reports. This was the information Commodore Harwood in *Ajax*, with *Achilles* and *Exeter*, had been awaiting, and which led to the Battle of the River Plate and the scuttling of the *Graf Spee*. The RANR ratings who manned the single guns mounted in *Doric Star* and *Tairoa* were the first of our men to be made prisoners of war.

As far as enemy raiders were concerned, the problem facing the Naval Staff was to position our ships around the Australia Station in order that, with the assistance of RAAF land-based aircraft, they would be able to ensure the safety of our sea communications against enemy action. With such a small navy, however, we were forced to concentrate our forces in focal areas and the entrances to main harbours. Ships outside this protection were routed evasively by our control service to, it was hoped, confuse the enemy. Our priorities were soon to change with the departure of troop convoys to the Middle East.

The Second AIF had been forming since September, and by December plans had advanced to the stage where transport arrangements were being made to ship the first brigade group to the Middle East. The New Zealanders also had a contingent ready to be moved and the Director of Sea Transport, Admiralty, was responsible for the provision of ships. Arrangements were made by a Transport Committee at Navy Office. The senior naval officers at Sydney, Melbourne and Fremantle received the added title of 'Naval Transport Officers' which gave them official authority in the Admiralty organization. No sooner had the governments agreed to the despatch of their troops than the Director of Sea Transport set about providing the ships for the first convoy, to be known as US 1. The decision was made on 1 December. Two weeks later the advance parties sailed in the P&O liner *Strathallan*, escorted by *Adelaide*, and forty days and forty nights after that, on 10 January 1940, US 1 was ready to sail. The work involved in organizing this was prodigious.

New Zealand troops to be transported numbered almost 7,000 and were allocated *Empress of Canada*,

Dunera II, *Strathaird*, *Orion*, *Rangitata* and *Sobieski*. Australia's 6,500 were to be carried in *Orcades*, *Strathnaver*, *Otranto* and *Orford*. With the exception of the slower *Dunera II*, it is seldom that such an array of the finest passenger ships in the Commonwealth had been formed into one operational unit, complete with its own commodore of convoy. The concern of the Naval Staff centred on the object of the operation, namely 'the safe and timely arrival of the convoy'. The New Zealand and Australian Naval Boards and the Admiralty all carried heavy responsibility. There could be no guarantee that the route to be taken would be a safe one and it would be unrealistic to assume that German intelligence was unaware that a big move was imminent, and that action would not be taken to impede it.

After prolonged discussion between the authorities concerned the escort arrangements were agreed. From Wellington to Sydney the New Zealand contingent was protected by HMS *Ramillies* (an elderly 15-inch battleship), HMAS *Canberra* and HMNZS *Leander* (cruiser). Joining with the Australian contingent off Sydney, the escort to Fremantle for the ten-ship convoy was *Ramillies*, *Australia* and *Canberra*; the eleventh ship, *Empress of Japan*, after embarking troops in Melbourne, joined in Bass Strait. From Fremantle HMS *Kent* and the French cruiser *Suffren* relieved *Canberra* and *Australia*.

US 1 arrived in Suez on 12 February. The following Sunday I was called into Navy Office to find a signal from the Admiralty mentioning that it was proposed to use *Queen Mary* and *Mauretania* as transports in a future move of Australian troops and requesting our views on harbours to be used for embarkation, observing the length and draught of *Queen Mary*. I did not have a ready answer. The simple first choice was Hobart with its deep water approach up the Derwent. Melbourne was not a starter but Sydney was a possibility. Discussions with army staff, however, made it clear that to move the troops across to Tasmania would be complicated and time-consuming. Port Jackson had to be considered seriously. The entrance channel had the necessary depth and could be negotiated with safety in all except gale-force winds but her draught precluded berthing alongside. The anchorage water available was a circle with the centre about halfway between Garden Island and Bradleys Head. If *Queen Mary*'s anchor was dropped accurately on that point, she could lie at anchor with about five shackles of cable. Swinging to the wind and tide, there was a small margin of safety before her stern would ground. After much thought I said that I would be prepared to recommend this only seamanlike solution, provided the anchor was dropped on the precise centre of the circle and a second anchor was used in a strong wind to reduce the ship's yaw. The commodore-in-charge in Sydney discussed my proposal with the Maritime Services Board and both agreed to it. A signal was passed to the Admiralty, adding that a dan buoy with flag would be laid to mark the anchoring position. Later in the year, when *Queen Mary* arrived, her anchor knocked the flag off the dan buoy. As far as I know, there were never any problems during that, or subsequent visits, but I was never completely happy.

Despite all our efforts to ensure secrecy, the imminent arrival of *Queen Mary* was known to too many people. She had sailed from New York on 20 March and after following the roaring forties in the South Indian Ocean, she arrived in Fremantle on 12 April and Sydney on the 16th. With two weeks to prepare for troop embarkation, the Cockatoo Island dockyard maties commenced work on converting the ship to carry the maximum number of troops and to give protection to the decor. This work was to progress on each successive visit to Sydney and before the end of the war I believe each bunk gave eight hours sleep to three bodies each twenty-four hours.

To return to events earlier in the year, towards the end of March intelligence suggested that German ships, which had taken refuge in the Netherlands East Indies, were preparing to break out. The nineteen ships concerned carried cargoes urgently required in Germany. To meet this contingency, the commander-in-chief of the China Station established 'Malaya Force' with two cruisers, two destroyers and two submarines. We assisted in this operation, with first *Manoora* and later *Westralia*.

On 9 April, Germany invaded Denmark and Norway. A close tab had been kept on Danish and Norwegian shipping in our area, and now there were twenty-eight of them to be taken under protection. Under Naval Board instructions, those not in harbour were intercepted at sea and were escorted in or had armed guards placed on board. The entire operation went very smoothly and the nett gain to the allied cause of about 3,000,000 tons was a welcome dividend.

A slow convoy (US 2 comprising *Ettrick, Neuralia, Strathaird* and *Dunera*) was due to sail from Melbourne on 15 April escorted by *Ramillies* and *Adelaide*. The day before sailing we were alarmed to learn that *Ramillies* was aground alongside Princes Pier. I immediately hopped into a car and drove to the pier. She had a list of about fifteen degrees away from the jetty, clearly because her bilge keel had caught on the shallower water ledge close to the piles of the jetty. The problem was not serious and it only required wider catamarans to keep her a few feet further away.

By early May, convoy US 3 was assembling. On the 5th, *Aquitania, Empress of Japan* and *Andes* sailed from New Zealand, being joined by *Queen Mary* and *Mauretania* off Sydney and *Empress of Canada* in Bass Strait. There could be no finer array of shipping. As it was evident that Italy was about to enter the war, it was deemed prudent to divert the convoy round the Cape should she enter the war before US 3 reached its destination. We kept a close watch on endurances of merchant ships and escorts, as there would come a point past which diversion would be impracticable. With one day to spare the decision was made by the Admiralty on 15 May to divert, but Italy dithered until 11 June before declaring war. The decision to divert can be questioned. If Italy had entered the war immediately, the Red Sea shipping lane would have been under threat from Italian aircraft in Eritrea and seven destroyers and eight submarines based on Massawa. However, during its diversion US 3, containing 8,000 Australian and New Zealand troops, was under threat in the Atlantic, and especially in the approaches to the United Kingdom, both entering and leaving. The diversion also tied up troopships and escorts for a longer period. I was involved in discussions on the proposed diversion. The Australian War Cabinet had asked if it would be possible for the troops to complete their training in South Africa or India, rather than go to the United Kingdom. This sensible course of action was overruled, I suspect, by Churchill who wanted the troops in Britain, possibly as an example of Empire solidarity in the face of an invasion of the home country.

The Naval Staff felt that the forces retained to protect our shipping around Australia were excessive and that we should offer additional assistance in the battle zones. The government agreed that *Australia*, then at Cape Town, could be placed at the disposal of the Admiralty. Accordingly she was sailed to Freetown and patrolled off Dakar for a period before joining the First Cruiser Squadron in Scapa Flow. The government also agreed that *Canberra* could serve under the commander-in-chief in the south Atlantic protecting troop convoys, and that *Westralia* and *Parramatta* could also assist in the Indian Ocean, outside the Australian Station.

By this stage, the Navy's initial permanent force of 5,400 officers and men had been doubled by the mobilization of reserves, who soon became indistinguishable from their permanent service messmates. Since the war started we had recruited a further 3,000 officers and men which enabled us to undertake additional commitments for ourselves and for the Royal Navy.

War Signal Stations for reporting movements of every ship sighted, and for passing and accepting messages to and from them, were now operating on appropriate headlands around our large perimeter. The extension of DNI's Coast Watchers to the islands to our north-east was also functioning and a building programme of seventeen corvettes (anti-submarine minesweeping vessels) had been authorized, as had the Captain Cook battleship graving dock. Australia's industrial capacity was being harnessed for war. We were making good use of the breathing space afforded us by the 'phony war' in Europe.

In June 1940 our forces on the Australia Station were *Perth*, *Adelaide*, *Manoora*, *Swan* and *Yarra*, with *Warrego* nearing completion, but our main units were playing their part in larger arenas — in the Mediterranean there was *Sydney* and the Scrap Iron Flotilla, and in the South Atlantic and Indian Oceans there were *Canberra*, *Hobart*, *Australia* and several others manned by the RAN. We realized that reducing forces on our Station carried with it a degree of risk, particularly to unescorted ships. However, fighting the known enemy justified this risk.

With the likelihood of Italy entering the war in June, we had a problem with the Italian ship *Romolo*. Attempts to delay her departure from Brisbane failed and AMC *Manoora* (Commander A. H. Spurgeon) was given the job of shadowing. Spurgeon knew the ship carried a Torres Strait pilot. After a cat and mouse game, *Romolo* switched off all lights and, this being before the days of radar, disappeared. Spurgeon appreciated that she would be foolish to continue inside the Barrier Reef and would make off to the north-east into the Pacific and so followed her probable course. At dawn there was *Romolo* in sight, but since the Italians were still wavering, it was decided by the Naval Staff on 9 June to call off the shadower. I cannot remember my part in this decision, but I hope I said, 'Is that wise?'. It turned out to be a mistake, and about six hours later, the order was countermanded, but with separation now approximately 150 miles, Spurgeon had another appreciation to make. He had already picked up the Torres Strait pilot from *Romolo* who had overheard that the ship's destination was Yokohama, so a course was set to pass eastwards of the Solomons. Aircraft searches proved unproductive and we informed shipping at sea to break wireless silence and report if *Romolo* was sighted. This brought an early result on the 11th, the day Italy declared war. *Trienza* of the British Phosphate Commission reported the position of a ship resembling *Romolo*, but painted half grey and half white. This was immediately passed to *Manoora* by our Combined Operations Room in Melbourne and on 12 June the captain of the *Romolo*, on sighting his adversary, decided to scuttle and set fire to his ship. The ship was beyond saving but *Manoora* closed and picked up her passengers and crew. Spurgeon did extraordinarily well under the circumstances, no thanks to our calling the dog from the rabbit, even if only for a few hours.

After the fall of France we could no longer rely on the

French Navy, which drastically weakened our naval strength. However, there was one bright spot when there arrived in our Operations Room the signal reporting the sinking of the Italian cruiser *Bartolomeo Colleoni* on 19 July by *Sydney*.

Having discovered mines off Cape Agulhas in South Africa in May, raider activity was expected in our area. These expectations were realized on 18 June when the New Zealand Naval Board reported the Pacific liner *Niagara* sunk by an underwater explosion five days earlier at the entrance to Hauraki Gulf, the northern approach to Auckland. A sweep brought a mine to the surface and so confirmed the enemy in our midst.

A minesweeping expert from the days in HMS *Pangbourne*, I now faced a problem which previously had been only a threat. Mines are a thoroughly annoying means of making war, the threat of which can be removed only by physical sweeping. Available sweepers were ordered to check Investigator Strait, near Adelaide, and routes in Bass Strait. Ships fitted with paravanes were ordered to stream them when in mine-able waters. We drew a blank.

Interest in Japanese activities increased in May and June, both in America and Australia. The French capitulation increased speculation that Japan might be given a free hand in New Caledonia which would have been a frightening menace to us. In April the United States had warned Japan against armed intervention there and a move was made to establish a larger fleet at Pearl Harbor to discourage any Japanese move.

It was quite clear that if Japan should enter the war Britain would be unable to send a battlefleet to Singapore, despite all the prewar rhetoric. An undertaking was given, however, that in the event of Japan invading Australia or New Zealand, Britain would cut her losses in the Mediterranean and come to our aid. We were anxious to sit down and discuss at a service level the military situation in the Pacific, especially the security of the Netherlands East Indies. Politically, President Roosevelt could not allow his service staff officers to take part. Discussions aside, one factor stood out: oil was a major factor limiting Japan's ability to wage a

Pacific war. If America should cease supplying oil, Japan would have to rely on oil from the Netherlands East Indies to survive. Therein lay a seed of war. Consequently it was decided that our garrisons at Darwin, Thursday Island and New Guinea would be built up. To enable this, and to continue to service them, in June we requisitioned the coastal steamers *Zealandia* and *Orungul*.

On 29 August the Naval Board was expanded to incorporate a Third Naval Member, Engineer Rear-Admiral McNeil, who would also be Chief of Naval Construction. This addition to the Board made sense, but was a departure from Royal Navy practice. Some excitement came to the Operations Room in the latter part of August. The New Zealand section of Convoy US 4 (*Mauretania*, *Empress of Japan* and *Orcades*) was preparing to sail with *Achilles* and *Perth* as escorts. All this time the French ship *Notou* due in Noumea on 17 August was overdue and three days later SS *Turakina* en route Sydney to Wellington shattered the air with a distress message, reporting that she was being attacked by a raider to the west of Cook Strait. (See the front endpaper map.) Accordingly, *Perth* was despatched from Sydney and *Achilles* from Wellington to her aid. Without air reconnaissance the chances of interception would be slim but luck had to be given a chance. As will be recorded later, *Orion* evaded *Achilles* and *Perth*, proceeded south of Tasmania and the Bight and then closed the Cape Leeuwin area. By this time Convoy US 4 was in the western Bight with *Canberra* as escort. *Orion* was then sighted by an RAAF aircraft on patrol south of Albany in poor visibility and reported as an 'unidentified ship'. A broadcast was made to warn shipping and perhaps *Orion* read the broadcast or had sighted the reconnaissance plane for she made off to the west to search for victims on the Fremantle to Cape Town routes. She failed in this, doubled back south of the Bight and north through the Tasman Sea, but she was to have no further success until December.

The New Caledonian worry grew in intensity until early September when the War Cabinet decided that we should send a warship there urgently. The object was to persuade the inhabitants to support the Free French and remove any chance of the Vichy French allowing the Japanese to use their harbours as bases. Accordingly, we ordered the light cruiser, HMAS *Adelaide*, then in Sydney, to proceed with the utmost despatch to Noumea, fuelling at Brisbane en route. During the early hours of the morning of 3 September, off the northern NSW coast, *Adelaide* collided with an unknown ship. *Adelaide* was steaming on a northerly course at twenty knots on a dark night with a clear sky and practically no wind. Obviously shipping carried no lights and there were no radar sets. Normally on the bridge were the officer of the watch (in this case a lieutenant in the naval reserve) a gunner as principal control officer (part of the main armament being manned), a leading signalman and two ordinary seamen as port and starboard look-outs. The ship was steered in a wheelhouse below decks by a leading seaman quartermaster and an able seaman helmsman.

Shortly after 1 am, *Adelaide*'s officer of the watch heard his port lookout report a ship right ahead. This was followed immediately by a similar report from the starboard lookout. In the evidence of the officer of the watch, he stated:

> I would say [the approaching ship's] distance would be approximately one mile. I took the glasses and ascertained that he was coming on and ordered the wheel to be put over to starboard. The vessel didn't swing. The [ship] was still ahead and I repeated the order 'Starboard the wheel'. The vessel was still ahead and I again repeated the order by which time the vessel was right upon us and she struck us on the bow just forward of the bridge; she bounced off and struck again with the bow.

The officer of the watch added:

> I couldn't say the Quartermaster did not give her the helm as the light on the Helm Indicator was not on, but the [ship] was right ahead all the time, the ship didn't appear to swing.[5]

84

Whether or not the officer of the watch had time to call the captain via the voice pipe is conjecture. The captain only became aware of anything untoward when he was shaken in his bunk by the impact. The next information available finds the two ships stopped about a mile apart, comparing notes by signal lamp.

These revealed the other ship was SS *Coptic*, a merchant ship of 8,333 tons, owned by Shaw Savill and Albion Company Ltd. of Southampton. She told *Adelaide* that she did not require assistance — 'Nothing serious, slight damage'. *Adelaide* suffered damage to her starboard bow but this did not affect her seagoing or fighting qualities.

To *Coptic*, the collision was a complete surprise. Her officer of the watch, a cadet on the bridge, and a lookout in the eyes of the ship, apparently saw nothing. In fact, both ships were on identical tracks and their courses were exactly reciprocal. In such conditions, above average efficiency by the lookouts in both ships was obligatory if a dangerous situation was to be avoided.

The captain of the *Coptic* in the preliminary inquiry conducted by the Deputy Director of Navigation and Lighthouses NSW, stated *inter alia*:

> The other vessel asked me our name. I gave our name and asked if she wanted any assistance. She replied 'No'. The other vessel gave her name as warship *Adelaide*, after which we proceeded on our respective courses.

One strange factor was the lapse by *Adelaide*'s officer of the watch (an ex-Merchant Navy officer) into a Merchant Navy wheel order which was not understood by the helmsman. Naval practice is to order the wheel to be put over to an exact number of degrees (for example, 'starboard 20' or 'hard-a-starboard'). The order 'starboard the wheel' meant little to the helmsman. It was a fortunate quirk, for had the officer of the watch, in obeying the rule of the road, given the correct order, 'hard-a-starboard', *Adelaide* would have been cut in two with great loss of life. That there was no loss of life or even limb, was miraculous. Initially damage to both ships appeared superficial, although later investigation showed that *Coptic*'s refrigerated holds had been damaged by *Adelaide*'s bilge keel.

At Noumea the noteworthy diplomacy of *Adelaide*'s commanding officer and Australia's assistance with economic problems were important factors in the discussions which influenced the inhabitants to follow de Gaulle. The worry of a hostile New Caledonia evaporated.

In October plans for the Pacific in a war against Japan landed on my desk. Anglo-American staff talks held in London in September had made little headway, but that the staffs met at all was an advance. The question of operational control of US, British and Dutch forces in the Pacific in a war against Japan was mulled over and another seed was sown. But it was presidential election time and Roosevelt would not answer the question whether a Japanese attack on British or Dutch Pacific possessions would bring the US into the war. Perhaps it is well that he did not as it might have lost him the election.

By the signing of a pact between Germany, Italy and Japan on 27 September, the Berlin–Rome–Tokyo Axis was established. This precipitated the Singapore Naval Conference in October under the chairmanship of Vice-Admiral Layton (Commander-in-Chief China) at which we were represented by Captain Burnett and Lieutenant-Commander Oldham. The Americans sent an observer, which at least was promising. The terms of reference were a review of the tactical situation in the Far East in the event of Japanese aggression and a list of points to be raised with the US in the event of full staff discussions eventuating. The conference reported the stark fact that, without a battle fleet in the Far East, the defence forces and their equipment were inadequate to meet a major attack by Japan. Not surprisingly, this caused much concern to our War Cabinet. The Naval Staff recognized that only evidence of an American threat would cause Japan to think twice before launching an offensive in the Pacific area. It was clear to me that Britain, despite the best will in the world, could not cut her losses in the Mediterranean and come to our aid

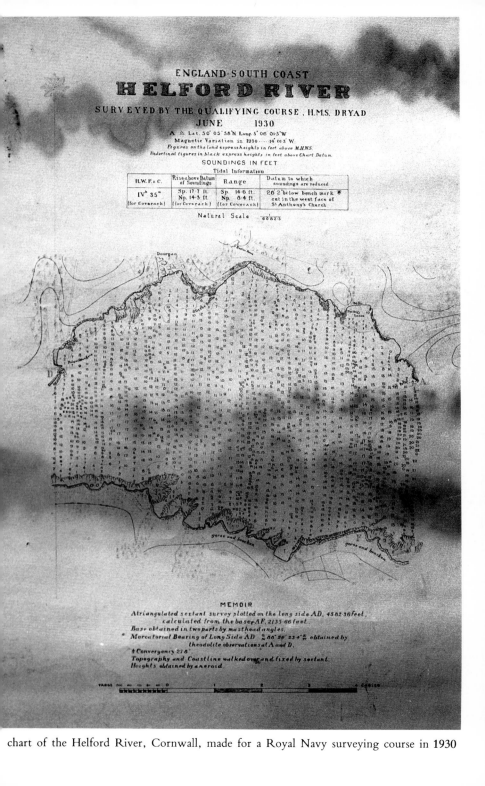

chart of the Helford River, Cornwall, made for a Royal Navy surveying course in 1930

Lieutenant Henry Burrell

In full dress (borrowed) for presentation at a royal levee, 1931

HMS *Pangbourne* with three ships of the 1st Minesweeping Squadron, at Odda, Sor Fiord, Norway

in the event of a major attack upon Australia.

My constant concern in 1940 was the presence of enemy raiders (armed merchant cruisers) in my area. I have already mentioned mines having been laid in Hauraki Gulf, the French merchantman *Notou* long overdue, SS *Turakina* having been sunk and an unidentified ship sighted south of Albany. German records, after the war, gave the first clear picture of the movements of their three powerful raiders, *Pinguin*, *Orion* and *Komet*, who operated with varying degrees of success from June to December whilst I worked and slept. The front endpaper map shows the movements of these interlopers.

The raider *Pinguin* left Germany in June, sank one ship in the Atlantic and crossed the south Indian Ocean where she captured one ship and sank four. On the Australia Station off Broome she seized the Norwegian tanker *Storstad* on passage from Borneo to Melbourne and shrewdly placed aboard her a prize crew and transferred to her some mines. Both ships then set off to mine Australian waters. *Pinguin* laid mines between Newcastle and Sydney on the night of 28 October and then the approaches to Hobart on the night of 31 October; bold moves indeed as the chances of detection were high. Meanwhile *Storstad* on 29, 30 and 31 October laid mines off Cape Otway, Wilsons Promontory and in Bass Strait. *Pinguin* proceeded to lay mines in Spencer Gulf after which both ships sidled into the Indian Ocean and never returned. From the enemy point of view, *Pinguin* made a successful departure, sinking SS *Nowshera* on 18 November, SS *Maimoa* two days later and SS *Port Brisbane* the following day, and then set course for the Antarctic. The latter two ships did send out the vital signals. The resulting action is described later.

It was not until 8 November that a sinking off Wilsons Promontory gave us the first evidence of the enemy mines. Air searches failed to find the minelayers, who were now well away to the west, and two minesweepers were sent to the area and swept two mines. On 9 November the field in western Bass Strait was revealed by the sinking of the USS *City of Rayville*, the first US ship sunk in the war. The minesweepers

Warrego and *Swan* were soon in the area and Bass Strait was closed temporarily until the limits of the fields had been established.

The second raider, *Orion*, entered New Zealand waters from the east in 40 degrees south in June and proceeded direct to Hauraki Gulf (approaches to Auckland, North Island) and, undetected, laid a minefield. This resulted in the sinking of SS *Niagara* on 13 June. *Orion* then sank the passenger liner SS *Rangitane* six days later. She then roamed the tropics for two months during which time (as already mentioned) she sank SS *Notou* close west of New Caledonia on 16 August and SS *Turakina* on 18 August. With no luck in her search, she then backtracked well south of Tasmania, before heading north to arrive at Ailinglapalap (Marshall Islands) on 10 October. Forty-eight hours later, with a supply ship, she sailed west to Lamotrek (Caroline Islands) sinking SS *Ringwood* en route — her first kill for a long time. There she joined forces with the third raider, *Komet*, who had left Germany via the Arctic Circle with the aid of Russian icebreakers.

The pair of pillagers, *Orion* and *Komet*, with a supply ship, set off on a long southward trek to the east of New Zealand and found themselves south-east of Chatham Island without a sighting. Reversing course they crossed tracks with *Holmwood* on 25 November and sank her before she could transmit the vital enemy report. Such a report might well have saved the well-known passenger liner *Rangitane*, on passage from Auckland to the United Kingdom.

Approaching the phosphate isle of Nauru, *Komet* went on ahead to survey the scene and happened upon the fully laden *Vinni* and sank her. *Komet* was actually sighted from Nauru on 7 December, but her Japanese disguise proved to be effective protection. *Triadic*, *Triaster* and *Komata* drifting, awaiting their turn to load phosphate, were easy pickings.

We sent radio messages from our operations room directing all shipping bound for Nauru and Ocean Island to disperse. After refuelling, *Komet*, *Orion* and the supply ship, *Kumberland*, proceeded to Emirau and landed 514 prisoners. *Orion* then proceeded to Maug in the Marianas to overhaul her engines and *Kumberland* sailed for Japan to replenish her stores. *Komet* appeared off Nauru on 27 December, hoisted the German ensign and bombarded the phosphate-loading gantries, before transferring her operating area to the Indian Ocean by way of the Antarctic. The island radio survived and reported the details to us in Melbourne.

The landing of prisoners at Emirau on 21 December was reported by the District Officer at Kavieng in New Ireland on Christmas Eve, and so we learned that no fewer than nine important ships had been sunk in our area in the previous calendar month. I was called into Navy Office about 4 am where we considered our predicament. We had no fighting units within thousands of miles of New Ireland so could take no immediate action, except to order *Nellore*, an Australian ship then in Rabaul, to recover the castaways and take them to Townsville. I then called at Cliveden Mansions (now the Hilton Hotel) to inform the Chief of Naval Staff, Sir Ragnar Colvin. It was customary to give the Minister for the Navy, Mr W. M. Hughes, classified information on one sheet of paper and non-classified on another. Unfortunately, on this occasion Billy handed the secret details of the raiders to the press. Fortunately, the sheet was returned and the press were kind enough to keep quiet about the contents.

With the possible exception of the Nauru tragedy, there was no practical solution to the raider problem. If more distress calls could have been transmitted before the ships' radios were made inoperable, the chances of interception would have improved greatly. On the other hand, I think the raiders could have increased their bags had they patrolled across the traffic routes instead of steaming rather aimlessly about the oceans.

With the information from the survivors, it was possible for me to piece together a blurred picture of the raider position. On the information available to us we immediately arranged for *Sydney* and *Westralia* to return to Australian waters, for *Adelaide*, *Westralia* and *Manoora* to patrol and escort in the Nauru–Ocean Island area, and for Tasman convoys to be instituted. With the knowledge of hindsight, perhaps this action should have been taken much earlier.

Meanwhile, convoys continued to carry New Zealand and Australian troops to the Middle East. Convoy US 6 comprised the rapid trio *Queen Mary*, *Aquitania* and *Mauretania*. This was to become routine, troops being discharged in Bombay or Colombo for transshipment to smaller vessels for the journey to the Middle East. *Canberra* was released from the convoy escort there and searched unsuccessfully for a raider who had sunk a ship in the Bay of Bengal. She then returned to Fremantle to await the arrival of Convoy US 5, approaching from the east. At 7.30 on the evening of 20 November, Captain Farncomb received a distress message from SS *Maimoa*, some 800 miles to the west of Fremantle. Anticipating directions from our Operations Room, he recalled his sailors from shore, raised steam and was at sea by 10.30 pm.

The captain of *Maimoa*'s first evidence that he was about to be a victim was the sighting of an approaching float plane, with British markings, flying directly towards him. Like the Queen Bee targets which operated from HMS *Devonshire*, a line with weight was being trailed with the aim of parting the main aerial strung between the masts, so preventing the despatch of the emergency signal. The plumbline failed, but the pilot severed the aerials with one of the aircraft's floats. During the three-hours chase which followed, a jury aerial was rigged and continued repeating the distress call. However, only nightfall or fog could have saved the merchantman and after abandoning ship she was sunk by *Pinguin*.

Pinguin then set off northwards and, presumably by some skilful shadowing that night, ranged up in the darkness on the beam of *Port Brisbane*, opened up her searchlights and fired at point-blank range. Commendably, the victim managed to transmit her distress signal before the ship was abandoned and sunk by torpedo.

Canberra picked up *Port Brisbane*'s distress signals containing the ship's position and, in the fading light on the day after the sinking, *Canberra* sighted three lifeboats under sail. Captain Farncomb was told by the second officer that *Pinguin* had made off to the north-west, so he continued to hunt in that direction. However, the time interval between receiving a report and arriving in the area was again much too long. *Canberra*, using her aircraft, searched for two days and returned to Fremantle on 22 November without success.

Looking back on my two years ashore, it is very clear that the naval liaison between the Admiralty, the New Zealand Naval Board, the commanders-in-chief of the various naval stations and our Naval Board was of the highest order. This is directly attributable to joint training in peacetime and the fact that the RAN and RNZN, both protégés of the Royal Navy, were in harmony with their mentor. Prewar, my brother officers and I received great experience during loan service in ships of the Royal Navy and much knowledge in their training schools which certainly enabled me to tackle this first shore job with confidence. I was not successful in handling the raider situation. On the credit side was the safe and timely arrival of all troop convoys. I was a cog in that big troop transport wheel.

At the end of 1941, the major units of the RAN were dispersed between Australia, the Red Sea, the Mediterranean and the Atlantic. Commander A. E. Buchanan was to relieved me as Director of Operations. Commander W. H. Martin had already relieved me as Director of Plans and in addition a specialist navigator was also appointed. My job had expanded threefold. Now I was packing my bag for Washington, DC.

5

Washington Interlude
1941

In the dark days of July 1940 the USA promised all aid to Britain, short of war. In the same month, President Roosevelt approved the gift of fifty venerable destroyers in exchange for the leases of British naval bases in Newfoundland and the West Indies. The astute President was moving public opinion away from the 'peace at any price' attitude in slow stages. He knew the American conscience was stirring but that it was impolitic to mention possible US participation, especially since the Senate was hostile to the actions already taken by the President to help Great Britain. Therefore, we knew that the President was likely to frown upon any open joint US–UK staff discussions, at least for the present.

This was the position as I understood it in October 1940 but, unknown to me, Mr R. G. Casey, our minister in Washington, became aware of a proposal for a top secret joint Great Britain–US conference, and, with our Pacific interests in mind, he saw the need for Australia to be represented. On 22 October, after some cabled discussion, Mr Menzies sent a message to Casey, which read:

> ... until more definite arrangements are made for Staff Conferences, it is considered inadvisable to send Commodore Boucher (Second Naval Member) to Washington. It is proposed, however, to send Commander H. M. Burrell RAN who has full knowledge of Australian plans and resources. He has been Director of Plans at Navy Office and has the full confidence of the Naval Board and is in a position to advise on Australian naval problems. Burrell will travel by air arriving San Francisco November 13 and Washington November 18.[6]

Roosevelt had made it clear that he wished to avoid any publicity about staff conversations. Casey was informed on 1 November that I would be attached to his staff 'ostensibly to investigate and expedite Australian orders in respect of Australian naval requirements'. The cable continued:

He is available to advise you on Australian naval problems. Subject to arrangement, he may undertake private and confidential talks on naval matters with officers of the United States America Naval Administration insofar as Australia station may be concerned. If possible desire to return leaving San Francisco by air on Saturday 30 November. Subject to New Zealand government's concurrence, he will bring summary of New Zealand naval information.[7]

The trip to Washington had come as a surprise because I knew that I was to be sent to England to take command of HMAS *Norman*, the fourth of the 'N' class destroyers to be manned by the RAN — my first command. However, a short interlude of intrigue had a certain appeal.

Accordingly, I was directed to travel in plain clothes, as a civilian. Under a false passport, I departed by flying-boat from Rose Bay in Sydney on 9 November. Short hauls by day were the means of progress in those days and so the first evening we landed in Noumea harbour and were accommodated in neutral territory which, as it turned out, was an expensive yacht at anchor. The second leg was to Canton Island in mid-Pacific, and from there to Pearl Harbor. The immigration control allowed me into the USA without demur, but unfortunately there was no time to visit Honolulu, the only place on earth where the locals converted the missionaries.

The remaining flight to the mainland was a long haul and once there I pressed on to Washington, via a domestic airline, where I was met by Alan Watt, the First Secretary to the Minister. He and his wife very kindly put me up at their house so that my presence would not be conspicuous. Alan's knowledge and experience was unique and to have learned then that he was to complete his career as the Secretary of the External Affairs Department would have come as no surprise to me.

Casey outlined for me the situation in Washington and stressed the need for security as the projected joint discussions could well be jeopardized by press speculation. From Australia's and Great Britain's viewpoints, it would be a giant stride if some principles for the conduct of the war could be established before the USA entered the fray. If such principles were to be agreed on at the planning level, they could well be accepted at higher levels.

During the next fortnight I accompanied the minister on his diplomatic rounds which were all carefully orchestrated. Usually the car would be parked behind the main buildings and we would go up in the service lift to avoid stray press-men looking for a story. Our first visit to Mr Berle, an Under-Secretary of State, was reported to the Prime Minister in a cable which clearly shows the Casey form:

From: Australian Minister in Washington
To: External Affairs
No. 379 Repeated to London 114.
Sent: 15 November 1940
Received: 17 November 1940.
I called on Berle today. I started by advancing argument in the penultimate paragraph of my telegram No. 358 repeated to London 109.

After referring appreciatively to the economic and other action taken by [the] Administration before [the] Election and to the understandable pre-election reluctance to pursue staff talks proposal, I said for our part we were now most anxious to revive the staff talks proposal originally made by the Secretary of State and also to pursue any lines designed to deter Japanese from further attempt to expand.

In latter regard it would seem that preventive dispositions of available forces presented most useful line. I repeated without quoting the Secretary of the

Navy the substance of his 'preventive' view reported in my telegram 358.

I reminded him also that it was the President who had first suggested the visit of the United States fleet units to Australia, Singapore etc., and said that we looked forward to [the] moment when his proposal should be revived. Such a visit would be warmly prized in Australia by Government and people.

As regards staff talks I said [Admiral] Ghormley's [naval observer in London] talks in London, the Singapore meeting and Burrell's visit here appeared to me to be nibbling at separate bites of the main problem which was that of all-embracing discussions between sufficiently senior and informed service officers on how to apply armed strength and re-sources so as to avoid war in the Far East and win war in Europe.

Berle received all this with understanding and said that he found little in what I had said with which he disagreed. In the absence of [the] President and Secretary of State he would discuss it with Sumner Welles [the Under-Secretary of State] at once. He agreed that these matters might turn out to have some urgency following on the recent Russian-German meeting.[8]

Alone I visited the head of naval intelligence, Admiral Anderson, the results of which Casey reported to Australia: 'Discussed with officer [Burrell] plans bases and facilities in Australian and New Zealand Stations. Great interest shown, particular reference being made to possible use of such bases and facilities'.[9]

A visit to Mr Sumner Welles was arranged for 23 November. The report to the Prime Minister read:

I took Burrell to see Welles and other senior State Department officials today. Very good reception. During talks with Welles, I said although Burrell's talks with Navy Office were most useful, they were oneway traffic and asked when he thought strategic Staff Conversations could begin. He said he saw no reason why they should not be undertaken at a very early date, the sooner the better. British Ambassador returns today and Welles hopes to see him tomorrow.[10]

While I was in Washington the minister took advantage of my presence and often chatted on into the night about defence matters. By this time it was clear to me that a continued naval presence was desirable in our legation as an energetic minister like Casey required ready advice. Cables to Australia for information took time and were a poor substitute, and so I told the minister he needed a naval attaché without delay. I said that judging by the questions put to me by the USN they knew there were large gaps in their knowledge of Australia's and New Zealand's defence establishments and the position in our part of the Pacific after fifteen months of war. I argued that an attaché would greatly alleviate this paucity of information. The minister asked what type of naval officer was best suited to meet his and the liaison needs and further requested that I write a paper for him so that he could get the Prime Minister's approval. I produced this the next day before we set off to call on Colonel Knox and Admiral Stark. That night Casey cabled Australia:

I took Burrell to call on Secretary of the Navy and Chief of Naval Operations today.

Secretary of Navy holds same views as expressed in first two paragraphs of my telegram No. 389 (No. 116 to London).

Five additional modern United States submarines are being sent to Manila making total seventeen.

China is seeking and will probably get additional financial assistance here. China also seeking aircraft here to enable air offensive to be conducted against Japanese.

Secretary of Navy and Chief of Naval Operations both agreeable highly confidential high level strategic staff talks early date. Secretary of Navy will see British Ambassador today on this.

Chief of Naval Operations agreed to show Burrell

American strategic proposals in Pacific area tomorrow.

Both Burrell and Goble have had useful discussions with all appropriate branches both services and have given all relevant information regarding Australian situation. Burrell will leave Los Angeles November 30. Navy Office suggest he see Admiral Richardson, Commander-in-Chief Pacific Fleet, in Honolulu, and are so arranging.

American Naval Attache (Commander Causey) is to be sent to American Legation in Australia.

I find on inquiry that State Department and Navy Office and British Embassy would welcome appointment RAN Naval Attaché to this Legation. It would enable me keep touch with Naval Intelligence and Plans Division in advantageous way that is not possible now. Grateful if early consideration could be given and if I have confidential opportunity expressing opinion regarding individual before appointment. Personality of individual most important here. Burrell has knowledge of type necessary.[11]

The posting of service attachés was usually a low-key affair, but Casey hoped to make as much political mileage from the appointment as possible:

Actually no formal announcement is made but in the present circumstances, I suggest there is value in so doing. If you agree in principle to send Australian Naval Attaché here, I suggest you authorize me to try to arrange with the Administration that simultaneous announcement of intention be made here and in Australia at an early date in the hope that significance will be exaggerated by the Japanese.[12]

I spent my final day in Washington at the Navy Department and then packed my bag, ending a heady few weeks for a junior commander. I retraced my steps across the Pacific, calling on Admiral Richardson in Honolulu. Once home I discarded my alias and false passport. While I was still in transit the President agreed to the staff talks and Casey reported as follows:

President has agreed to completely confidential strategic staff talks between Great Britain and United States. President had some misgivings arising out of possibility of leakage of information that they were taking place.

Officers mentioned in my telegram No. 400 will represent Britain. Admiral and general leaving England very shortly. Arrival date uncertain.

British Ambassador believes unwise in view President's hesitant attitude to suggest expanding numbers involved by adding Australian representation.

However, I understand from Burrell that Boucher likely to be travelling Australia [to] England at early date. If at all possible I suggest his coming here en route as soon as possible. Once he is here I have little doubt I will be able to work him in. In any event he will be able see United States Naval plans division confidentially.

Above regarded as completely secret.

If you decide agree proposal naval attache here you might appoint Boucher temporarily and relieve him by another with or without intervening interval of time.[13]

I note that the British Ambassador deemed it unwise to suggest Australian representation but Casey was in no doubt he could find some way of following the discussions and learning of the conclusions. I think that the above account of my visit to the United States shows that Casey's efforts helped to convince the State Department (and possibly the President) of the need for UK–USA staff conversations and that, if held, Australia, Canada and New Zealand should be privy to them. As for me, I enjoyed being the pawn on the chess board.

Meanwhile my passage to England was being organized. My future command, HMAS *Norman*, was being built by Thornycroft's at Woolston, on Southampton Water. For some time Portsmouth and Southampton had been pulverized nightly by heavy bombers, and during one of these air-raids a bomb fell close to *Norman*, delaying her completion by a couple of months. This coincided with government approval for the appointment of a naval attaché in Washington and I was told that, as I had suggested the job, I should go there and establish the office before crossing the Atlantic to command *Norman*. New Zealand was to be kept informed at the top secret level and their Prime Minister requested that copies of my reports be sent to him. Eventually, it was agreed that, although I would not be present at the joint meetings, I could attend the UK delegation meetings and report to both the Australian and New Zealand governments.

The notification of my appointment was signed on 19 December by the Minister, W. M. Hughes. Things then began to happen quickly. I was required to leave on 2 January 1941 but this time with a diplomatic passport. Before my departure, my three duty commanders (Eddy, Price and Knight) decided to give a farewell party for me at the Chevron in St Kilda Road. The hosts hired some gear from J. C. Williamson and greeted the guests attired as the 'three wise monkeys', a point which was well taken. We had been a happy team, but I was pleased to be leaving with a command in prospect.

My Pan American Clipper took off from Sydney harbour on the morning of the 2nd. The flight was uneventful but the navigational safety worried me. I had a chat with the crew and asked them how they would manage to find Canton Island if the direction finding set became unserviceable in flight. The answer was to fly until the dead reckoning position was close to the destination and then carry out a square search. I was not impressed. A fellow passenger was Mr Pitt, a senior man in the Aspro pharmaceutical company, who was on his way to Newfoundland to discover how olive oil could be obtained from shark. To me the whole thing smacked of 'Heath Robinson', but perhaps the chemistry was similar. This chance meeting was to have an unusual sequel about a year later.

At San Francisco, it had been arranged for me to visit our Consul and then to proceed to Washington by train. At Chicago, to my surprise, I was subjected to a minor press conference. How the press managed to track me down there I will never know, and that I could be of any interest was even more baffling. However, they were more interested in life in Australia than in the reasons for my presence in the USA.

Arriving in Washington, I found that I was booked into the Wardman Park Hotel, where my overseas allowance permitted me to remain provided I went without lunch. I reported to Mr Casey and then carried out the arrival procedures for diplomatic staff. A stack of visiting cards had been engraved for me, which in some cases had to be delivered personally, but for most the minister's driver spent several weeks delivering them around the capital.

My first important call was on the Secretary of the Navy, Colonel Knox. I was ushered into a big room to be confronted by the Secretary standing before a festoon of flags, flanked on both sides by many admirals. I advanced, shook hands and a pause followed. Then it dawned on me that I was supposed to present my credentials. Credentials! I hastened to explain that I had not been provided with any and quickly went on to apologize for my juniority. I explained that the Royal Australian Navy was a young service and officers passing through our equivalent of Annapolis had not yet reached flag rank. 'Admirals you want!' said Colonel Knox, and, pointing to the array of gold braid, said, 'You can have any of these if you like'. That broke the ice, and after words of welcome the tableau broke up and we chatted for a while about 'down under'. It was a good start to a short period of service which I often think constituted my most valuable contribution to the war.

The normal difficulty in a liaison job is to find points of interest which will justify a visit to a specific person or department. Busy staff officers often prefer to send a written reply to a question rather than ask one to call but it is only by personal contact that one can feel out the climate surrounding a difficult subject or prepare the ground for subsequent action. However, I was in an enviable position because my local knowledge was required on subjects such as entry into defended ports, enemy mines, raiders, the hydrographic situation in New Guinea waters, to name a few items which, in the past, had only been of passing interest to the United

States Navy. It was becoming clear to the Americans that a war in the Pacific could not be averted and the chat about entry into Australian ports was not idle. It transpired that the President wished to demonstrate to Japan the solidarity between the USA and the Commonwealth by sending a task force to visit his antipodean friends. Admiral Stark was not enthusiastic but in late March, with little warning, two cruisers and five destroyers visited Sydney, Brisbane, New Zealand, Fiji and Tahiti.

The normal attaché work in addition to the 'conversations' which were to begin on 24 January was to keep me occupied. On 20 January the minister attended the President's reinauguration held in below-freezing conditions. As he had omitted to wear an overcoat on that occasion, pneumonia put him out of action until mid-February.

I had been given an office in the Residence and the official car was at my disposal. The driver entered into the nautical spirit which had pervaded the Legation atmosphere by trying to mimic the whistle of a boatswain's pipe when reporting, 'Barge alongside, sir'.

Once again, the Caseys were very kind to me. Their dinner parties, where even the misplacing of name cards could cause international incidents, were full of interest and intrigue. Sometimes I would be asked to keep one diplomat engaged in conversation to avoid his interrupting Casey's discussions with another. Occasionally the minister would invite me for supper or coffee to discuss some of his bright ideas, and often I would find on my desk in the morning two or three chits in his handwriting outlining the pros and cons of various courses of action. I supposed that he retired to bed with a pad on his knee.

The Caseys were an astounding couple. Both were pilots and in a private plane they would fly in and out of America's crowded airports. Mr Casey was not only a good diplomat but a good Australian. If such a man's ability is known by the calibre of his staff (with the exception of his first naval attaché) he must have been a reasonable performer. The staff was still Alan Watt and Peter Heydon, who were soon to be joined by John

McMillan as Third Secretary. I regret that I did not question the minister on his staff days in Gallipoli. As a captain he had been ADC to Major-General Bridges and was with him in Monash Valley, where he was mortally wounded while on his way to visit Brigadier-General Harry Chauvel.

The cable traffic between Australia and Canberra was on the increase. There was a duty officer to work the ciphers, and a duty typist to be called in when required and it was obvious that I should volunteer to join the roster. One of the secretaries was a very attractive Canadian girl reputed to have won skating championships in Canada. I must have been slow not to realize why the fair Naomi was never rostered on my duty days. It was not until I received a wedding invitation late in the year that I realized that Peter Heydon had rigged the system.

The staff conversations were imminent. We learned that the United Kingdom delegation and the new ambassador, Lord Halifax, were taking passage in the recently commissioned battleship *King George V*. The team, known as the Bellairs' Mission, comprised Rear-Admirals Bellairs and Danckwerts, Major-General Morris, Air Vice-Marshal Slessor and Captain Clark, RN. On 24 January, *King George V* arrived at Annapolis where President Roosevelt's welcome to the new ambassador was meant to be noticed. Lord and Lady Halifax were entertained and dined on the President's yacht on the Potomac, and finally driven by presidential limousine to the British Embassy. The embassy staff had arranged Lady Halifax's spare bedroom as a conference room so that the mission's activity would be inconspicuous. It had been agreed that Commander Barry German, Royal Canadian Navy would, like me, be privy to the mission's activities and be present at its meetings.

The talks began on 31 January and through amicable and frank discussions, in an unhurried atmosphere over five weeks, Allied thinking was brought into the open and broad areas of agreement found. By the time of Pearl Harbor the USA had entered into an Allied strategic policy which had been well considered, at least

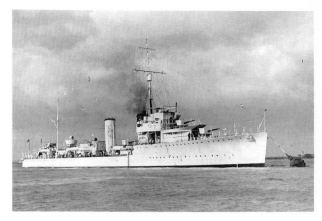

HMAS *Stuart* at Sheerness

HMS *Coventry* after conversion to an anti-aircraft cruiser

HMS *Devonshire* off Malta, testing 8-inch guns by firing 52 broadsides

RMS *Queen Mary* riding at single anchor in Sydney Harbour *(Courtesy the late Captain (E) R. G. Parker)*

The Naval Board, 1941. Left to right: Mr R. Anthony, Finance Member (obscured); Engr. Rear-Adm. P. E. McNeil, 3rd Naval Member; Admiral Sir Ragnar Colvin, Retiring 1st Naval Member; Mr G. L. Macandie, Secretary Naval Board; Vice-Admiral Sir Guy Royle, 1st Naval Member; Mr A. R. Nankervis, Secretary, Department of the Navy; Commodore J. W. Durnford, 2nd Naval Member; Mr H. G. Brain, Business Member. *(Australian War Memorial)*

up to the level of the chiefs of staff. This was of inestimable value to the war effort.

The instructions to the United Kingdom delegation were made available to Barry German and to me at the outset, and I cabled a summary to Australia and New Zealand (see Appendix I). The hypothesis was war between Germany, Italy and Japan on the one hand, and the British Empire and the United States on the other. The important foundation was that Europe was to be the vital theatre of war — beat Hitler first. Nevertheless, the security of the Far East, including Australia and New Zealand, was to be considered essential and the retention of Singapore was to be assured. It was hoped that employment of Allied forces could be fully co-ordinated to achieve these ends. Political commitments would not be recognized, nor would any agreement reached be binding until ratified by the British government.

In reporting the start of the conversations, Alan Watt reiterated to Australia and New Zealand the need for the utmost secrecy, particularly in view of US government discussions on the Lend-Lease Bill,[14] but in early February there was a security scare. The *New York Times* asked the State Department and the Australian Legation for confirmation of a report from Wellington that an 'understanding' existed between the USA, Australia and New Zealand in which we had agreed to grant 'refuelling facilities at ports and flying fields' in return for some unspecified American 'limited guarantee', allegedly connected with the defence of Singapore. The incident, very disturbing for the Americans, passed but it showed the tense atmosphere prevailing.[15]

After a US–UK joint session, Barry German and I would attend the wash-up in the British Embassy which would continue until about 6 pm and occasionally after dinner. I reported by cable to Australia and New Zealand in nine progress reports which are included in full in Appendix I. In the first report I noted that the US would not reinforce their present Asiatic Fleet, based on the Philippines, and that some portion of their Pacific Fleet, based on Pearl Harbor, would be transferred for operations in the Atlantic and Mediterranean areas. The latter strongly suggested that there would be agreement over the 'beat Hitler first' strategy and there were indications that the reduced US Pacific Fleet would not move far from Hawaii and would not be a threat to Japan. This of course would not help ease our Far East position. The cards were on the table.

My second report showed the picture filling out. That the US main contribution should be in the Atlantic and Mediterranean had been agreed, but the US would not agree to the value placed upon Singapore by the UK. Furthermore, they would be prepared to abandon the Far East in order to concentrate on the Atlantic and Mediterranean. The US held the view that the existence of the Pacific Fleet in Hawaiian waters would deter a major Japanese operation against the Singapore–Netherlands East Indies area. Consequently, the idea of reinforcing their Asiatic Fleet fell on deaf ears. I reported that the prospect of a US capital ship force in the Singapore area was not even remote. Once more the UK delegation suggested a temporary reinforcement of the US Asiatic Fleet but this did not get to first base. The Americans considered that the Japanese would be provoked rather than deterred by such action. I could only note in my third report that satisfactory progress was being made as far as the Atlantic and Mediterranean theatres were concerned.

The fourth progress report contains the UK appreciation of the strategic importance of the Far East in relation to the object, the defeat of Germany and Italy, and points made in relation to it during discussions. The appreciation and the arguments it engendered do not lend themselves to paraphrasing. Many strong, perhaps wild, statements were made. In the second paragraph it was said that, acting alone, Britain 'should [would] be prepared to send a fleet to the Far East, even if this would compromise or sacrifice the position in the Mediterranean'. Presumably this was to cajole the Americans into sending ships to Singapore, but with the low priority they placed upon it, such attempts by the British were destined to be of little avail. In the fifth paragraph the UK delegation returned to the charge strongly: 'We consider issues at stake so fundamental that loss of Singapore would be disaster [of] first magnitude, second only to the loss [of the] British Isles'. The final paragraph 'invited the Americans at least to accept that the security of the Far East position, including Australia and New Zealand, is essential to the maintenance of the war effort of the associated powers. Singapore is the key to the defence of these interests and its retention must be assured'.

The reply by the United States is contained in my fifth report. It had received the approval of the US chiefs of staff, but not the State Department. It stated that in their view the retention of Singapore was 'very desirable, its loss would be 'unfortunate' but its loss would not have a decisive effect upon the issue of the war'. Such a reply ruled out any possibility of sending US capital ships to Singapore or of reinforcing their Asiatic Fleet. It also stated that it would be a serious mistake to count upon prompt military support by the United States if Singapore were attacked.

The sixth report outlined agreed areas of responsibilities in the Pacific and noted that local commanders in the Far East were to collaborate on formulation of strategic plans. The responsibilities of the British C-in-C, China Station, and the US C-in-C, Asiatic Fleet, were defined, which was a constructive development.

The seventh report was even better. It covered agreements to collaborate continuously on the formulation of plans governing the conduct of the war by the establishment of military missions in London and Washington, and the early convening of conferences, especially in the Far East. The Dominions were to be represented on the British military mission in Washington by their service attachés. The next report envisaged the possibility of a Hawaii-based Pacific Fleet showing the flag in the Caroline Islands area. It also touched on interest expressed in the defences of Rabaul.

My final cable noted the probability of a joint conference at Singapore on 18 April and that it was hoped that the final report of the Washington discussions could be made available to delegates. The final agreed report is known as the ABC 1 Staff Agreement. I had to leave Washington before the 'Top Secret' document was released.

While talks were taking place in Washington, the Australian chiefs of staff had prepared a further appreciation of the Far East situation in the event of Japanese aggression. It stated that our vital interests were the security of Australia, New Zealand, the Singapore Base and Malaya, the Netherlands East Indies and the Indian and Pacific Oceans' sea communications. The British chiefs of staff supported this view in their appreciation outlined in my fourth report.

In February the Australian War Cabinet discussed the Australian appreciation with the Commander-in-Chief, Far East, Air Chief-Marshal Sir Robert Brooke-Popham. Not long before this meeting the British chiefs of staff had warned the Far East authorities to be on the alert for a Japanese attack as the Dominions Office had reported the landing of Japanese troops near Hong Kong, the doubling of troops in the Tonkin area, and the appearance of Japanese warships off Hainan and Indo-China. Brooke-Popham is recorded as speaking in confident tones about his ability to meet a Japanese attack. He stated that in his opinion Hong Kong could defend itself for at least four months and Singapore for six months until capital ships could arrive. Britain's ability to despatch a large proportion of her naval forces to the Far East while Germany and Italy were still in the fight was at the very least questionable, and assurances that this could, and would, be done were unrealistically optimistic.

Later in February an Anglo–Dutch–Australian conference was held at Singapore at which Rear-Admiral Crace (RACAS) was our representative. The US Navy sent two captains as observers but their silence was evidence that the United States had conflicting views on the value of Singapore. The conference drew up a list (later approved by our War Cabinet) of Japanese moves which would require offensive action by the Allies. The list included a direct act of war on Allied territory; Japanese forces in Thailand west of Bangkok or south of the Kra Isthmus; convoys appearing in the Gulf of Siam;

and attacks on Timor, New Caledonia (including the Gilbert Islands) and the Philippines.

We could only hope that such moves would not occur since the reports emanating from Washington confirmed the US attitude to the Far East which was that it took second place to the war in Europe. Undoubtedly the US view was correct but if a bushfire is closing in on your house, it is not pleasing to be told that the fire brigade is at the manor house and will be along later.

The Singapore Conference was held from 21–26 April. The Commander-in-Chief, Far East, presided and the aim was to formulate plans in the event of a German-Italian-Japanese war against the British Commonwealth and its allies, including the United States. Captain Purnell of the US Navy represented Admiral Hart (Commander-in-Chief, Asiatic Fleet) and we sent a high-powered team led by Admiral Colvin. Captain Purnell naturally followed the Washington line, namely that the US could best assist in the defence of the Malay Barrier (Kra Isthmus to Timor) by using their Pacific Fleet to attack the Marshall Islands. Some local defence plans were worked out, but the conference achieved little. The US chiefs of staff rejected the conclusions of the conference mainly because they pivoted on Singapore.

I take some satisfaction in having played a minor part in arriving at a basic strategic concept for a hypothetical war, which, in the event, was put into practice. There was no binding agreement requiring sanction by the US Congress or UK Parliament and although the joint chiefs of staff and UK chiefs of staff were consulted on some items by their delegations, the final document was a signed Staff Agreement.

The significance of the ABC 1 Staff Agreement has been noted by Herbert Feis:

The report of these Joint Staff Conferences in Washington was submitted by the two delegations, subject to confirmation by both military and civil authorities. It was to be passed upon first by the Chief of Naval Operations of the United States Navy, the Chief of Staff of the United States Army, and the

Chief of Staff Committee of the British War Cabinet; and, second, by the government of the United States and His Majesty's government in the United Kingdom.

The named American and British military authorities approved it quickly. Then it was endorsed by the Secretary of the Navy on May 28 and by the Secretary of War on June 2. The President did not approve it formally and explicitly. This fact, however, is not conclusive as bearing on the American obligation to carry it out. To all intents and purposes, the President permitted it to be understood that he approved; and he allowed American military plans and arrangements to be guided, if not governed, by the plan. The Navy at once set about the making of a new basic war plan based on the joint reports, and soon it was issued (Rainbow No. 5). The operation plans of all three main American fleets were revised to fit. The President knew everything that was being done in this, his natural field of interest.

Beyond that, American participation in these staff conferences had consequences — practical and moral. To give effect to the jointly approved strategic conception, warships were moved over the seven seas, and planes were shifted between combat points. Scarce fighting units and weapons of other countries were distributed in accordance with its term. Had the American Government refused to play its part in their execution, loss and trouble would have followed. The British and Dutch would have felt themselves wronged. The problem is not peculiar to this instance. If a nation (or individual) enters deeply, as adviser or sharer, into the troubles or dangers of others, it must accept the duties of partner or name of shirker. Public figures in their public statements and memoirs do not usually enter into subtleties such as this. But the President and Secretary of State were perceptive men; and I think it safe to conclude that they appreciated this point.[16]

To me, it is remarkable that the agreement, the work of two teams of officers, none higher than rear-admiral (or equivalent), should be accepted without amendment by all interested parties up to the level of Head of State. Great credit must go to Rear-Admiral Bellairs. It was with some relief that his mission completed its work without attracting press attention.

During the first six months of 1941 the President was keeping our cause progressively in a timetable of his own choosing; that is, he was going as far as he thought the majority of his countrymen would accept. During this period he approved the Lend-Lease Bill, made the gesture of presenting fifty geriatric destroyers in exchange for bases in British territory (Newfoundland and Bermuda), extended the US Defence Zone towards Britain (from 60 degrees to 20 degrees west longitude), allowed our warships to be refitted in US Navy yards, and sent a mission to the United Kingdom to select naval and air bases for possible American use. As an immediate consequence to ABC 1, three battleships, one carrier, four cruisers and two destroyer flotillas were transferred from the Pacific to the Atlantic.

Roosevelt, Secretary of State Hull, and Under-Secretaries Welles and Berle deserve great credit for agreeing to these staff conversations. For Roosevelt's part, it was the act of a statesman, all the time fully aware that public knowledge of the talks could do him serious political harm. In the event, immediately after the Japanese attack on Pearl Harbor the machinery for Allied military co-operation was already in place, to mention just one of the benefits accruing from the joint UK–US discussions.

I consider it a privilege to have seen Casey at work but I hope it is not presumptuous of me to agree with Alan Watt's view that 'Casey's work in Washington and the United States generally has been underestimated in his own country',[17] or to state that I thought then, and do now, that Australia was fortunate to have him as our representative at the right time and place.

My brief but fascinating frolic in the diplomatic field was over and I had not committed murder or parked a car in a prohibited area although I had acquired the American way of saying 'yes'. At this time I received word that my marriage, which had failed, had been terminated. I had been ashore for three years and now the finest job in the naval world was awaiting me, provided more bombs did not fall at Woolston. My relief, David Harries, arrived and a train was waiting to take me to Halifax, Nova Scotia.

6
HMAS *Norman*
1941–42

At Halifax I joined the battleship *Rodney* for a fast, unescorted journey to Rosyth. It was more than interesting for me that my friend, Lieutenant-Commander Gatacre, who had relieved me in *Devonshire* and *Stuart*, was the navigating officer. It was a welcome opportunity for me to learn about navigating during wartime around the British Isles.

After an uneventful passage *Rodney* anchored in the Firth of Clyde and I took the night train to London. I had of course heard about the blitz but I was not prepared for the scenes of destruction which greeted my arrival. I spent a couple of nights in a hostel while visiting Australia House to glean information about my new command, such as officer complement, ship's company details, the courses being undertaken, and the courses organized for me.

Norman carried six 4.7-inch guns in three mountings, ten 21-inch torpedo tubes and forty-five depth charges; and her 40,000 horsepower turbines were expected to produce thirty-five knots. Her radar, asdic set and communications were said to be the latest available. I thought one could not ask for more than this within a most graceful ship of 1,760 tons. Gunnery and torpedo doctrines and methods had changed little since my destroyer days but the modern methods of submarine attack and the capabilities of the radar set, although abysmally limited, had to be learned.

The Portsmouth train transported me into the midst of a ravaged town. I was accommodated at the Portsmouth Barracks, which by now were well known to me, but this time, as a commander, I received treatment very different from my days there as a midshipman. The shortages of equipment in the United Kingdom after Dunkirk were indeed severe as I realized when I asked the hall porter about a row of staves with bayonets lashed to them. He said that they were the best weapons available to provide the necessary welcome for enemy parachutists.

I had a quick run around the gunnery school at Whale Island and HMS *Vernon*, the torpedo school. The 'Wreckers' Rest' had moved out to Southwick in Hampshire after my old navigation school and the adjacent commander-in-chief's house had both received direct hits. Admiral Sir William James described the bombing on 10 March 1941:

> ... a real blitz yesterday. The raid lasted seven hours and it was estimated that about 300 planes came over. They did a lot of damage in the yard ... One bomb knocked out the centre of the Navigation School but another arrived in one of their shelters and rolled down to the wall where I saw it in the early morning. I was told that the Wrens in the shelter lifted their feet to let it pass.[18]

Naturally, I was keen to be away from such an accessible target and to get on with my anti-submarine training. I was quite out of date as far as the latest attack procedures were concerned, but I knew that success could only come from an efficient team and efficiency required knowledge and practice. A training unit of destroyers and submarines was in operation on the west coast of Scotland, and there my anti-submarine team and I went through our paces. The operators had previously experienced a great deal of simulated practice, training their ears to interpret the varied types of echo against a noisy background. It took experience to distinguish whales, wakes of ships and wooden wrecks from submarine echoes and noises. Even so, the submarines still had the advantage as we quickly realized.

Thus primed for the part I would have to play in action, I returned to Portsmouth and obtained permission to move to Woolston to stand by during the final stages of *Norman*'s construction. I found some accommodation at the Botley Grange Hotel and I bought for

£45 an ancient, and not very sporty, sports car to get to work. I now attended ship No. 235 daily at Thornycroft's on Southampton Water and learned my way around. Fortunately I was in time to have the many bridge instruments aligned so that fighting the ship from a position beside the pelorus (the main gyro compass) I could see the remainder without having to move. Not far away Southampton was still receiving the attention of bombers from time to time and I was relieved each morning to find No. 235 in one piece. The air-raid sirens wailed most nights and, as the hotel had no shelter, the staircase was accepted as the safest place to congregate. Nobody appeared frightened, but somehow the corniest of jokes became extremely funny.

As always in new ships, ten days before completion it appeared that it would require a miracle to be ready on time. Towards the end fifty women with buckets and scrubbers descended on the ship and managed to produce an air of respectability. The builders made it on time, the ship's company arrived from Portsmouth Barracks, and HMAS *Norman* was commissioned on Monday 15 September 1941.[19]

The ship's company quickly settled in and each officer and man set about getting to know the ship and the equipment peculiar to each specialization. Drills of every description were carried out from gunnery to damage control and all equipment was tested and calibrated. Many men of the engine room department had been allowed on board some weeks earlier and had watched boiler and engine trials, which was of some assistance to us.

I had a pleasant day-cabin aft, though it received little use. Nevertheless I brightened it up with portraits of the King and Queen, R. G. Casey and President Roosevelt, as well as a framed copy of the 'King's Quotation' which had been read over the BBC during his Christmas broadcast. It had a strong appeal for me:

I said to the man who stood at the gate of the year — Give me light that I may tread safely into the unknown and he replied — Go out into the darkness and put your hand into the hand of God. That shall be better than light and safer than a known way.

113

By default I was the ship's parson and so acquired a suitable calendar that I might not get All Saints' Day mixed up with the second Sunday after Epiphany or give the sailors fifty days of Lent.

On the day following commissioning I gave a lunch party to the managing director and senior officials of Thornycroft's and the Admiralty overseers, and in the evening had a drinking session with the firm's foremen and charge-hands. After the bomb damage, some nine months previously, they had had to repair and complete the ship under trying conditions.

Curiously, I found that my orders were to carry out sea trials inside the protected waters of Spithead. This was quite impracticable so I drove over to Plymouth and whispered in the ear of the staff officer operations. After apologies for thinking *Norman* was a sixteen-knot frigate, the orders were changed. The new plan was to carry out the full powered acceptance trial down the Channel to Plymouth under fighter escort and then, if the ship was accepted, to go west about England, Wales and Scotland to Scapa Flow. I received permission to have two preliminary canters in Spithead, still inside the boom protection.[20]

On Thursday, 18 September, we came to life and steamed down Southampton Water. On either hand dumb barges had been moored, each flying a barrage balloon to discourage enemy aircraft approaching Southampton at low level. For two days in the Solent we carried out the prescribed equipment trials down to testing the anchors, cables and capstan. The magnetic compass was adjusted by turning the ship slowly through 360 degrees a number of times while the correcting magnets were adjusted. The final result was a deviation table showing the compass error on all points of the compass. Normally the gyro compass would be used for navigating, but as machines break down, bolts unscrew and rum evaporates, gyro compasses wander. Without checking against an unerring magnetic compass, navigation using a single gyro compass could only be disastrous. Without a magnetic compass, three gyros would be required since the wanderer would be difficult to pick with only two. Now that we could navigate safely, we calibrated the W/T direction-finding set and the chernikeef log, a small propeller which records the distance run through the water.

We turned in semi-circles and circles with varying degrees of rudder at varying speeds, noting times, distances and diameters. Results of such turning trials are most important for it is essential to have an accurate idea of the ship's capabilities, especially when ships of vastly different sizes are manoeuvring together. During these activities the degaussing (the demagnetizing procedure which renders a ship safe from magnetic mines) depth charge and firefighting trials were carried out. We approached the boom at the eastern end of the Solent where one round was fired from each gun as a preliminary test. Where the shots fell was of no consequence and I would not be surprised if a few are still on their way.

Our two days of trials completed we returned to the maker's yard. On the way an incident occurred which taught a lesson to my inexperienced navigator. The shipping tracks through Spithead and Southampton Water were marked by buoys of distinctive shape and colour and at night by lights of differing characteristics. As we passed a buoy on the starboard hand I noted a distance from the chart and, knowing our speed, calculated that it would be nine minutes before the next major alteration of course. After about five minutes, as we came abreast of a buoy, the navigator requested permission to make the big alteration. I said no. We both looked at the chart and he realized that the buoy in the channel had tricked him. He had taken no precaution by calculating time, by taking a check bearing from a land object near the beam, or by noting the markings of the buoy. However, he was to become an efficient navigator as the commission progressed.

The Australian High Commissioner, Mr S. M. Bruce, and his wife visited us with the Flag Officer-in-Charge, Southampton, Rear-Admiral R. G. Tillard. It was a pleasing gesture on the part of His Excellency, and I think too that he wanted to show Australia's appreciation of Britain's action in allowing the RAN to man five of their latest destroyers. He handed me a silk ensign which was a gift from Sir John Thornycroft, in whose yards *Norman* had been built.

After the weekend we proceeded again to Spithead, this time for further preliminary and acceptance trials, and intensive armament training. However, low visibility caused delays and so I took the opportunity to pay my official call on the Commander-in-Chief, Portsmouth, Admiral Sir William James. As a child he had been the model for a famous painting by his grandfather, Millais, which was used later as a Pears soap advertisement on the hoardings. More recently he had been bombed out of his office and had established his headquarters in HMS *Victory*, which always bore his flag. So it was a special moment in my life to be piped over the side of *Victory* and to be received in Nelson's cabin.

The weather cleared, enabling me to fire ten rounds per gun from the shelter of the boom before returning to Southampton. After a further steaming trial the gear casings were lifted for inspection. The ship's turbines were fast revolving and had to be geared down to speeds within the practical limits of the ship's propellers. Gears are a vital link in the propulsion chain and so even the circulating lubricating oil had to be thoroughly filtered, and partially refined, before re-entering the gear casing. The blades of the turbine could not be reversed for the ship to go astern. Thus a separate astern turbine was required.

With turbine blading and gearing 100 per cent effective, Monday, 29 September, was to be the real start of the commission. We did our high speed trials on passage to Devonport with air cover provided. The trials showed everything up to specifications and the Hun failed to interfere. Near our destination Thornycroft's manager came to me with a crumpled piece of paper on which was written 'Received Warship No. 235', and asked me to sign, which I did, gladly.

We sailed up the Hamoaze, past Drake's bowling green and duly arrived at Devonport dockyard where the few Thornycroft foremen disembarked. That evening the Commander-in-Chief at Plymouth invited me to dinner. I was flattered that my host, Admiral of the

Fleet, Sir Charles Forbes, had a cap full of headaches, yet found time to interest himself in RAN matters. The scenes of destruction as we drove up to the residence were indescribable. Plymouth had taken some hard knocks and there were many more to come.

The following day we raised steam before leaving harbour to escort the cruiser HMS *Kent* to Scapa Flow. With cold steam turbines it was not possible to get under way until they were heated and expansion had taken place, otherwise there was every chance that the turbine blades would be stripped. There was an incident during the middlewatch after our departure. The rods for the engine room telegraphs and the revolution indicator from the bridge to the engine room pass through the captain's sea cabin and so, even seated half asleep in an armchair, it did not take a Sherlock Holmes to know when something unusual was afoot and, judging by the turning shafts, something was. I was up the ladder in a bound and found that we were doing high speed to get back into station. I could not get a satisfactory explanation of the incident or why *Kent* had made a signal 'Stop skylarking'. This brought home to me forcibly that the holding of watchkeeping certificates by the younger officers did not mean that they were experienced. In time my trust in my very young officers increased, but in the months ahead my seniority usually made me senior officer of the escort, or some other activity, which gave added responsibility to me and therefore to my young officers of the watch. Fortunately I too was young and fit enough to keep an eye on things in the early days. Without further incident we entered Scapa Flow and secured to buoys.

I was to be given time and all facilities to convert a fine ship and 226 fine men into an efficient fighting unit. I was surrounded by enthusiasm and all seemed eager to learn. I too had a lot to learn, for although I had been well trained in peace, the war had been going for two years with me behind a desk. I had to adapt rapidly and get my 'worrying' priorities right — half of the worries would not occur, but to know which half was a problem.

We were progressing well until the end of the first

week in October when low visibility in the Flow caused the cancellation of our sub-calibre gunnery practice. It was the rule always to be full of fuel so I topped up from a tanker on the way back to my buoy. In the middle of my evening meal a signal arrived from Rear-Admiral Hamilton to repair on board. Hamilton informed me that the destroyer *Antelope*, with Sir Walter Citrine and a Trade Union Council delegation embarked, had broken down in Iceland en route for Archangel and that I was to proceed immediately to Seidisfiord to take over from *Antelope*. I was to arrive there before sunset the following day as the minefields were set to fire in the dark hours. The admiral inquired if I had the necessary charts. I admitted that I did not know, but said that I would pinch *Antelope*'s set if necessary. I hastened to remind him that my sub-calibre firing had been cancelled that morning and that in no way could I be considered battleworthy. He replied that he knew the position and that I was to let him know at what time I wanted the boom gate opened. He wished me God speed and I departed with the suspicion that I might well need some divine assistance.

The turbines were still hot and we had steam in one boiler, so we were able to get going while steam was raised in the other. It was pitch dark and the channel was narrow, but our night sight soon came good as we passed other ships at distances too close to be comfortable. The boom gate lights appeared and we were away. Fortunately the sea and swell were kind, but the reason for this generosity was soon obvious as we ran into a thick fog at thirty-two knots. The gunner (T) was officer of the first watch from 8 pm until midnight and appeared nervous, but I reassured him that as there were no friendly ships in the area, anything we rammed would be an enemy. By midday the following day the fog lifted and eventually a glistening Iceland appeared. Before sunset we had refuelled and were anchored close to *Antelope*. The average speed for the passage had been thirty-one knots, which at least was evidence that the main engines were fully effective.

It was late when *Antelope* hustled her VIPs on board *Norman*. Apparently the British government, in other

Right Hon. R. G. Casey

Commander Burrell, Director
Plans and Operations

HMAS *Norman* in tropical camouflage with 'signs of the sea showing plain' *(Australian War Memorial)*

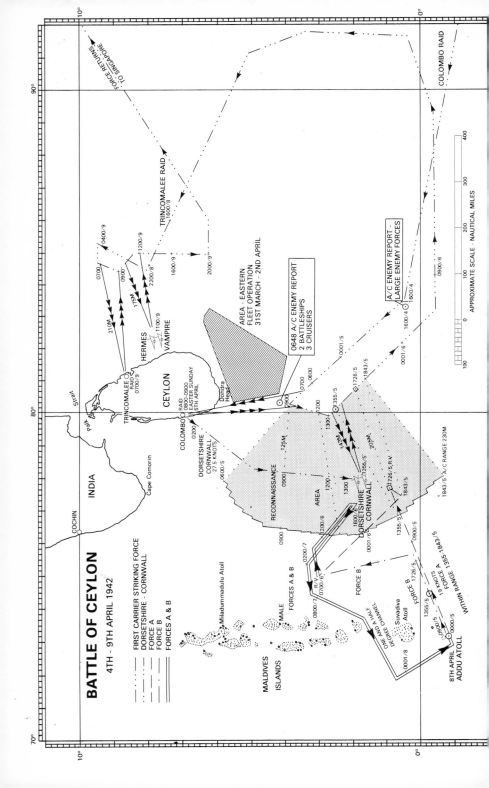

BATTLE OF CEYLON

4TH - 9TH APRIL 1942

- FIRST CARRIER STRIKING FORCE
- DORSETSHIRE - CORNWALL
- FORCE A
- FORCE B
- FORCES A & B

INDIA

Cape Comorin

COCHIN

Palk Strait

CEYLON

Dondra Head

COLOMBO RAID
0800-0900
EASTER SUNDAY
5TH APRIL

TRINCOMALEE
RAID
0700/9

TRINCOMALEE RAID
1600/8

COLOMBO RAID

FORCE RETURNS TO SINGAPORE

HERMES

VAMPIRE

0400/9
0700/

1100/9

1200/9

0900/

2200/8*

1600/9*

2000/9*

210M

175M

1100/9

AREA - EASTERN
FLEET OPERATION
31ST MARCH - 2ND APRIL

0648 A/C ENEMY REPORT
2 BATTLESHIPS
3 CRUISERS

A/C ENEMY REPORT
LARGE ENEMY FORCES

0700

0600

0900

1200

1355/5

1300

145M

202M

125M

RECONNAISSANCE

AREA

0900

1200

1300

1726/5, R.V.

1843/5

0001/6

DORSETSHIRE
CORNWALL

0001/5

0700/5

1726/5

1843/5

1600/4

1600/4

0001/6 *

0900/6

0001/5

DORSETSHIRE
CORNWALL
27.5 KNOTS

0600/5

1200/6

0200/7

R.V.
0700/6

1800/7

DORSETSHIRE
CORNWALL

1355/5

0900/5

1843/5 A/C RANGE 230M

FORCE B

FORCE B

19 KNOTS
FORCE A 1355-1843/5

1726/5

FORCE A

WITHIN RANGE

MALDIVES
ISLANDS

Miladummadulu Atoll

MALE

FORCES A & B

FORCES A & B

0800/7

Suvadiva
Atoll

ONE AND A HALF
DEGREE CHANNEL

0001/8

1355/5

0900/5

8TH APRIL
ADDU ATOLL

0000/5

APPROXIMATE SCALE - NAUTICAL MILES

100   0   100   200   300   400

words Churchill, considered it would be good for the Trade Union Council to have discussions in Moscow on employment problems. I was sufficiently narrow-minded to think that the value of such talks would not be commensurate with the loss of my precious ship and crew. I gave over my day-cabin to Sir Walter while the other five delegates dossed down on the wardroom settee and camp stretchers.

Setting sail at the crack of dawn on 8 October, I decided to give the Norwegian coast a wide berth, still keeping south of Bear Island (74 degrees north). With the arrival of the delegation in Russia already delayed I was required to go at my 'best speed', which was as fast as weather conditions and endurance would permit. We soon ran into rough weather and I found that the easiest method of judging the 'best speed' was by sitting in my sea-cabin where I could feel the reverberations of the main bulkheads and increase or decrease a knot or two as the situation required. I took the earliest opportunity to drop a homemade floating target and use it for some practice by the main armament, which at least removed any gun shyness from the younger hands.

At sea, to avoid being surprised, the forward gun mounting was kept manned day and night. As the magazines would not be manned until the 'alarm' rattlers were sounded, projectiles were kept in racks around the mounting. However, racks and ammunition soon became frozen. I had the bright idea of rigging up a steam hose to melt the ice but the weather had quite different ideas: it simply froze the steam.

My guests were not enjoying life in a destroyer. Sir Walter would come forward for a chat each day but I resisted the temptation to question the importance of his Russian visit. On the other hand, he complained that while the Admiralty had only allocated him a destroyer, in August the Prime Minister had been given the comfort of the new battleship *Prince of Wales* for his 'Four Freedoms' and 'Atlantic Charter' talks with Roosevelt in Newfoundland. After entering the White Sea the problem was to find the entrance to the Dvina River. The light vessel marking it had been removed, but things became clear when we sighted two Russian patrol boats coming downriver. They turned at the entrance and returned upstream and I followed. Approaching Archangel a Russian officer embarked and pointed out our jetty which was really just a mass of timber without bollards. I said goodbye to Sir Walter and his team and it was quite clear that he hoped for a bigger ship for his return. The cruiser HMS *Suffolk* and destroyers *Impulsive* and *Escapade* were in another arm of the harbour.

Two days later I was ordered to carry out an anti-submarine patrol off the entrance to the river and the next day received orders to return to the United Kingdom. However, near Bear Island, my cipher team produced a signal ordering me to return to Archangel — with such poor fighting ability it was no occasion to cheer. Apparently I was required to await the return of the trade union delegates. Instead of languishing in port while awaiting their return I was sent to patrol the entrance to the White Sea (there had been a report of a submarine sighted there on the surface) and to inspect Ionkanka and report on its suitability as a winter convoy anchorage.

I had difficulty in getting to sea — winter was setting in and the Dvina River had started to ice over. Fortunately the ship was heading down-stream when the engine room reported that the engines had to be stopped because the condenser inlets had become blocked with ice. This possibility had not crossed my mind. I set the chief on the technical trail regarding the design of condenser inlets. It was clear that the fitting of any ice-clearing arrangement by ship's staff was impractical. The locals informed us that the phenomenon only occurred during the first two weeks of the freeze when small floes tend to float at varying depths. The practical answer was to use very slow speed. Should choking occur, the ship should gather slight sternway and run the main circulators as slowly as possible. This should result in almost immediate clearance. If this failed, the Lord's Prayer might help. Perhaps casting four anchors over the stern and praying for dawn would have been a more seamanlike answer.

We eventually made it to sea and I returned to

harbour two days later with still no word of Sir Walter Citrine. There was nothing for it but to wait, but there were better places than Archangel in which to stay, especially with *Norman* guarded by rifle-carrying sentries who, incidentally, were women. I had a single run ashore and found it a thoroughly depressing town. There were no men to be seen and the women shrouded in black all seemed very old. The town's roads were made of wood. The chief and I tried a café and ordered fried eggs in sign language and we were each given a frying pan with four small eggs sizzling away. My medical officer recently reminded me of another incident. He wrote:

> We drank quite a lot of the local Vodka in a small cafe following the example set by some friendly Russians seated nearby. It seemed to be quite innocuous but one of the party fell flat on his face in the snow after we left. He then became quite violent, mounted a boy's bicycle, and despite all our efforts disappeared at high speed into the night. We ran after him but he had gone, heaven knew where! We got him back eventually, courtesy of the local commissars.

At last, on 27 October, Sir Walter and his team were seen approaching. Sir Walter embraced me and, not a little taken aback, I said that I thought that we were the last people he would have hoped to meet. He replied, 'Commander, you do not know the sanitary situation in Russia'. The imminent capture of Moscow had caused the Russian government and the Trades Union Convention to retreat to Kuibyshev where apparently things were rather primitive. At least my bathroom facilities were new. Victor Kravchenko, in his book *I Chose Freedom*,[21] stated that he happened to travel in the same train as the delegation and that attempts were made to protect it from the truth of Russian living conditions, but that nothing could hide the tattered and hungry peasants to be seen from the carriage window.

We departed on 27 October and were thankful that the voyage back to Scotland was without incident and the weather almost benevolent. Before landing the delegation in Scrabster Roads, Sir Walter presented me with a black lacquer cigarette box, embossed with a Pushkin fable scene. He said it was the first time the Trades Union Council had made a presentation. I have yet to learn if the conference in Russia achieved anything, and I still doubt the wisdom of sending out into enemy waters a ship whose only fighting attribute was high speed in retreat.

Back in Scapa Flow I sent a parcel over to Admiral Hamilton with some samples of vodka and caviare (it was rather like giving an apple to the teacher, but I was not to know that I would serve under him as his deputy when he was Chief of Naval Staff after the war). The admiral asked me to supper on Sunday night with several of his contemporaries who wanted to hear first hand the story of the Archangel affair. With the serving of Russian delicacies, it was a warming evening after the nights in Archangel.

At Scapa Flow 'working-up' continued in earnest, culminating in full-calibre high-angle and low-angle firings, day and night torpedo firings, anti-submarine exercises and efficiency tests, damage control exercises and seamanship drills — in fact a thorough run-through of our various capabilities. At this stage there was every indication that my 226 officers and men would develop into a fine fighting unit. An unusual day's activity was to proceed to Wick and bring His Royal Highness Prince Olaf of Norway to Scapa Flow. He took a lively interest in everything aboard and thoroughly enjoyed the battle with the elements as we passed through the Pentland Firth.

The finale was to proceed to the appropriately named Bloody Foreland on the extreme north-west of Ireland where, with destroyers *Icarus* and *Faulkner*, we rendezvoused with the mighty *Nelson* and escorted her to the Scapa Flow entrance. I was then detached to Gourock for a boiler inspection as some minor defects were getting beyond our repair facilities.

At Gourock, on about 1 December, we received news of the loss of *Sydney* on 19 November, about 150 miles off Carnarvon in Western Australia. The story is well known: the armed merchant cruiser *Kormoran*, posing as the *Straat Malakka* with Dutch colours, had sunk *Sydney* without one survivor. *Kormoran* too had sunk as a result of the short action, but 315 of her crew survived. I knew Captain Burnett very well. He was particularly careful and efficient, which made the course of events quite inexplicable to me.

The day before we left Gourock was 7 December 1941 — the day that Japan attacked Pearl Harbor. I, and many others, were infused with renewed confidence that the Axis would now be defeated and I knew that the staff conferences in which I had played a small part while in Washington would begin to pay great dividends. However, the immediate future brought disappointing local news.

It was found necessary for *Norman* to return to Thornycroft's at Southampton to make good defects at the shipbuilder's expense and we arrived back at the yard two weeks before Christmas. The defects in the boilers turned out to be serious and were to take three weeks so I was able to give seven days' leave to each watch. It was surprising that serious defects should have arisen in such a new ship. The 'N' class was a new design with extremely long boilers and this seemed to have caused unexpected stresses and strains. However, it was fortunate that these showed up early in the commission.

The opportunity was taken to give me four extra Oerlikon short range anti-aircraft guns and to change my 286M radar set to a 286P. Changing the letter did nothing to increase efficiency but, to its credit, the one day it was really needed it earned its keep.

This enforced pause gave us time to take stock. The Admiralty plan was to form the 'N' class destroyers into the Seventh Destroyer Flotilla under Captain (D) Steve Arliss in *Napier*. Commander Max Joshua Clark commanded *Nizam* and Commander Rosenthal *Nestor*. *Nepal*, to be commanded by Commander F. B. Morris, was still under construction.

The day after our return to the shipyard we learned of the loss of the *Prince of Wales* and *Repulse* and the Japanese landings on the Malay Peninsula. In December Burma was invaded; Guam, Wake Island and Penang were occupied and Hong Kong capitulated. Those weighty events are not part of my story but I can admit that the skill of the first line Japanese pilots and the range of their aircraft surprised me and many others. In many spheres we badly underestimated the expertise of our opponents and paid the penalty.

My short refit and leave period ended on 4 January 1942. After checking my degaussing coils on the range and the main armament director, I was ordered to escort HMS *Ascania*, an armed merchant cruiser, to Milford Haven in Wales preparatory to forming part of the escort of troop convoy WS 15 to Freetown. The old 15-inch gun battleship *Resolution*, the flagship of Vice-Admiral Tait, was to give the heavy protection to the convoy and the destroyers *Norman*, *Garland* and *Anthony* screened her as we left on 12 January to join the convoy which had already been bombed in the south Irish Sea. We ran into heavy weather and the composition of the escort kept changing until on 17 January we joined the convoy; the anti-submarine screen was then *Norman* (with myself as senior officer of the escort), *Boreas* and *Demirhissar* which was later to join the Turkish Navy. It was very weak protection for a battleship and troopships.

Oil-fuel for destroyers was always a problem on a long voyage, and it was decided to release one destroyer at a time to proceed at high speed to Ponta Delgada in the Azores to fuel and then rejoin as quickly as possible. I was the second destroyer to be detached. My record of the visit sounds refreshing but was tempered by an intelligence report that two U-boat wireless transmissions placed them within a hundred miles of the convoy. I wrote:

It was a beautiful day, in striking contrast to the gales of the preceding week. Sunshine, green fields and Portuguese colouring combined with the prospect of fresh fruit and eggs gave new life to the ship's company, not entirely fresh after keeping alert in two watches under exposed conditions for some time. The Consular Shipping Adviser was most helpful. Calls were exchanged with the Portuguese destroyer

Lima. Her captain, a keen student of Nelson, made us feel welcome and left no doubt as to his sympathies. The moment fuelling ceased I was off at speed in ideal conditions to rejoin the convoy. It was obvious that the providor had heavy trading in oranges, bananas and pineapples.

Earlier we had passed the island of Flores and I recalled the brave naval action of Sir Richard Grenville in HMS *Revenge*, immortalized by Tennyson. I was soon to be in company with the latest HMS *Revenge*, another of the senile 'R' class battleships.

When it was *Demirhissar*'s turn to nip into Ponta Delgada there occurred a most stupid accident. While the captain was ashore talking to the consular shipping adviser, the harbour master required *Demirhissar* to shift berth. The first lieutenant took the pilot up to the bridge. The pilot ordered, in merchant navy language, 'Full ahead' — 40,000 horse-power was being built up before 'full astern' could be ordered. The ship's stem hit the dock wall and changed its knife edge into an S-shape. It was a most inconvenient time to learn such a lesson. When she rejoined she had to report that the sea noises from the bent bow made her anti-submarine set useless.

However, luck was on our side and WS 15 arrived in Freetown on 25 January without loss. Throughout the voyage I had been considering the right action to take if one of the troopships were torpedoed, a topic discussed at the staff college. I had an admiral in *Resolution*, so the responsibility was his, but there could be some occasions when the onus was on me. I knew the unpalatable answer was to leave the men in the boats and rafts to their fate and, when safe to do so, inform the operating authority so that help could be sent.

It became clear that the Seventh Destroyer Flotilla was to serve in the Indian Ocean, which cheered the ship's company for they would meet the enemy directly threatening Australia. *Norman* was full of fuel by sunset and was ordered to sail next morning for Simonstown at best speed, fuelling at Point Noire in French Equatorial Africa en route. This was pleasant sailing with a tanker awaiting our pleasure in a French outpost of the Empire. We embarked provisions, including goat's meat. The thought of fresh meat was cheering until at sea a day later I noticed the goat's meat being fed to the sharks. On inquiry the medical officer had declared it unfit for human consumption owing to its strong smell. I was able to pull Dr Simon's leg many times when, some years later, I discovered that freshly killed goat characteristically has a strong odour. Averaging twenty-two knots, I rounded the Cape of Good Hope and entered the Royal Navy dockyard at Simonstown on 3 February 1942.

The world war was being waged furiously, but I was living in a very restricted realm, oblivious to many happenings elsewhere. The medical officer was the ship's informer, listening to the BBC radio and disseminating anything of importance. Our immediate concern was the Japanese advance through Malaya which had now reached Singapore city itself.

I had orders to sail for Addu Atoll, fuelling at Mauritius and the Seychelles en route. Addu Atoll was well placed strategically at the southern end of the Maldive Islands, about 450 miles south-west of Colombo, and was being developed as a fleet base. Secrecy regarding its existence as a base was tight and we were to have good reason to be thankful that it remained so.

I did not make Port Louis in Mauritius but instead was ordered to Durban. The reason became obvious as I approached the channel on 13 February. My old convoy WS 15 was entering harbour and I was to join the escort for part of the convoy's next leg through the Mozambique Channel where U-boats were having some successes.

The ocean escort for WS 15 was an armed merchant cruiser, *Worcestershire*, and the light cruiser *Ceres*. I was bound for the Seychelles and oil-fuel consumption was a problem but Captain Hopkinson of *Worcestershire* wanted me to stay with him for as long as possible. His ship had diesel engines and so we discussed fuelling at sea which in both our navies was in its infancy. We had no special equipment and therefore the only method available was to use lengths of canvas water hose to transfer the diesel. While fuelling, station-keeping was maintained by the use of a hemp spring with a towing point abreast my bridge. The operation was a success and although there may have been little strain on the spring, there was much on the chief quartermaster and me, for keeping a safe distance without parting the hose did not permit any lapse in concentration.

I was able to remain as escort until 22 February when I had to break off for Port Victoria in the Seychelles. I had only 21 per cent fuel remaining on arrival which meant that I had no margin for an emergency en route.

There was no time to enjoy the beauty of Port Victoria, though it seemed to have all the quiet attributes of a delectable tropical isle. When we had fuelled I pressed on to Addu Atoll where on the 26th I was ordered to retrace my steps and join convoy DM 3 the following day. No sooner had I joined than I had to escort *Ramillies* (another aged 'R') to Addu Atoll to fuel. We were at sea again before dark and saw the convoy safely to Colombo, with only one incident: at dawn action stations one morning, a suspicious shape was seen ahead; but first light revealed it as a Maldive Island dhow. That time of day is the most critical. To be silhouetted against the light of dawn is precarious in the extreme. Later in the war, efficient radar reduced this danger considerably.

Arriving at Colombo on 4 March, we were surprised to find in harbour ships returning AIF troops of the 6th and 7th Divisions from the Middle East. *Hobart* had arrived that day and I made a signal to Captain Howden requesting a convenient time to pay my respects. I had breakfast with Harry and talked to a few officers, but they obviously were too busy for a long chat. The atmosphere, from the captain down, seemed somewhat strange and, later on, when the facts were made known, I realized that there had been good reason for it. I was completely unaware of the ordeals *Hobart* had been through and the naval disasters connected with the Japanese occupation of the Netherlands East Indies. I did not know of the Battle of the Java Sea, the loss of *Perth*, the heavy bombing of *Hobart* before breaking out through Sunda Strait, or that *Hobart* the previous day had landed refugees recovered from Padang and that they were lucky to be alive. It was no wonder they were all a little different.

After the debacle at Singapore and the Netherlands East Indies, it was clear now that Ceylon was under direct threat. Admiral Somerville, who was to assume command of the Eastern Fleet being formed there, was very conscious of the strategic value of Ceylon. In enemy hands communications to the Middle East and India from the Cape, and from Australia, would be in grave danger. The same lines of communication would be in great danger too if the Japanese gained a foothold in Madagascar.

Soon Admiral Somerville would have under his orders the old, but recently modernized, battleship *Warspite*, two large carriers, *Indomitable* and *Formidable*, the small carrier *Hermes*, the Third Battle Squadron of battleships *Resolution*, *Ramillies*, *Royal Sovereign* and *Revenge*, five cruisers, sixteen destroyers (including *Norman*), and seven submarines. Although endowed with aggressive spirit, it was not a formidable array, especially since the air component was only about one hundred planes. In Colombo there were a few long-range reconnaissance aircraft. Recently arrived Hurricane fighters would be able to provide some air protection.

As far as the other 'N' class destroyers were concerned, my knowledge was sketchy, but I knew that *Napier* and *Nizam* were in the eastern Mediterranean in late 1941, and I had been in company with the third 'N', *Nestor*, in Gourock. I did not know that these sister ships had left for the Indian Ocean after bombarding Bardia on New Year's Eve, and were the last RAN ships to leave the Mediterranean.

I departed Colombo and arrived in the attractive tropic harbour of Trincomalee on 12 March to find that I had joined my flotilla at last — there were *Napier* and *Nizam*. I played some tennis and had a good chat at the Naval Officers Club with Captain Steve Arliss, RN, on Sober Island which was, of course, a most inappropriate name.

Meanwhile, the Eastern Fleet was congregating and

fleet exercising was the order of the day. (See the back endpaper map.) At first I was operating with *Royal Sovereign* (the 'tiddly quid') and *Ramillies*, but later we rejoined the Third Battle Squadron at Addu Atoll.

On 28 March the commander-in-chief at Colombo received an intelligence report which confirmed that an attack by a heavy Japanese force including carriers was imminent. As yet air reconnaissance from Ceylon had nothing to report, but all units of the Eastern Fleet were ordered to rendezvous south of Dondra Head, the most southern point of Ceylon, on 31 March. I have since gathered that our battle plan was to inflict damage by night air attacks, with the help of the radar of the two carriers, and that surface action was to be avoided. In fact the British official history states that Admiral Somerville 'was determined at all costs to avoid being attacked by the enemy's carrier aircraft and, because of his inferior strength, to decline fleet action. He knew that, whatever the weakness of his present fleet might be, it was the last that Britain could send into the Indian Ocean.' [22] It is my contention that Admiral Somerville's actions conflict with that statement. *Warspite*, the carriers, two cruisers and six destroyers were formed into Force A. Force B comprised the 'Wobbly Rs', *Royal Sovereign*, *Resolution*, *Ramillies*, *Revenge*, three cruisers and five destroyers (including *Norman*). *Dorsetshire*, refitting at Colombo, joined us on the first day of April. The next day, with no further enemy information, the main body set course to the south-west to replenish at Addu Atoll, *Dorsetshire* and *Cornwall* being despatched to Colombo and *Hermes*, with *Vampire*, to Trincomalee.

Arriving at the atoll at noon on 4 April, Force A was ordered to fuel first, but no sooner had ships started to replenish than an enemy report was received. A Catalina reported a strong force 360 miles south-east of Dondra Head, but was shot down before transmitting details of the enemy. (See the Battle of Ceylon map.) Force A got away by midnight but Somerville knew that he could not get back in time to prevent the bombing of Ceylon. However, he stood a chance of making night torpedo attacks if air reconnaissance could find the enemy. He was in a most unenviable position as he did not know the strength of the opposition, but there could be little doubt that it was considerable. Furthermore, if our fleet reconnaissance aircraft were sighted, then obviously the Japanese would know that we were not far away. Force B sailed the following morning to rejoin Force A, and *Hermes* and *Vampire* were ordered to sea as were the remaining shipping in Colombo so that they might not be trapped in harbour. *Dorsetshire* and *Cornwall* were ordered to rendezvous with Force A.

On Easter Sunday morning, 5 April, Force A was making ground to the east-north-east in the general direction of the enemy, whose exact position was not known. It was to be a great day for the Japanese, but it could have been greater. Between 8 and 9 am the balloon went up: Colombo was attacked by over a hundred aircraft. Fortunately, neither the city, the airfield, nor the harbour facilities were seriously damaged. The Hurricane fighters from the last ferry trip by *Indomitable* proved invaluable and, although not fully appreciated at the time, their efforts seriously affected the Japanese carrier operations for the remainder of the war. Many Hurricanes were lost but only after shooting down at least an equivalent number of enemy aircraft. Force B had sailed from Addu Atoll as the report on the bombing of Colombo was being received and set course towards Force A, about 120 miles distant.

Judging by the number of aircraft in the Ceylon attack it should have been clear that a strong carrier force was about. Force A was closed up at action stations all day. At about 7 am Somerville had received a report of two battleships and three cruisers about 100 miles south of Dondra Head but he was still in the greatest need of accurate intelligence, which was not forthcoming. He had no idea where the enemy carriers were, but pressed on towards the rendezvous with *Dorsetshire* and *Cornwall*. It was not until 3 pm, when a reconnaissance aircraft reported sighting survivors in the sea, that the admiral realized that the two 8-inch cruisers had been sunk.

At 5.26 pm, with little daylight remaining, Somerville ordered Force A to retreat to the south-west for an hour and then for both forces to join early next morning, Monday, 6 April, some 230 miles to the north-west. It required the breaking of wireless silence to pass this order to Force B. I am surprised that the enemy did not pick up this coded message and obtain a bearing using their direction-finding sets. That Easter Sunday both sides were surrounded by a dense fog of war. The true picture, one which would have shocked all of us from Somerville down if we had known, was that we were in close proximity to Admiral Nagumo's First Carrier Striking Force, the same force, with the exception of one aircraft carrier, that had crippled Pearl Harbor and more recently had decimated Darwin. (The movements of this force are shown on the back end-paper map.)

Nagumo's force comprised five aircraft carriers, with 105 fighters and 123 bombers, four battleships, three cruisers, and eight destroyers; with only one exception the carriers and battleships could make twenty-six knots. It is certain that the Eastern Fleet would have been overwhelmed in an encounter with this strong and experienced force. I have plotted the relative positions of the Japanese force and Force A to see how close it was to disaster. (See the Battle of Ceylon map.) Assuming 230 miles as the enemy air reconnaissance range, my estimate is that Force A came within range at 1.55 pm and was at its closest, about 200 miles, at 5.26 pm. The range then continued to open until it passed out of range at 6.43 pm. It was lucky not to be sighted in those four and three-quarter hours. I would have thought the position and course of *Dorsetshire* and *Cornwall*, accurately marked by their conspicuous javelin-shaped wakes, would have given Nagumo a clue to its position. After the Colombo raid Nagumo steered to the west-south-west for four hours, no doubt searching, but it is not known whether, when he turned to the south-east at 1 pm, he was still searching for us or retiring. Having rendezvoused early Monday morning, Forces A and B boldly set course to the south-east. Somerville's intention seemed clear and there was a chance of a fleet encounter. In the situation report to his force, he concluded with his famous sentence: 'There is many a fine tune played on an old fiddle'. The tune would have had to be fine indeed if our fiddles were not to be drowned out by the orchestra opposing us. However, by sunset there had been no sign of the enemy and course was reversed. I could take off my battle bowler. We continued to the west, passed through the Vieman-du Channel in the Maldives, and returned to Addu Atoll from the north-west. Fortunately, the bold advance to the eastward on the Monday turned out to be without risk. Admiral Nagumo had continued his south-easterly course and so the two forces were drawing apart at a fast rate. Had Admiral Nagumo known of the fleet base at Addu Atoll, we would have been in great trouble.

In the meantime Vice-Admiral Kurita, in the carrier *Ryujo* and accompanied by a cruiser force, had a field day in the north-west of the Bay of Bengal, sinking twenty ships unopposed. The loss that week of valuable merchant ships, warships and their ship's companies, and the damage to shore installations, were hard blows.

On 9 April Trincomalee naval base came under heavy air attack. Although shore-based aircraft had detected the Nagumo carrier force eastward of the base in time for *Hermes* and *Vampire* to put to sea again, they were detected and sunk. It was now obvious that a very powerful force had been in our vicinity on Easter Sunday. Admiral Nagumo and his force left the Bay of Bengal never to return. The Battle of Midway on 4 June saw to that.

We can be thankful that Nagumo's search patterns were sketchy. His aim was to damage Trincomalee and Colombo, and to sink merchant and war ships in their harbours. His aim, therefore, should have been to find and destroy the Eastern Fleet. At 4 pm on Easter Saturday he knew that his force had been sighted and from that could have deduced that harbours would be cleared of shipping. Nagumo could have spent days searching for the Eastern Fleet since his fleet had refuelled at sea only a few days earlier. It was providential that the existence of the base at Addu Atoll had remained a well-kept secret.

The circumstances surrounding the sinking of the two cruisers *Dorsetshire* and *Cornwall* are still somewhat clouded. As shown on the map, they departed Colombo at 2 am on Easter Sunday with orders to join Force A. From dawn they were well within enemy reconnaissance range and their chances of remaining undetected were slim. They were sunk at 1.55 pm.

At Addu Atoll, I learned, from speaking with survivors, that without warning dive bombers had come out of the sun and sunk both ships without a shot being fired. Historians cannot agree whether they were sighted during the forenoon. One has stated that *Cornwall* knew she had been sighted, but that the senior officer, *Dorsetshire*, did not pass the information on to Somerville because he was following 'the orthodox principle of maintaining wireless silence at sea'.[23] This is nonsense. Why keep silent when the enemy knows your position, course and speed! If Somerville had known of the sighting he could have diverted the cruisers to the west; he needed something positive to be able to estimate the enemy's position. However, considering all the evidence, including material in the Public Record Office, London, it appears that the cruisers were unaware that they had been sighted[24] and that *Dorsetshire* did open fire and began to report the attack before sinking. Battle Summary No. 15 (BR 1736 (9)) is not yet available to the public.

To substantiate my earlier contention that Somerville's actions were in conflict with his determination 'at all costs to avoid being attacked by enemy aircraft', I draw my evidence from an examination of the map. This shows the area which could have been covered by Nagumo's reconnaissance aircraft. Force A was within that range from 1.55 pm until 6.43 pm on 5 April. It was fortuitous that the enemy altered course to the southeast at 1 pm, for had it continued on the SSW course, Force A would have been only about 160 miles from the enemy by 5.26 pm. Enemy aircraft were appearing on British radar screens. Force A escaped disaster only by faulty Japanese air reconnaissance.

The next day, Forces A and B combined and, without the slightest knowledge of the enemy's whereabouts, sallied forth to the south-east looking for trouble. Once more, a sighting from the air would have meant annihilation. Somerville was quite unaware that the enemy had withdrawn eastward. The comment from the British official historian neatly encapsulates the affair:

> Thus, when the need to build up an Eastern Fleet arose, it had to be done hurriedly, and could only be done with what ships could be scraped together from other sources. The first attempt ended in disaster, and the second very nearly ended in a greater one...and one may feel that the goddess of fortune aided his [Somerville's] escape.[25]

With the fleet in Addu Atoll, some vital decisions had to be made by the Admiralty and Admirals Somerville and Layton (C-in-C Ceylon). It was clear that the battlefleet would not be given adequate air protection in the Ceylon and Addu Atoll area and 'Wobbly Rs' age was showing badly. To further hinder us, U-boats were appearing off the west coast of India. As a first measure, it was decided to send the old battleships to Kilindini (the port of Mombasa), while Force A went to Bombay. I joined the latter and sailed on 9 April for the city with the ornamental Gateway of India. During that short time in Bombay the plans for basing the Eastern Fleet on Kilindini were put into effect. This was an admission of defeat, but a wise move nevertheless. Before returning to our new base at Kilindini, I was included in a force required to operate to the north of Madagascar to provide distant cover for a combined operation.

The Battle of Ceylon: the last minutes of HM ships *Cornwall (top)*, *Hermes (centre)* and *Dorsetshire (bottom)*. All three were photographed by Japanese dive bombers from 1st Carrier Striking Force. *Imperial War Museum/W. P. Trotter)*

Operation 'Stream-Line-Jane'—*Norman* escorting the troop convoy

HMAS *Bataan*

7
HMAS *Norman*
1942–43

In February 1942 Britain could not have been sure that pressure exerted by the US Fleet in the north Pacific would require the Japanese to retain significant naval forces there. Consequently, there was a strong possibility that the enemy would return to the Indian Ocean in force. The first class anchorage at Diego Suarez in northern Madagascar, could they obtain it, would allow them, in conjunction with the base at Singapore, to control the sea communications of the Indian Ocean. Supplies and reinforcements to the Middle East and India could easily have been seriously disrupted. It is not surprising that General Smuts described Madagascar as the 'key to the safety of the Indian Ocean'.

Vichy French forces were in control of the island at that time. A Free French expedition to capture the island was considered impracticable but reinforcements en route to the Middle East could do the job without much loss of time. Accordingly, Operation 'Ironclad' was put in train to capture the main asset of Madagascar — Diego Suarez and its fine harbour. The rest of the island could be captured later. The operation was to be commanded by Major-General Sturges, Royal Marines, with Admiral Syfret as the naval commander. The naval component was *Ramillies*, *Illustrious*, two cruisers, eleven destroyers, some minesweepers and fifteen assault ships. I was to be in the distant covering force, an Eastern Fleet responsibility.

The first troops, including commandos, landed on 5 May 1942. The main landing was on the west coast, enabling the troops to march nine miles across the isthmus and approach the town from the rear. Although 400 lives were lost, the operation was considered a success.

With Diego Suarez now in our hands, we of the covering force returned to Kilindini on the 10th. At this time Malta was under siege and an operation was planned to break it. The plan provided for some store ships departing Haifa in Palestine, to join others from Alexandria and, under escort, to try to force an entry. A similar operation was to be carried out from Gibraltar in the hope that this would cause some dilemma in the Italian command and so enable at least one of the convoys to get through. To assist, it was decided to borrow units from the Eastern Fleet. *Birmingham*, *Newcastle* and nine destroyers (including we three 'N's) were detailed.

On 25 May I left Kilindini in the first group with *Birmingham*, *Pakenham*, *Fortune* and *Nizam*. The reason for steaming north was kept a secret from us all and it was only at Aden, when the navigating officer returned from shore with the latest notices to mariners affecting the Red Sea, that we knew our destination. The Suez Canal pilot reminded me that the ships' names were secret and that I had failed to cover up a brass name plate by the jacob's ladder. An unexpected sight at Suez was the old battleship *Centurion* (which had been embarking a load of flour). With wooden stage props to alter her superstructure she was supposed to resemble *Nelson* or *Rodney*. We all thought the subterfuge would not fool anyone, but we were wrong. It was also strange to see wooden anti-aircraft guns on the banks of the Suez Canal at frequent intervals. I assumed that from the air they would appear to be the real thing.

At Alexandria there was little time to check on the Yacht Club or Pastroudi's cakes, but we did see many of our Australian friends. I had an opportunity to call on my old commander, Eric Bush, then a captain in command of the cruiser *Euryalus*. It felt strange while reading the church service on Sunday to see contrails of enemy photo reconnaissance planes above us. Nothing could be done as our fighters could not get up to their height in time. We no doubt appeared in the photographs.

The orders which had brought me to Alexandria concerned Operation 'Vigorous', the code-name for our endeavour to supply Malta from the east by eleven supply ships. Simultaneously, Operation 'Harpoon', a similar operation from the west, was to be launched. It was hoped that the two convoys would reach Malta on successive days. 'Vigorous' required four merchantmen to sail from Haifa and be joined off Alexandria by three others and *Centurion*. A four-ship diversionary convoy would precede the main convoy, which it would later join. The combined escorts were seven cruisers, one anti-aircraft cruiser (my old ship *Coventry*), twenty-six destroyers, a few corvettes and minesweepers. Rear-Admiral Vian was in command in the cruiser *Cleopatra*, with Acting-Admiral Sir Henry Harwood (of River Plate fame) as commander-in-chief ashore.

It was an ambitious project when one considered geography, the state of the land war, and the strength of the opposition. We were without battleships or carriers, and dependent upon shore-based aircraft for distant reconnaissance, attacks on enemy surface craft and air cover for the convoy. We expected to have to contend with Italian heavy warships based at Taranto, continuous German and Italian air attacks, enemy submarines and motor torpedo boats (MTBs). However, we did have nine submarines and expected assistance from them in reporting enemy movements and perhaps sinking a worthwhile target.

I was allocated to the Haifa part of the convoy. We sailed, escorting four merchantmen, on 13 June and were to join the other seven supply ships and *Centurion* in the middle of the night. However, this manoeuvre was facilitated as night turned into day with the aid of enemy flares. The deception had not worked.

Throughout the next day the convoy was bombed. One ship was damaged and returned to Alexandria and a straggler was sent back also, but it was sunk by German bombers en route. At night the MTB threat developed from Crete. By 11.45 pm Vian knew that the Italian heavy ships had left Taranto and could make contact early next morning. He was ordered to hold on until 2 am and then to reverse course.

The presence of *Duke of York*, alias *Centurion*, was of great benefit to all except *Centurion*. Her appearance from the air was so realistic that she copped more than her fair share of bombs: we would see her disappear in a great cloud of water spouts, and then, after an interminable time, her bow would appear and she was seen to be steaming serenely on.

A bomber was shot down near me on this first day. I was ordered to recover the pilot and check for codes and ciphers. I was not particularly happy about stopping even for a minute and nothing of value was found. We buried him after dark, when I read part of the burial service by the light of a small torch. Afterwards I realized that I had read the wrong passage — 'ashes to ashes and dust to dust'.

At 2 am on the 15th our large formation turned through 180 degrees as ordered. Two hours later our cruiser *Newcastle* was torpedoed, but struggled on. The destroyer *Hardy* suffered the same fate, but had to be destroyed to prevent her falling into enemy hands. By dawn two Italian battleships and four cruisers were known to be 200 miles to the north-west. The commander-in-chief ordered the convoy to turn and carry on towards Malta. Then our bombers from Malta attacked the enemy fleet with some success. However, with the enemy only 150 miles away, at 9.40 am we were ordered to retreat again. Before noon, after an optimistic assessment of the attack on the battle fleet, we were once more ordered to resume onward passage. Shortly after turning, the cruiser *Birmingham* was hit by a bomb. She was able to continue, but the small destroyer *Airedale* was not as fortunate and had to be sunk.

When a particularly heavy raid was in progress, screening ships would be ordered to fire an umbrella barrage over the convoy; consequently, as the operation progressed, anti-aircraft ammunition became an important factor. Individual ships were allowed to ration their ammunition and keep a reserve for self-protection.

Destroyers on the screen took individual action to avoid torpedoes. The tracks were clearly visible and usually it was safer to turn and steam parallel to them in the same direction as the torpedo. In the commotion of a bombing and low-level air attack, often the sighting of approaching torpedo tracks was the first indication of danger. The torpedo is actually some distance ahead of its track, so a split-second decision is required on whether to turn towards it or away from it. On one occasion I turned away on a course parallel to the tracks, moving out of the screen. I then had to decide when it would be safe to turn back and regain station. The size of the screen provided good anti-submarine protection for the main body. Although our position was known accurately, no concerted effort was made by U-boats. Later there was one successful, undetected attack.

At midday, the commander-in-chief, lacking solid intelligence reports, came to the conclusion that Admiral Vian should be left to decide whether to continue. This direction was not received until 2.20 pm; we continued westward. Admiral Vian no doubt was cheered by a reconnaissance report that the enemy fleet was retiring towards Taranto. The commander-in-chief had signalled: 'Now is the chance to get convoy to Malta' [26] and asked for the state of fuel and ammunition. From 5.20 pm to 7.20 pm air assaults, as well as torpedo attacks, were particularly heavy. *Nestor* received a direct hit from a high-level bomber. When Vian reported that less than one-third of the ammunition remained, the commander-in-chief stepped in and ordered the return to Alexandria. Our original eleven supply ships were now down to seven plus *Centurion*. On our way back on the 16th, the cruiser *Hermione* was sunk by a U-boat — a depressing finale.

I was adjacent to *Nestor* on the screen when she was hit and it was obvious that her back had been broken. I half expected to be ordered to render assistance and I heard later that some of my sailors were disappointed that I did not break off to help. However, my captain (D) was the screen commander and so made the decisions. I knew Commander Rosenthal well and his engineer officer, Commander (E) Roger Parker, even better, and it was not pleasant to see *Nestor* stopped in the water, being passed by the entire convoy.

Commander Rosenthal told me later in Alexandria that he had made a silly mistake when he was taken off his stricken ship. On the bridge he kept two handbags, one with his mechanical treasures, such as automatic station keeper, screwdrivers, small spanners and minor inventions in the making, and another which contained his bank and cheque books, pens and papers. He picked up only one bag so that his treasures were now on the floor of the Mediterranean. Needless to say, he was not pleased.

The effort put into our operation was very great but we had failed. Poor *Centurion*, though still afloat, was so down by the bow she had to wait outside the harbour till her draught could be reduced. I know that we were all pleased to be on the other side of the screen to her. I have nothing but praise for my ship's company. During those exciting days we had no time to dwell on the risks that abounded, being fully occupied doing what we had been trained to do.

Our losses in the escort were heavy — *Hermione*, *Hasty*, *Airedale* and *Nestor*. While in actual convoy, only one supply ship was sunk. On the credit side the enemy lost her cruiser *Trento* and the battleship *Littoria* was damaged. I cannot find an estimate of air losses but they could only be slight, despite the high expenditure of ammunition. Apart from any close-range successes, kills would be sheer luck. Our submarines, through no fault of their own, did not happen to be at the right place at the right time.

A study of historical accounts shows that Operation 'Vigorous' was undertaken with all the risks involved well known and accepted. I am not, however, entirely happy with part of the execution. I hesitate to blame the commander-in-chief for his decision to abandon the operation, but I am far from sure that, with the enemy fleet no longer a menace and only one supply ship sunk when in convoy, it was a correct one. I can envisage three or four transports and *Centurion* surviving to be released for a night run to Malta. We escorts would not be hampered by slow shipping on a hurried run back to Alexandria. Admiral Vian simply obeyed orders, but I think a message to ships to keep their ammunition expenditure under close scrutiny could have been beneficial. I know I was quick on the 'check fire' buzzer. I lay blame on ships' captains for expending two-thirds of their ammunition in the first third of the operation. The umbrella barrage over the convoy, ordered by Vian, was obeyed too enthusiastically. All that can be said for the barrage is that it may have forced bombers to release their bombs at a greater height and therefore with less accuracy. While serving in the AA cruiser, *Coventry*, and carrying out 'Queen Bee' operations in *Devonshire*, I had realized that there would be no solution to the anti-aircraft problem until a proximity fuse became available. The principal value of the main armament when dealing with an air attack lay in a rapid-fire close barrage. This minimized the amount of ammunition used. With the possible exception of the cruisers, I cannot think it was the close-range weapons ammunition that had been expended heavily. There were very few low-level attacks. With the operations planned in full knowledge of the risks involved and with the acceptance of the losses which would result, I can only conclude that Operation 'Vigorous' should have been allowed to continue. The misinterpretation of Vian's reply that 'less than one-third of ammunition remained' is possibly to blame. Searching for a morsel of comfort, history shows us that aircraft withdrawn from Rommel's forces to knock us about became a valuable bonus to our Eighth Army in North Africa and thus helped its successful withdrawal.

R. G. Casey was now the United Kingdom Minister of State in Cairo but unfortunately there was no time for me to pay my respects. At the time things were going badly in the desert and within days Tobruk was to capitulate, with Major-General Klopper and the Second South African Division being taken prisoner. Alexandria and Cairo were already under threat.

We moved out on 22 June to pass through the Canal and rejoin the Eastern Fleet, and returned, rather crestfallen, to base on 8 July. The only bright spot about this time was the news that on 27 May the *Bismarck* had been sunk in the North Atlantic, unfortunately at the expense of the battle cruiser HMS *Hood*.

I mentioned earlier that I shared the flying-boat passage to the United States with an official of the Aspro company. He must have talked to the firm's ladies' auxiliary, for each month I would receive a parcel of goodies including a tin of toheroa soup and of course a packet of Aspro tablets. Gastronomically, my dinner parties were deemed a success as RAN ships were supplied with tinned salmon — toheroa soup followed by salmon mornay made a pleasant change. However, to this day I cannot stand the smell of herrings in tomato sauce!

Back now in the Indian Ocean, our minds turned once more to the Japanese. In early July 1942, Admiral King, United States Chief of Naval Operations, asked the First Sea Lord, Admiral Sir Dudley Pound, if he could create a diversion in the Bay of Bengal to draw attention away from an American offensive in the Solomons in early August. So was born Operation 'Stab', in which *Warspite*, *Illustrious* and *Formidable* with cruisers and destroyers (including *Napier*, *Nizam* and *Norman*) were to proceed to Ceylon and there simulate the departure of an expeditionary force to recapture the Andaman Islands. Dummy convoys were to sail from Colombo and two Indian ports.

We sailed on 20 July for another long trek across the Indian Ocean. En route, hurrying up a ladder through a hatch to the upper deck, I slipped and my shin struck the combing of the hatch. This gash took a couple of months to heal which made it clear that, apart from the shin being poorly supplied with blood, the lack of fresh food was slowly taking its toll. I wrote to my captain (D) and suggested that, if we could get hold of vitamin pills, the medical officer each week could work out the deficiency in the diet and prescribe the right number of pills for each man. I was told politely not to be frivolous and yet later in the war, that is exactly what happened in the US Navy in the Pacific.

On the way to Ceylon, Nobby Clark, commanding *Nizam*, achieved a dubious reputation when a bright light suddenly appeared ahead of him. His forward 4.7-inch mounting was closed up and the order to fire was given but, despite several shells, the rising Venus continued to climb.

Occasionally, when replenishing at sea, I would be ordered to fuel from the flagship. At Kilindini the commander-in-chief had noticed my speedy skimmer and told me that his barge was playing up and that he was thinking seriously of procuring my skimmer, which certainly looked smart at high speed. On one occasion while fuelling, I draped a 'negative' flag over it, hoping to avoid being distracted by the Admiral's habit of chatting by semaphore during replenishment — I had enough to worry about without thinking of snappy replies. There came the retort: 'Despite the negative, I will have her yet', which at least amused the bridge personnel. Admiral Somerville was known throughout the Navy for his ability to raise a laugh and particularly for his personal signal to Admiral Sir Andrew Cunningham. Already a knight, Cunningham received a second knighthood in the honours list. In a plain language message over the ether came Admiral Somerville's: 'Congratulations — twice a night at your age'. Italians, *loro comprendate*!

We called at Colombo before moving to Trincomalee for the start of the great deception which was to begin early in August. All forces headed in the direction of the Andaman Islands for most of two days and then retired to Colombo. Later *Warspite* and *Illustrious* made a 'radio diversion' but whether we assisted Admiral King has not been established. I helped escort *Formidable* back to East Africa and visited Zanzibar before returning to Kilindini on 18 August. There we had to prepare for unfinished work in Madagascar.

Ships were being sunk in the Bay of Bengal and Arabian Sea area in the first half of 1943 by Japanese submarines. They also indulged themselves in a brief sortie into our area — the Mozambique Channel — in July, but for the rest of the year spread their Arabian Sea activities into the Gulf of Aden and the Persian Gulf. Australian-built corvettes played an important part there, as in other theatres. An account of the combined German and Japanese submarine offensives in South African waters and throughout the Indian Ocean would make interesting, but depressing, reading.

At this time we were stunned by the news of disaster in the Solomon Islands — the Battle of Savo Island had claimed many ships including HMAS *Canberra* which suffered heavy loss of life. Due to *Canberra*'s high upper deck, and therefore prominent silhouette at night, she was bound to be sighted before she could sight a ship with a lower freeboard. At night, and especially at short range, the first to sight is the outright winner.

Nepal, the last of the 'N' class, finally arrived and joined the Eastern Fleet. She was a welcome addition as U-boat and Japanese submarine attacks were on the increase in our area. More than 94,000 tons of shipping, all unescorted, had been sunk in June and July, and we had to keep on our toes.

By now it was considered prudent to gain control of the remainder of Madagascar from the Vichy French. The risk was too great that Tamatave and Majunga might be taken by the Japanese and used as submarine bases from which to disrupt essential traffic to the Middle East, India and Ceylon. The operation, code-named 'Stream-Line-Jane' after a shapely comic-strip character, provided for a force to be landed at Majunga ('Stream') and then a drive east ('Line') to the capital Antananarivo. This was to be followed by a landing on the east coast at Tamatave so that other troops could move west to the capital. This other arm of the pincer had the code-name of 'Jane'.

The landings were under the command of Rear-Admiral Tennant in the cruiser *Birmingham*. Ships taking part included *Warspite*, *Illustrious*, *Albatross*, cruisers and destroyers including *Nizam*, *Nepal* and *Norman*. *Napier* was detached initially to land a commando troop on the west coast at Morandava to seize the aerodrome, wireless station and other key points and rejoined us later.

Before dawn on 10 September, the 29th Brigade landed a few miles north of Majunga, seized the local airfield and entered the town against only minor opposition. The 29th Brigade was re-embarked and replaced by the 22nd East African Brigade which began the long trek towards the capital, unmanned roadblocks providing the main opposition.

While the heavy ships were standing off to prevent any interference, we were close inshore in shallow water where Nizam picked up a contact and dropped depth charges. When the water subsided, we found ourselves awash in a sea of stunned fish. The temptation of this manna was too much for us and we hastily provisioned ship. Thus supplied, and with 'Stream' completed and 'Line' on the move, we returned to Diego Suarez to prepare for 'Jane'.

Intelligence photographs showed coastal defence guns surrounding Tamatave harbour and town and resistance was expected. The plan was a bold one: on 17 September, while the big ships kept the area clear, the cruisers and destroyers were to enter the harbour at first light, when we hoped the French would be asleep, issue an ultimatum, and, if that was refused, annihilate the defences at close range. Then the troops, again the 29th Brigade, would be disembarked and set off inland to the capital.

To facilitate this ruse, I was detailed to go ahead of the convoy and place myself close to the leading line into the harbour and show a red light to seaward. The idea was that if the leader passed close to me, by the time there was sufficient light she would find herself with the leading marks in line. It was a navigational problem requiring some thought. Not far from the leading line was a small island and if I could find this in the dark all would be well. The soundings on the chart would be little help, and my radar set, like all of that vintage, might give me an indication of the presence of an island but I could not count upon it. The *Sailing Directions and World Currents* were vague, but suggested a southerly set, so my last daylight fix would give me ten hours in an unknown current — I could be miles out in my reckoning by morning. *Norman*'s speed through the water was another important factor. My 'engine revolution/speed through the water' table by now was fairly accurate, provided due allowance was made for the state of the bottom. I had borrowed a chernikeef log (a small distance-measuring propeller) from *Nizam* as mine was unreliable, and calibrated it.

Soon after sailing on 16 September, I found myself closing Admiral Tennant's flagship and receiving by line amendments to the operation orders to distribute to all ships. This really was a chore: it required steaming close to each ship, firing a coston gun line and then easing the package over. Before I finished, I had to ask for some coston gun cartridges to be sent back on the line. Eventually at sunset I was detached and increased speed to allow myself as much time as possible to find the spot marked X. I was thankful that calculated guesswork was not far out and, finally, feeling my way close to the coast, the thoroughly unreliable radar set suggested an object on the bow. Approaching from a different direction it showed up again, so I could now be bolder and move in to pick it up with binoculars. The problem was solved; it was only a short distance to the spot where the anchor was lowered as silently as possible so as not to disturb the Frenchmen. The red light was trained to seaward and the operation went as planned.

The cruisers and destroyers of the armada entered harbour and the ultimatum was broadcast. There was no reply but gunfire was withheld. A power boat with a white flag was sent in shore, but when fire was opened on it, the order to bombard was given. I have never heard such a racket in my life and was not surprised when a white flag appeared ashore. We ceased fire; the troopships entered and landed men and equipment. They began the west-bound trek to the capital, which soon was declared an open city. The Japanese had been forestalled.

In late September *Norman* was in for boiler cleaning at Kilindini and I took the opportunity to go up to Nairobi by train for a break and some fresh food. In the train were three RAF types who asked me to make a four for bridge. I had forgotten mother's advice but soon recalled her words after I had lost a couple of pounds. In Nairobi I stayed at one of the country clubs in true colonial splendour; I kept mostly to myself, recharging my batteries.

October marked a new phase in the U-boat campaign in South African waters, and particularly in the Cape Town area. The 'Polar Bear' group consisting of four of the most modern boats arrived in the area, supported by a tanker submarine known as a milch-cow. At one stage the four were within 100 miles of Cape Town, sinking ships at their leisure. On 7 October six ships were sunk.

Four destroyers including *Nizam* were in the area, more occupied in picking up survivors than finding and destroying the enemy. The destroyer *Active* alone had a success.

I operated from Simonstown, Durban and Walvis Bay during the last three months of the year. From Cape Town I was ordered out to the north-west in the hopeless search for a U-boat. The orders then current were that submarines were to be sunk by depth charge, not by ramming, as destroyers were in short supply. At last light on the first night, I sighted a dark shape dead ahead; quickly I pressed rattlers (action stations), and increased speed, intending to ram — conveniently, the latest ruling had slipped my mind. When within about two ship's length, the object was identified as a ship's lifeboat under sail, heading for the West Indies. I just missed it, reduced speed and put the ship alongside the boat. The survivors, who had been a long time at sea with little to eat, had no strength at all. The doctor, to put it mildly, took them all in hand and adjusted their diet. From the two officers I learned that their ship had been torpedoed three weeks earlier and that they had tried to steer north-east to find land. I asked why they were therefore steering north-west, to which the reply was, 'Were we?' The elements and shortage of food and water had caused a mental blackout. However, they were soon bright and breezy with no wish to be rushed to the shore — they enjoyed being in a ship with some real offensive power.

The answer to the U-boat problem was to use escorted convoys. The trouble was that there were too many ships at sea and too few escorts, but a pattern had emerged. History records that these U-boats had no wish to take on warships or convoys with escorts. Obviously, to sink a fleet carrier would be a great success, but they clearly preferred the easy pickings with little risk.

A constant worry for us was the continual failure of ships when torpedoed to make the all-important enemy report. It had been a serious problem when I was Director of Operations and I still find it hard to believe that in so many cases the power of a ship should fail

147

with the first explosion. It does not take thirty seconds to press the morse key to send, for example, SSSS 4021S530E, and keep on repeating till the power fails. I continued to operate in South African waters and was fortunate to pick up another two batches of survivors. One lot had not been long on their carley rafts, which was just as well since the rafts gave no protection from water, wind and weather. My plain-clothes wardrobe was being depleted rapidly.

At the end of October the 'Polar Bear' group departed for home, with a score of thirty ships, totalling about 200,000 tons. Its place was taken by three U-boats who concentrated on the Durban–Lourenço Marques area. In those days all the advantages were with the submarine as it could steam on the surface with little risk of detection at night and only slightly more by day.

Having had little success, on 18 December, at which time I was operating from Durban, I was ordered to proceed to the sabotaged graving dock at Diego Suarez. In the Mozambique Channel I ran into fog, and I knew that at some point at the northern end of the Channel I would have to make off to the north-east. This was not a serious problem but I did study the current charts, which showed a permanent southerly current varying between a half and one knot. I made all due allowances and at a specific time altered course for north Madagascar. At my next fix, after leaving the fog astern, I found to my consternation that I was ten miles to the north of my dead reckoning position, and plotting back I discovered that I had missed an island at the north end of the Channel by only five miles. For some odd reason, possibly a distant cyclone, the current on that day was to the northward at half a knot, which in a fog for ten hours could make a difference of between ten and fifteen miles. I had been lucky and although the sounding machine would have saved me, it was a black mark. Only my navigator and I knew.

Arriving Diego Suarez on 20 December, I secured alongside the jetty at Antsirane where the destroyer *Anthony* landed her Royal Marines in Operation 'Ironclad'. We were still in dock on Christmas Day, but the locals did not welcome us with open arms, so the festive season was rather dull. New Year's Day 1943 saw us safely out of dock and on our way back to base. At least we started the year with a clean bottom.

At Kilindini the fleet needed constant exercising. On one occasion I was part of the anti-submarine screen for a carrier out for a day's flying, with my commodore (D) as a spectator. An aircraft suffered engine failure and crashed close to me. I brought the ship to within about ten feet of the pilot in the water and allowed the wind to drift the ship so the scrambling net was abreast the man, when a couple of sailors hauled him inboard. Then I was off and back in my station with alacrity. I felt rather pleased with myself, only to be brought back to earth with a bump — a signal from the commodore waved in the breeze for all to see: 'Manoeuvre badly executed, sir', chirped my yeoman of signals. When next I spoke to Steve, I asked him the reason for the admonition, to which he replied that my manoeuvre was unseamanlike. He said I should have lowered a whaler to pick up the pilot as he might have had a broken leg and required careful handling. At least the pilot was happy.

At the end of January I took part in Operation 'Pamphlet' which was to ensure the safety of our 9th Division returning home in a magnificent array of vessels: *Queen Mary*, *Ile de France*, *Nieuw Amsterdam* and *Queen of Bermuda*. This was an uncomplicated operation but covered many miles; we returned via Addu Atoll and the Seychelles.

I was due for a refit at Simonstown but before leaving Kilindini, as was our custom, we tested all circuits and equipment. While checking the pompom, a rapid-firing close-range weapon, the rating in charge pressed the trigger and there was a loud bang. A round which had been left in the barrel was on its way towards the inhabitants of Mombasa. I made an urgent signal about it. However, I never received a justified 'bottle', and there was no word of any fatality or damage.

On the way to Simonstown I picked up another batch of survivors, all in good health, and landed them at East London. The refit started on 3 March and I was able to give some long leave to the ship's company. I felt well but boils had started to develop on my neck so I spent a short time in the local naval hospital to recuperate. A refit is a very thorough affair, during which opportunity is taken not only to do the normal maintenance, but to make 'alterations and additions' which experience had shown were needed to improve a particular class of ship. The compilation of the list of defects was the key to its success and that required close scrutiny by the head of each department. We had kept such a list and looked forward to a much improved *Norman*. Every ship using the graving dock at Simonstown was expected to paint her ship's badge on the dock walls, which made an interesting sight. At the Officers Club, ships were expected to leave a photograph. I did so but asked that it not be mounted opposite the bar as every ship on that wall had been sunk.

During the refit one of the alterations carried out was to place a bearer arm across a circular hatch. At sea, soon afterwards, Chief McGuire tried out this new bar which was held in place by a split pin. Unfortunately it gave way and he crashed head first on to the deck eight or nine feet below. He suffered concussion and serious shock and we had to land him at the next port for treatment. He was returned to Australia and recovered, although it took a long time. Always calm and efficient, he was one of my few seasoned officers and one whom I could ill-afford to lose.

With the ship and the ship's company in renewed vigour, *Norman* and *Nizam* were turned over to the control of the Commander-in-Chief South Atlantic in Cape Town. In April there were no U-boat sinkings, but a fresh team of the 'Cruiser' class were on their way and created havoc in May from Walvis Bay to Madagascar.

We had our work to do and no time to take an interest in the war progress elsewhere. Indeed we had little information about it. We were losing our battle and scarcely noticed the happy ending of the Tunisian campaign on 12 May.

Whilst at Cape Town I had an unusual request from a rating for permission to marry a black girl, and it was not the Cape brandy talking. It was a dilemma, but I could see only one answer. There was a ship in harbour sailing for Australia the next day and the rating was given an immediate draft back to Australia. There was not a discordant note from any higher authority.

My last major job was to fuel at Pointe Noire on 9 June and then join as senior officer of the escort of a south-bound convoy. Naturally I dared not trust my theory that U-boats kept clear of the escorted convoys. One day out from Cape Town there was an alarm. My starboard lookout reported: 'Green 30 — periscope sighted — periscope dipped — medium range'. The drill was carried out: the convoy was ordered to do an emergency turn away and the appropriate destroyer joined me in the hunt and carried out the search procedure, but without result. The convoy was ordered to resume course. We were soon to sight many such periscopes; all in fact were seals. My theory, which is probably incorrect, is that it was mating season for seals and that this required one flipper in the air, which they dipped promptly on hearing propeller noises.

My time in *Norman* was now all but over. Earlier in the commission we had the depressing experience of losing a man overboard. I was on my own in a long but heavy swell with a gentle breeze. I received orders which required me to reverse course and I knew that at least once during the 180-degree turn the ship would roll heavily so the pipe went round to clear the upper deck during an alteration of course. This was done and the turn made during which there was one heavy roll, followed by a shout from the lifebuoy sentry: 'Man overboard'. My chief was sick in bed and attended by a stoker who, not having heard the precautionary pipe, hurried up the ladder from the cabin flat at the precise moment when the ship lurched, and he was flung overboard. I manoeuvred the ship just to windward of the man in the water and was drifting down on to him as a life-buoy, with heaving line attached, was thrown to him. It almost splashed him in the face. Safety was but an arm's length away when he disappeared. Perhaps he had been hurt on his way over the side.

The only other loss during my command happened in Cape Town dockyard. The ship was moved into the drydock. After we were on the blocks and the gangway in place, I told the first lieutenant to put guidelines on either side of the brow (gangway) so that there would be no doubt as to its position at night. About midnight, a rating who was returning from the heads on the dockside fell into the drydock and was killed. This was a heartache. Of course there was the usual Board of Inquiry but I felt no dereliction of duty. I am still upset that, months later, I received the displeasure of My Lords Commissioners of the Admiralty for failing to enclose the entire dock to prevent such an accident happening. My correct action was to have stopped the dockyard from pumping out the dock until safety chains had been placed around the dock. At the time, I was left with the impression that safety chains had not been used around that dock for years. These two incidents, together with the injury sustained by Chief McGuire, spoilt an otherwise happy and lucky commission.

On arrival at Kilindini on 24 June, Commander H. J. Buchanan was waiting to relieve me. I turned over the ship to him, having steamed 124,000 miles, more often than not 'at best speed'. *Norman* had had a refit and now her late captain needed one. My time in *Norman* had provided some exciting experiences which money could not buy and for which I was paid. My meagre expenses were paid by the rate of exchange. It is seldom that a naval officer is 'in funds'.

There was one scar on my late ship that I avoided mentioning to my relief. It is a captain's aim to keep his ship free from evidence of mistakes in ship-handling, particularly the stem. I was not prepared to admit to a slightly imperfect bow. Berthing at Simonstown in a strong wind I had made a miscalculation. The dockyard maties hauling a catamaran along the jetty fouled things up so my bow touched the lip of the dockside wall and bent it slightly. The dockyard straightened it with great skill and made it difficult to detect.

The best command job in the Navy is captain of a destroyer and I hope I have made it clear that no captain of a ship could have been better served than I. When I left the area, unknown to me or my relief, there was a group of seven U-boats in south-east African waters and eleven U-boats (the Monsoon Group) had left

Europe and would pass through the area on their way to their Penang base. ULTRA does not seem to have helped us with submarine rendezvous positions and the like. With an increasing number of escorts available, later Commander Brooks of *Nizam* was landed at Durban to organize convoys and escorts and Lieutenant-Commander Bill Cook assumed temporary command. Meanwhile I took passage in *Nizam* across the Indian Ocean and was landed at Geraldton. Somehow, leaving Scapa Flow for Archangel seemed an aeon away.

8
Final Stages of World War II
1944–46

After landing in Geraldton, I was driven south to Fremantle, where I had to report to the Naval Officer-in-Charge, Commodore Cuthbert Pope. I was to report on the prospect of developing Cockburn Sound as a harbour as ships anchored off Fremantle provided tempting U-Boat targets. Many years before, work had been started on dredging an entrance through broad sandy shallows. I was now able to report that silting of the channel had not taken place over time so further dredging would be a practical proposition.

I was due for leave, but it soon became evident that the paucity of green vegetables, lack of sleep and general strain had taken its toll and I was required to enter Caulfield Repatriation Hospital. I dislike hospital and not being able to laugh cramped my general outlook. Twice I almost recovered but it was clear that nature would not give in without a fight. After another relapse it was decided that I needed a change of scenery and so I was bundled off to the requisitioned Naval Hospital at Elizabeth Bay in Sydney. There I complained that I was receiving treatment without any efforts being made to find out the cause and suggested blood tests. A few days later, early in the morning, I was whisked off to Macquarie Street in my pyjamas where blood samples were taken. After some days I called over the chief sick-berth attendant and inquired as to the result of the tests. He replied, 'You are all right, sir. You don't have V.D.' I mumbled that I could have told them that and saved a lot of trouble.

Time, fresh food and solid sleep were the great physicians and eventually I was able to make my way to Melbourne to take up my appointment as Director of Plans, in relief of Commander A. S. Storey. First it was necessary to get up to date in the progress of the war for whilst at sea one suffered a world news blackout, and understandably so for the only concern was one's immediate operational area. It was in several ways a pleasant change to have a shore job, devoid of pressing operational responsibility. Of course planning meant long hours, but they were rewarded with uninterrupted sleep.

I was surprised to learn of the submarine attacks on the New South Wales coast during the twelve months prior to June 1943. Twelve submarines had operated during that period and had compiled a score of eighteen ships sunk, including the hospital ship *Centaur*, and a dozen more attacked. However, convoys were in operation and air cover was provided which kept the score low. The submarines were not to reappear again, probably because the tide in the Pacific war had begun to run in the Allies' favour.

Late in September came the first detailed news of the loss of *Perth* and USS *Houston*, sunk in the northern approaches to the Sunda Strait on 1 March 1942. Four survivors from *Perth* had arrived in Saipan in the Marianas in late September 1943 and, after a few days in hospital, were returned home to Brisbane where they gave their accounts of a sea battle against overwhelming odds and some of the vicissitudes and tribulations of their incarceration. The full story could not be pieced together until the release of our prisoners of war at the end of the war. Nevertheless, the revelations gave some hope to wives and families who, like the rest of us, had been very much in the dark.

The general position in the Pacific and Indian Oceans at the end of 1943, soon after I took up my new post, was encouraging. Admiral Nimitz had captured the Gilbert Islands in the Central Pacific Area and was about to attack the Marshalls. (See the back endpaper map.) From there he planned to strike westward through the Marianas to Palau and Mindanao by the end of 1944, bypassing, and thus isolating, the Carolines and Truk in the process. In SWPA (South-West Pacific Area) General MacArthur, after his success at Guadalcanal, had captured west New Britain and was making plans to capture the Admiralty Islands. The Australian Army's successes in New Britain had effectively neutralized Rabaul and on the mainland of New Guinea Lae and Finschhafen had been taken and further offensives were imminent.

To the west, our naval strength in the Indian Ocean had increased. After the surrender of Italy in September, the Admiralty had been able to send reinforcements to the Eastern Fleet. These included *Renown*, *Queen Elizabeth*, *Valiant*, *Illustrious*, *Unicorn* and appropriate cruisers, destroyers, submarines and minor war vessels.

In the approaching months of 1944 great and stirring events were to be enacted — the invasion of mainland Europe and the consequent breakout across France towards Germany; the recapture of the New Guinea mainland and MacArthur's advance through Manus to Hollandia and Morotai to Leyte; and Admiral Nimitz's westerly progress across the Pacific. But it was SWPA which most concerned me.

The Admiralty Islands were captured on 29 February 1944, to the surprise and delight of many, particularly General MacArthur, as the target date had been the first day of April. Advances were being made within the Navy at this time, too. Our most senior RAN college graduates, Collins and Farncomb, were by March 1944 experienced captains. Collins became Commodore Commanding the Australian Squadron and Farncomb was detached to command a British aircraft carrier, HMS *Attacker*, and took part in the D-Day landings.

I found that my job as Director of Plans, while concerned with our part of the Pacific and Indian Oceans, was at times greatly affected by high-level discussions held thousands of miles away. From the Sextant Conference in late 1943 to the Second Quebec Conference in September 1944, planning was dogged by disagreements at the highest level on the strategy to be adopted in the Indian and Pacific Ocean areas, and the use to be made of Commonwealth forces within that area. Initially great pains were taken to avoid involving us in the controversies.

In the midst of this rash of planning activity, the greatest good luck came my way. Somehow I made time to persuade Ada Theresa Weller to marry me, on Princess Elizabeth's birthday, 21 April, after a three-week acquaintance. As well, I changed her Christian name to Terry.

Strategy for the Pacific and South-East Asia

I will not attempt to go into intricate details on the nine months of high-level squabbling. Regarding the serious confrontations between Churchill and his chiefs of staff, the British official historian has written: 'It is difficult at times to trace a pattern in the discussion, for the arguments pursue many by-paths and the protagonists return to positions they had previously abandoned'.[27] As it suited his ideas, Churchill had the Supreme Commander S. E. Asia, Admiral Lord Louis Mountbatten, on his side. Among the Combined Chiefs of Staff (UK and USA), the *bête noire* was the American, Admiral King. His clearly stated obstinate view was that the American Fleet needed no assistance for its Pacific operations as additional strength would merely add to the difficulty of supply.

Amidst this high-level turmoil, Australian service and civilian planners were kept busy answering logistic questionnaires regarding the basing of British naval, army and air forces in Australia. One of the many chores concerned a 'Middle Strategy' — to strike north-wards from Darwin towards Amboina and North Borneo. This resulted from the only Prime Ministers' Conference held during the war. The forces envisaged in this Strategy were three Australian Divisions, sixty-eight Dominion and three British squadrons of aircraft and, from the Royal Navy, three battleships, three aircraft-carriers, ten cruisers and twenty-eight des-troyers with fleet train (logistic) support. The operation was practical if the US could supply the necessary landing craft. An October date for the operation was overly optimistic. Early 1945 seemed a more realistic date.

Considerable doubt has arisen as to whether this 'Middle Strategy' was but a pie in the sky. I took part in many planning sessions. I discussed the problems with the naval officer-in-charge, Captain C. C. Baldwin, upon whose shoulders a heavy responsibility would fall as Darwin became a hive of activity. A study of the chart enabled me to work out the number of anchor berths for ships of different draughts and then the requirements for lighters, barges, small oil tankers, water-boats and communication could be deduced. The trickiest problem was to select suitable places for the establishment of 'hards' — slopes used by landing ships and craft to embark tanks, land vehicles and stores.

When the various aspects of equipping Darwin for its new role were drawn together, an important factor limiting the operation was discovered to be the supply of fresh water to the shipping involved. In those days ship evaporators were not very efficient and the consumption rate for boilers and normal ship use was high. It became clear that the existing pipeline from the inland reservoir and the storage tanks in Darwin would need to be doubled to meet the requirement. As this would take time to construct, it was decided to anticipate events and get on with it.

Planning for the Final Defeat of Japan in 1946
Australia as a Main Base

Early in May, the Dominions were informed that massive forces would be required after the defeat of Germany to conquer the Japanese on their own ground in 1946. Hence there would be a need for base facilities on a large scale either in Australia or India. We were invited to assemble details of our capabilities without commitment, the naval aspects of which fell on my plate. It was a mammoth undertaking by all government departments as well as the services. Churchill had proposed sending out parties of experts to do the job, but Curtin replied that liaison officers would suffice.

Australia was required to state the extent to which we could meet our estimates and the additional assistance, particularly shipping, which would be required to make up the differences. Briefly, Britain would provide five divisions, two armoured brigades, and four commandos. This would complement the six Australian divisions and the one from New Zealand. One hundred and fifty air squadrons were to be provided and the Royal

Navy contribution would be four battleships, twenty-eight carriers, twelve cruisers, sixty destroyers, forty-six submarines, a large number of auxiliaries and, to make it self-sufficient at sea, a vast fleet train.

Darwin was envisaged as one of the advanced bases and Sydney was to be the main base. The troops were to be trained in Brisbane, Newcastle and Sydney areas and the RAAF was to set up reception points and bases at Adelaide, Melbourne, Sydney and Townsville. Naval facilities, airfields and army depots would need major additions. The UK requirements listed nine floating docks and the construction of three graving docks requiring an additional labour force of over 100,000 men. On the naval side, the main force would arrive by July 1945 and comprised 120,000 RN personnel, including 29,000 shore-based.

John Ehrman has remarked that:

> ... had the war continued into the spring of 1946, the position might have been different. A larger fleet, an air force of perhaps two hundred heavy bombers, and either three or four Commonwealth divisions with fifteen squadrons of supporting aircraft, might have been present at the final assault on Japan, while to the south British land and air forces from south-east Asia and a part of the East Indies Fleet, allied with the Australians and New Zealanders remaining in the south-west Pacific and perhaps reinforced by French and Dutch troops, would have been released for operations in the Netherlands East Indies and possibly up the China coast, under new British and Australian Commands embracing the former South-West Pacific Area.[28]

The position was gratifying. In the early years of the war the distant members of the Commonwealth had made great sacrifices far from their shores, so it is pleasing to note the magnitude of the effort which was planned for our area. Although it seemed obvious to us that we could not provide base facilities of the magnitude in the time allowed, the job was taken seriously, for no one at that time could say that massive forces

159

would not be required to defeat Japan at some later stage.

Demise of the Middle Strategy

In mid-June official talks in London with US officials were prefaced by the statement that Americans would not be prepared to discuss officially their part in the Pacific war. However, they did divulge their Pacific planning timetable — by 15 June, they were to have occupied the Marianas; by 15 September, Palaus; by 15 November, Mindanao; and by 15 February 1945, Luzon or Formosa. They remarked that by the time the Australians were in Amboina in 1945, they would be astride the path to Tokyo, and pointed out that our 'Middle Strategy' effort would be of little benefit.

To cut short a long, complicated story, the planning information regarding the basing of massive forces in Australia, for the final defeat of Japan, was sent to London. General MacArthur's rapid advance towards Japan changed the strategic picture in South-East Asia. Churchill caved in and magnanimously stated that he proposed to make 'The greatest offer of naval assistance, which is within our power, to the United States, ascertaining from them in what way it can be most effective'.[29] His object was to share in the main operations against the mainland of Japan or Formosa, with the British forces operating under United States command. In a cable to Washington on 18 August he stated, *inter alia*:

> If for any reason the United States Chiefs of Staff are unable to accept the support of the British fleet in the main operations (which is our distinct preference) we should be willing to discuss an alternative. The suggestion that we would make in this event is the formation of a British Empire task force under a British Commander, consisting of British, Australian, and New Zealand land, sea and air forces, to operate in the South-West Pacific area und General MacArthur's supreme command. This alternative, if decided upon, would still enable the British fleet to be well placed to reinforce the US Pacific Fleet if this should later be desired.[30]

The Joint Chiefs' reply, not despatched until 9 September (a long delay), accepted part of the British proposal but the inference that the British Fleet should operate in the Central Pacific was ignored. However, the US Chiefs of Staff appreciated the great value of British long-range bombers which could help in pulverizing the Japanese homeland after the collapse of Germany. By this time it was clear that the assumption that the war with Germany would be over in October 1944 would not prove correct. This realization, the cable to Washington on 18 August, and the surprising speed of the US forces' advance towards the Japanese homeland, put paid to the 'Middle Strategy'. So ended nine months of discussion, confusion and at times illogical conclusions, but as it turned out, no great harm resulted. The mounting of the Darwin–Amboina phase of 'Middle Strategy' could now be forgotten. At my low level, there was no doubt that the 'Middle Strategy' was taken seriously. I believe that even the selection of the Australian Force Commander came up for discussion.[31]

With Darwin no longer liable to be used for mounting an expeditionary force, the government called a halt to any preparations in progress. However, I thought it would be a shame if no advantage could be gained from our preparations and I proposed that at least the second pipeline should be completed, the more so since the pipes had already arrived and workmen were available. I added that Darwin could be 'the garden city of the North'. To my delight my recommendation was approved. I travelled to Darwin after the war, but could not find my name engraved on the second pipeline.

Plan for Basing a Reduced British Pacific Fleet on Australia

At long last, Admiral King's rejection of the offer of British assistance in the Pacific was overruled by President Roosevelt so another planning chore appeared in my 'In' tray. Britain's naval contribution in the Pacific in 1945 was to be reduced to a more practical level, the main units being two battleships, four fleet carriers, cruisers and destroyers. However, the preliminary work in planning for the employment of Australia as a main base for the final defeat of Japan had not been wasted. A Joint Administrative Planning Sub-Committee representing government and service departments was established to tackle the problem. Detailed work on the main base and logistic requirements naturally fell to the RN and RAN. We had Admiral Daniel on the spot to give decisions on behalf of the UK to the many queries that arose. The naval planning assumptions were that the main force would arrive between December 1944 and July 1945, that there would be a fleet train comprising supply, repair, hospital and accommodation ships, that by July 1945 Royal Navy personnel would total 120,000, of which 29,000 would be shore-based, and that of this total 47,000 would arrive by January 1945. Assistance to be provided by Australia included items such as ship maintenance, refitting and docking, aircraft assembly and repairs, works, food, and medical stores.

My job was to be the co-ordinator of naval requirements and, with Commander R. C. M. Duckworth, RN, to produce an administrative plan with which the Royal Navy agreed so that all authorities in Australia, both RAN and RN, and at the Admiralty had available all the administrative details.

We produced the skeleton of a volume capable of infinite expansion known as the *Detailed Overall Administrative Plan (DOAP)*. The preamble outlined the assumptions and the forces involved for which administrative arrangements had to be made, and then each Navy director progressively was to build up his section in consultation with his representatives in the various shore establishments.

Additional pages to *DOAP* were added almost daily and despatched to all Australian holders and to the Admiralty, where they were copied and similarly distributed to Admiralty directors. Every four or five weeks Duckworth would fly to England to clear up points on the spot and to bring back any amendments and additions desired. The book grew at an ever-increasing rate, but, to my delight, everything was running smoothly.

The British Pacific Fleet came into being on 22 November 1944 when Admiral Sir Bruce Fraser hoisted his flag in a 625-ton gun boat at Trincomalee. On 2

December his flag was transferred to the battleship *Howe*, which sailed for Fremantle with an escort of four destroyers. It was 4 February 1945 before the main body (the battleship *King George V*, four fleet carriers, three cruisers and ten destroyers) appeared. It was gratifying that the support arrangements for the fleet had met with little difficulty, and pleasing to think that we had contributed to the work carried out by the British Pacific Fleet, which included the bombing and bombardment of the Japanese mainland. Unlike the other two services, naval logistics ashore are administered by civilians. They deserve high praise for their efficiency in replenishing the fleet train, providing the additional base facilities, repairing action damage and the refitting of fleet units.

In the meantime, while my head had been down over the planning table, the advances of the forces of Admiral Nimitz and General MacArthur had continued. On 15 September 1944, Nimitz captured Palau at the same time as MacArthur seized Morotai. However, where they would strike next was a continual guessing game, for at Navy Office we had no 'need to know'.

Events in mid-October had put us in good spirits. The battles for Leyte included RAN ships in the midst of action. There was bad news too — on Trafalgar Day, *Australia* suffered from a kamikaze attack and, sadly, thirty-one were killed, including Captain Dechaineux and Commander Rayment, both friends of mine; Commodore Collins was severely wounded and was brought back to Australia to recover. Captain Farncomb was recalled from his carrier command in the United Kingdom to take the place of Commodore Collins. With increasing speed our senior naval college graduates were ascending the promotions ladder. With Farncomb now in command of our task force, Captain Showers became Second Naval Member and the first graduate to be a member of the Naval Board.

Christmas was near when I was told by Captain Parker that I was to command the third 'Tribal' class destroyer, *Bataan*, then under construction at Cockatoo Island in Sydney Harbour. Naturally, I was elated. Before taking up the command I had an appointment in hospital and so I retired to Flinders Naval Depot, having been relieved by Commander Claude Brooks. Despite some prolonged treatment I recovered, and without the slightest discomfort have been able to sit upon the coldest of marble slabs ever since. While I was recuperating, my wife gave birth to our daughter Fayne.

Completely refreshed, I moved to Sydney to prepare *Bataan*, and myself, for a June commissioning. While I had been out of commission, the administrative plan to succour men, ships and aircraft of the British Pacific Fleet, from all accounts, had been working well.

HMAS *Bataan* 1945–46

Bataan was the third and last of the British-designed 'Tribal' class destroyers to be built in Australia. My *Norman* was handsome, but I thought that *Bataan* might even share the prize for good looks, particularly at speed. She carried six 4.7-inch guns, two 4-inch anti-aircraft guns, a close-range anti-aircraft weapon, one mounting with four 21-inch torpedoes, and two depth-charge throwers. Her three boilers produced 44,000 horsepower, making her capable of thirty-six knots at full power. The extra boiler required the ship to have two funnels. Originally *Bataan* was to have been named *Kurnai* but as a tribute to General MacArthur his wife was invited to launch the ship and name her *Bataan*.

I arrived in enough time to get to know my new command, particularly the new equipment. Once again, I saw to it that the instruments on the bridge were in the appropriate places and pointing in the right directions, and familiarized myself with the latest anti-submarine gunnery, torpedo and radar techniques. However, my main concern were the signal books and procedures. I was to join the US Seventh Fleet in the Philippines area and so US books, rules and phraseology had to be learned. Circular screens, for example, were new to me. One such screen was designed to give complete anti-submarine protection to a force, irrespective of its course, and was particularly effective in the defence of aircraft carriers. The main force would be manoeuvred so that a flying programme could be carried out safely; that is, if a carrier wanted to turn into the wind to recover planes, all ships would be turned together to the appropriate course. Interpreting US Navy signals could take time for a newcomer and time would not be available because as soon as an 'Executive Signal' was made, each ship had to set off in the right direction and at the right speed immediately. Not only had I to be familiar with such things as procedures, rules for zig-zagging, and screening diagrams, but also all officers of the watch had to acquire the same information quickly. A lifetime's knowledge of Admiralty signal books and procedures had to be forgotten.

During the two years I had been ashore, serious defects in damage control procedures had been revealed to me. Officers and petty officers had been given short courses but often in action a fire would break out and there would be no trained person around to tackle it in the best way — water may not be the right answer in a compartment with electric leads and switches. Consequently, it was decided that every man in the ship be given training in damage control so that the fire-fighting equipment could be used to the best advantage, especially since kamikaze attacks were becoming more frequent.

The main armament director now carried radar which revolutionized spotting the fall of shell. A small proportion of my anti-aircraft ammunition was fitted with the long-awaited US proximity fuses — the answer to killing aircraft moving in three dimensions. Even at that stage of the war they were still in short supply. The greatest technical advance was the main surface radar, mounted at the masthead and scanning through 360 degrees with a range of about twelve miles. This British invention, in American hands, had developed dramatically since my *Norman* days, and a reliable set could turn night into day. The result appeared on a circular display (Plan Position Indicator — PPI) on the bridge, the ship being in the centre. Radar displays at airport control towers are now basic equipment. The interpretation from a moving ship is quite different and is another of those relative triangle problems with the moving ship stopped in the centre of the picture. Failure to under-stand this has given rise to many 'radar-controlled collisions', as the human element sometimes fails to keep pace with improved technology.

My ship's company of 260 men comprised a high percentage of reserves but, as I mentioned earlier, they were indistinguishable from permanent servicemen. I was thankful that I was blessed with experience watch-keepers and a secretary. I was also given two lieutenants (junior grade) USN. They were embarked to operate the USN secret coding machine after we came under US operational control, for which purpose they were given a small locked office. They were a pleasant couple and tactlessly I asked them about their nautical experience — it was nil. The tremendous expansion of officers in the USN was achieved by narrow specialization to the exclusion of broader nautical knowledge.

Great events were happening while *Bataan* prepared to take her place in the field. Among these were the German surrender on 7 May; the death of a good friend to Britain and the Commonwealth, Franklin D. Roosevelt; the capture of Okinawa; and the landing of Australian troops in Balikpapan. We were not to know that the new President, Truman, had approved a combined operation on a breathtaking scale — the landing on Kyushu, timed for 1 November. This stipulated a head-on assault with the Japanese on their homeland, potentially involving some five million men. Originally the Americans did not want any Commonwealth assistance on the ground for the operation. However, after much discussion, the US agreed in principle to a deployment of a Commonwealth Land Force in the final phase. This was expected to be at least a division each from Britain, Australia, New Zealand and India.

Sydney, then the main British Pacific Fleet Base, was a hive of activity as far as the DOAP was concerned. Reloading ships of the fleet train was a continual process. It surprised me to discover that between March and May 1945 the train numbered fifty-eight ships, and by the end of the war ninety-two.[32] On one occasion, the heavy units of the fleet returned to Sydney for rapid repair of war damage and refit. The naval dockyards at Garden Island and Cockatoo Island completed the work in very smart time. It was controlled by the Garden

signing of the Japanese Instrument of Surrender on board US Battleship *Missouri* in Tokyo 2 September 1945. Japan's Foreign Minister, Mr Mamotu Shigemutu, representing the eror Hirohito, is at the head of the Japanese delegation.

-prisoners of war being cheered as *Bataan* passed down the lines of warships in Tokyo y

HMAS *Australia (Australian War Memorial)*

Captain Henry Burrell

The Burrells about to attend a royal garden party in London

Island manager, Engineer-Captain G. I. D. Hutcheson, a former shipmate. As the ships berthed, the dockyard maties were over the side with their steel cutters and welding sets, while the foremen inspected items requiring urgent attention. Hutcheson was the moving spirit and his attitude was: 'To hell with defect lists requiring approval: let's get on with the job'.

Many USN ships had been repaired in Sydney. Hutcheson had been given a portrait of General MacArthur; two American naval officers, seeing it, turned its face to the wall and told a story about the difference between Moses and MacArthur: Moses said to his people, 'Load your asses, mount your camels, we're off to the Promised Land', while the Supremo said to his forces, 'Sit on your asses, smoke your Camels, we're in the Promised Land'.

As with *Norman*, there was again a frantic last-minute rush by the shipbuilders but the commissioning date, 26 June 1945, was kept. The usual tests and trials of everything that moved were carried out. Acceptance trials off Sydney, including a run over the measured mile south of Port Jackson, showed the main propulsion up to specifications, so for a second time I signed a receipt for a ship and then set off to Jervis Bay to 'work-up' in quick time.

Soon we sailed from Sydney carrying with us Commodore Collins; he had recovered from his wounds and was rejoining his squadron. I was routed through Jomard Strait to the east of Samarai, on New Guinea's eastern tip, where I was confronted with a navigator's nightmare: I was unable to find the entrance to an approach channel through reefs and small islands. Bad horizons had prevented me from fixing the ship by celestial objects. Here was I, with my commodore watching, having to take the way off the ship until I knew my position. God's gift to mariners, the radar set, was quickly in operation, and ranges and bearings of five or six islands were plotted on tracing cloth to the same scale as the chart. One was then placed on the other and we were once more on our way.

At the Admiralty Islands I paused only long enough to fuel from an American tanker. Vice-Admiral Sir

Bernard Rawlings (second-in-command of the British Pacific Fleet), on his first visit to these islands, found the equatorial climate unattractive to Europeans and in his report to the Admiralty expressed bewilderment regarding 'under what circumstance and by whose whimsical conception these islands should have been named in honour of Their Lordships'.[33]

During a pleasant voyage to the Philippines, we continued to familiarize ourselves with American procedures. I joined the US Seventh Fleet at Subic Bay and had scarcely refuelled before a vast secret tome arrived by special messenger. The Seventh Fleet was about to carry out an exercise which looked much like a rehearsal for a major amphibious operation. The American format for operational orders was new to most of us and time in which to assimilate them was short. I was one of eight ships in one of three flotillas. On departure, not far from the entrance to the Bay, destroyers were ordered to form a screen of twenty-four ships around the flagship on a circle with a radius of several miles. Captain, navigator and yeoman of signals each set up a screening diagram and then, as soon as the screen commander allocated screen numbers, we hoped we knew where to go. Each ship in the screen had different areas to cover with her asdic set to ensure detection of enemy submarines. The whole operation made me feel like a new boy at school. Three days later we were back at Subic for a pause and my flotilla decided on a Sunday afternoon to have an officers' party on a small island as US Navy rules do not allow the consumption of alcohol on board. I was no longer a teetotaller (I took to the stuff when I was thirty) but was still out of my class and so returned on board without my absence being noticed.

During July projectiles from surface ships were exploding on the mainland of Japan and on 6 August the first atomic bomb was dropped on Hiroshima. I cannot remember how the word came to us but we discussed the effect it would have on Japanese morale. I was boiler-cleaning alongside USN *Dobbin* when the second bomb devastated Nagasaki on 9 August. We two captains decided that 13 August, my birthday, would see the end. Ashtrays were made and suitably engraved but we were two days out and the war ended on 15 August. We were all overjoyed. Without knowing any details of the devastation and the suffering, we were in no position to judge the ethics involved. My view now is that the dropping of the bomb was justified. The Germans and Japanese had attempted to achieve their aim of world domination by going to war, killing millions in the process. We were entitled, if not bound, to thwart such aims, even if that, too, would mean killing. In the short term, at the cost of many Japanese lives, it stopped the war and saved millions of lives on both sides, probably including my own.

Signalled congratulations were many. The following two are of special significance to *Bataan* and the RAN. One read:

Shropshire, Hobart, Bataan, Warramunga, Arunta from CCAS (Commodore Collins)
I wish to congratulate every officer and man of His Majesty's Australian Squadron on his share in our final victory announced by the Prime Minister of Great Britain this morning. I rejoice with you that the Japanese have been forced to surrender. We have every reason to be proud of the part played by the Royal Australian Navy during six years of war across the seas of the world and I say again to all 'well done'. Let us remember with sad pride our lost ships and their companies and thank God that their sacrifices were not in vain. 15 August 1945.

The second is a message from the King to General MacArthur:

I send you my heartfelt congratulations on overwhelming success which have crowned your efforts from the first day of the treacherous attack on the Philippines up to this last glorious moment. Your military skill your dauntless courage and your inspiring leadership have gained universal admiration and esteem. On behalf of all my people I would ask you to convey a special message of thanks and congratulations to the Forces of the British Commonwealth who have had the honour to serve under your command in the series of operations now so brilliantly concluded.

While deliberations regarding the surrender were under way, we awaited orders. It was decided that the main surrender ceremony would take place on board US battleship *Missouri* in Tokyo Bay early in September but when the list of ships to be present for the occasion was drawn up, Australia was forgotten. I do not know the details but I was ordered to proceed to an anchor berth off battered Manila where *Bataan* would provide a venue for a conference between General Blamey, an Air Vice-Marshal and Commodore Collins on the subject. I provided food, drink and bunks and at the end of it all I presume a message was sent to the government stating the minimum acceptable representation. In the event, Task Force 74.1 *Shropshire*, *Hobart*, *Warramunga* and *Bataan* with *Ipswich*, *Ballarat* and *Cessnock* standing in for our small ships, were to represent the RAN by being anchored in Tokyo Bay. I was a ring-in, having taken no offensive action against the Japanese in the Pacific and felt that an abortive foray into the Bay of Bengal and being in dangerous proximity to Admiral Nagumo's carrier force hardly deserved a jersey.

We entered Tokyo Bay on 31 August and were given anchor berths by an American port director. The Bay is vast and our berths were well placed for seeing Fujiyama but little else, with the exception of some buildings at Yokohama. I was one of 258 ships of war in the anchorage. The carriers remained at sea so that the might of their aircraft should be seen in the air during the surrender ceremony on 2 September.

I was too far from *Missouri* to see anything except the flypast of literally thousands of aircraft, but the ceremony was broadcast to all ships. General Blamey was to represent and sign for Australia, supported by Commodore Collins, Captain Dowling, Lieutenant-General Berryman, Air Vice-Marshal Bostock and Air-Commodore Brownell. It appeared to be a fine piece of staff work which organized the rapid transport of

Generals Percival and Wainwright from their POW camp in Mukden to the quarter-deck of *Missouri* in time for the ceremony.

An organization had been set up to handle the liberation of prisoners of war and internees and their return to their homelands. The Americans were responsible for the collection and evacuation of an unknown number of people in an unknown physical state. I can only mention the Japanese area. To help the USN, thirty-eight RN, RNZN and RAN ships in the area were made available. Other RN ships were dealing with the China coast including Hong Kong, Shanghai and Formosa.

The first requirement was to identify the prisoner of war camps. The international Red Cross had some information, the Japanese disclosed the whereabouts of some of their camps and carrier-borne aircraft revealed further enclaves. Food in 44-gallon drums was dropped by air to some places. The general plan was for the released men, women and children to be transported to Yokohama by the best means available — foot, car, train and ship. (Two escaped prisoners swam out to be picked up by the first ships entering Tokyo Bay.) Hospital ships were placed so that each person could be medically examined, bathed, clothed and fed. Evidence of war crimes was collected for use at a later date. Ships to take evacuees to their homelands were standing by and on sailing were cheered on their way as they passed down the lines in Tokyo Bay. One of the American hospital ships, *Tjitjalenka*, collected very sick Australians and eventually sailed for home with over 400 cot cases.

To mention one ship in particular, RN escort carrier *Ruler* sailed away with a passenger list of 400 officers, servicemen, civilians and children of all nations of the British Commonwealth and many of the colonies. The flightdeck was marked for many kinds of games and a Royal Marine dance band cheered people up as did the decorated hangar. The ship's daily routine included '6 pm: Children to supper'. The US rapidly organized an air evacuation to the USA and were soon flying out more than a thousand men a day. I was required to send off a 'contact team' who did good work at Hainanako and Sendai. Lieutenant D. H. Stewart, RANVR, was in charge. His main job was to meet trains at the local station and send the repatriates off in Japanese trucks to appropriate wharves. Stewart was most impressed with 300 men from the 9th Northumberland Fusiliers (Captain Thornehill) who, despite their weakened physical condition, marched off the platform with regimental smartness. Lieutenant Stewart's team helped over 2,000 (including seventy-two Australian servicemen) on their way.

On 11 September *Bataan* and *Warramunga* were ordered to proceed north-east to Sendai to co-operate with the American hospital ship *Rescue*. My Letters of Proceedings covering almost all my time in *Bataan*, including this month, cannot be found. I therefore rely on the official historian, Herman Gill, for the account of *Bataan*'s involvement:

It was on the Sendai operation that Commander Burrell in *Bataan* learned that among the prisoners of war taken from Tokushima Camp were some from HMAS *Perth*.

'Later that forenoon [on 12 September] I received word that Lieut-Commander P. E. Carr had just arrived on board *Rescue* together with Lieut-Commander P. O. L. Owen, Engineer Lieutenant W. C. Warner, Lieutenant W. L. Gay and Engineer Sub-Lieutenant T. F. Robbins. The news was the greatest thrill for all of us. With Lieut-Commander Dine I boarded *Rescue*. The Commanding Officer was most helpful in giving them top priority in the "processing" routine and arranging for them to embark in *Bataan* pending their departure. My words cannot express their joy at deliverance, to say nothing of ours. Provisions and clothing had been dropped at their camp by Naval aircraft so signs of extreme malnutrition had begun to wear off. However their reports will show their lot in Japanese hands was not different to those which have shocked the civilized world.'

On that Sendai trip *Warramunga* embarked 179

persons, including 32 women and 15 children. Of the total, the largest number of those of any one nation were the 79 English, which included 21 women and 10 children. In all, 13 nationalities were represented, including 5 Australians, African natives, Indians, Malayans, Americans, Spaniards, Armenians, Greeks, Arabs and Javanese. Commander M. J. Clark, commanding officer of *Warramunga*, described the ship's passenger list as 'a very mixed bag, but in many ways reminiscent of the "Tobruk Ferry"'.[34]

My officer passengers, wearing shoulder straps made from golden parachute silk, were all *Perth* survivors except Warner, who was on board the motor vessel *Hauraki*, taken in prize by Japanese merchant cruisers in 1942. Our guests were well up with news but they wanted to be assured that the *Queen Mary* was still afloat. At dinner the sight of butter seemed to give them the greatest pleasure and although we turned on a short film, they only wanted to sleep. The return to Tokyo Bay was uneventful until we passed down the lines of warships, when the ships' companies lined the upper decks and cheered the ex-prisoners of war up to our berth. To have survived was indeed a great feat. They deserved every cheer and more. Lieutenant-Commander Owen, on his arrival in Sydney, wrote a very touching letter of thanks in which he said, 'My wife told me all — or most of the solid comfort that our service and its womenfolk, both, have provided during these past hard years and with that knowledge one cannot but have great faith in our society and great and happy hopes for the future. From the moment we met *Bataan* on our release until our reception at Balmoral [a naval establishment in Middle Harbour, Sydney] nothing more than has been, could have been done'.

Commodore Collins was required to set up residence in one of the houses in the grounds of the United Kingdom Embassy and I was asked to send an advance party to prepare for his arrival, cut the lawn and organize a deck tennis court. The First Lieutenant discovered that the Ambassador's Rolls-Royce was still in the garage and had been cherished as befits that type of car — surely one of the strangest, warped, applications of protocol.

Soon *Hobart* and *Warramunga* were released to return home but the flagship and I were to be part of the Occupation Force for a further two months. At anchor in Tokyo Bay, the urge to remove our war-paint was strong. We scraped the paint from the gun muzzles, brass stanchions and name plates. I would have settled for some bottles of Allie Sloper sauce which was very good for bright work. In days past, this had been an RN issue and was a blood-red type of Worcester sauce, named by the sailors after a Ms Sloper who was brutally murdered. Nevertheless, it felt that we were getting back to normality. Commodore Collins invited me to join him on a drive in his jeep to Miyanoshita, where we lunched at a well-known hotel which had been commandeered by the Americans. As we sat on the large terrace amid drooping trees, wistaria, cascades and trout ponds there approached a lone individual in plain clothes who seemed out of place. He turned out to be a German who, much to his bewilderment, had been interned in this comfortable setting — surely a precession of the Axis (which will make sense to those familiar with the antics of a gyroscope).

A few days later I landed in Yokohama and was driven part of the way to Tokyo. To my eye the devastation was complete and the few people walking amongst it were all dressed in dull overalls. In some areas the only recognizable landmarks were Chubb safes which alone had withstood the fiery hurricanes generated in a fashion similar to the Hamburg holocaust.

The American fleet kept a lending store of the latest Hollywood films which they were kind enough to allow us to borrow. It was a peaceful evening for our cinema show on the upper deck with snow-capped Fujiyama visible in the moonlight. The film showed a US submarine breaking into Tokyo Bay, scraping mines and obstructions on the way, and emerging unscathed near Yokohama where it put up its periscope and sank three or four ships. The next day we were back to reality as the barometer started to drop. Cyclone warnings were being made at regular intervals and there was still a mass of shipping anchored in Tokyo Bay with a heavy concentration around me. As night fell steam was raised and an anchor watch set. By midnight the already strong wind was increasing — I was on a lee shore and most unhappy. If I started to drag anchor I would then have to steam with the anchor and cable trailing astern. The chart showed an underwater telegraph cable to seaward but I was prepared to risk cutting that. The inevitable moment arrived when we started to drag so there was only one answer — half speed ahead both. I found a bare patch in the middle of the bay and eventually was riding to one anchor at long stay and a second at shorter stay, so placed to prevent yaw. I was surprised I had not lost my anchor and was never to know if it had severed the telegraph cable.

To give the ship's company a chance to visit Tokyo itself, I was ordered to a berth up the Tokyo River which until then I did not know existed. The chart was an insufficient guide so I asked for a Japanese pilot but wondered if he would steer me to disaster and then commit hara-kiri. However, we arrived safely and soon my sailors were embroiled in a welter of bartering. When a packet of cigarettes and a Japanese camera were of equal value, it would have been difficult to prevent, although it was the general plan that I should remain ignorant. One day the first lieutenant reported that all cigarette stock had been stolen from the ship's canteen. What would we (meaning I) do about it? This theft was grossly unfair to the relatively honest ship's company. I decided to condone a felony and let it be known that replacement stock was not available, but that if the loot was returned, I would not take steps to track down the guilty party. On my paper-rack at breakfast the next morning was an envelope containing a note with a sketch attached showing a dotted line over the gangway and under the godown to a spot marked 'X'. The note said that if any cigarettes were found missing, the value should be put on the notice board and it would be refunded. The master-at-arms recovered the cigarettes and pinned 'deficit £3' on the notice board and the money duly appeared.

It would soon be time to return to Australia as the loot which had accumulated aboard was putting the ship deeper in the water. It was deemed appropriate for me to expound my view on the probable Customs approach to spoils of war which, I explained, was that items which were to be sold in Australia should be liable to tax and that presents should be allowed. Therefore, six strings of pearls destined for mother, two sisters, one cousin and two girlfriends should not attract duty.

On our arrival in Japan the paymaster had changed Australian pounds into yen. It seemed fair before departure to change any remaining yen back into our currency. A time was piped for this to occur. After a very short time, the paymaster came to me to say that he had exhausted the original money outlaid and only a third of the ship's company had been to the well. I was not popular in deciding that the matter could not be settled until we returned to Sydney. I cannot remember the outcome but no one was prepared to reveal the many means of getting rich. In non-naval ships, there were stories of bags of sugar, for example, being bought in Hong Kong, sold in Japan at enormous profit and, say, mushrooms being taken back to be sold in Hong Kong at even greater profit. Even without a slide rule, the profits sounded astronomic.

On 18 November, in the company of *Shropshire*, we left Japan bound for home. Navigation lights could now be burned and this, coupled with my reliable Sugar George radar, made steaming at night a pleasure. At Manus to fuel, the time had come to say good-bye to our two lieutenants USN. Before they left I told them I would pay their mess bills if, on return to the States, they would send to my wife a gold watch up to that value. They agreed; I paid the mess bills and thought no more about the watch.

Shropshire was diverted to Wewak and I was sent to Madang to pick up fifty-nine officers and men from the three services for passage to Sydney. On 30 November, my Letter of Proceedings read: 'The return to a home port in time of peace (an uncommon experience) was most exhilarating.'

While on leave in Melbourne I reflected on the great

part played by reservists in our naval war effort and the irreparable losses of our senior permanent naval officers. The strength of the Navy at the outbreak of war was 5,440 men in the permanent forces and 4,400 in the reserves. At the end of June 1945, these figures had increased to 7,057 and 32,593 respectively, the permanent forces being only eighteen per cent of the total.

By January 1939, the original 179 who had entered the Naval College between 1913 and 1918 had been reduced to 120 by normal wastage and retrenchment in 1922. Omitting those who found their metier in the non-seamen branches, the number of executive officers was forty-four. By the end of the war, heavy losses had cut a swathe through the executive list; that is, Captains Burnett (*Sydney*), Getting (*Canberra*), Dechaineux (*Australia*), Waller (*Perth*), A. H. Spurgeon (natural causes), Commanders Walker (*Parramatta*), Rayment (*Australia*) and Moran (*Vampire*). The number was now down to twenty. The two most senior were Captains Farncomb and Collins. In the 'whirligig of time' ahead, the wastage factor is seldom taken into account. So many unknown factors will arise, be they fate, bad or good luck. I did not give this any reflection at the time.

After leave, with changes in the ship's company, it was necessary to go through the 'working up' routine once again at Jervis Bay. This honing of fighting efficiency had little bearing on my next unusual assignment. The Commonwealth Government set out to raise £70 million from a security loan and, to attract business, anyone contributing £50 within a particular three-day period would be entitled to a few hours at sea in one of HMA ships. My name came out of a hat to meet obligations at Brisbane, Newcastle, Sydney and Melbourne. Brisbane was the toughest as four trips to Moreton Bay was required and so I came to know well the tortuous Brisbane River. This jollity came to the notice of the Brisbane *Courier Mail* cartoonist, Jack Lusby, who presented me with the original 'More Government Competition', with myself as a hirsute ferrymaster.

The Newcastle folk did not take full advantage of inspecting a fine destroyer at sea and only one trip was required, but Sydney and Melbourne required three each. In all we entertained 3,298 passengers, who, I trust, were better informed on nautical matters as a result. The director of the loan felt the cruises were 'a great success'.

On 2 April I was given the acting rank of captain and appointed Captain (D) 10th Destroyer Flotilla comprising *Arunta* (Commander G. G. O. Gatacre), *Warramunga* (Commander M. J. Clark), *Quickmatch* (Commander J. K. Walton), *Quadrant* (A/Lieutenant-Commander W. F. Cook) and *Quiberon* (Lieutenant-Commander G. F. E. Knox). This was encouraging. I thought at the time that the key to this promotion rested on my performance in *Norman* but discovered later that my confidential report and 'flimsy' from Commodore Arliss had been lost at sea. My mind floated back to my days as a two-striper when even a commander (D) seemed an ogre. The ship's company were only too pleased to paint a black band on the forward funnel, which at least ensured a good berth in any harbour.

I was not to see much of my team, let alone give any flotilla training. It was really a paperwork job and I had a secretary to take the load. My orders were to visit Portland, Victor Harbour and Adelaide.

At Victor Harbour on Easter Saturday evening, my commissioned signal boatswain told me that Easter Sunday, 21 April, was Princess Elizabeth's birthday and that we should 'dress ship' on the morrow. A weak brain cell had taken its time to remind me that it was my wedding anniversary and that I had done nothing about it and it was now almost too late. I landed at breakfast time and borrowed a telephone, said my piece and my wife mentioned the arrival of a gold wrist-watch. My two American lieutenants (junior grade) should have been promoted to senior grade.

After visiting Adelaide, I arrived back in Sydney at the end of April. V. E. Day was to be 10 June and HMA ships were spread around Australia to assist in the celebrations. I was allocated Devonport in Tasmania and it turned out to be a very jolly affair. A contingent from the ship was to join a Victory March through the town, led by the Devonport Municipal Band and the

178

culmination was a cocktail party on board to be attended by the Mayor and Corporation.

Returning north, I spent some time on the Queensland coast, ending at Mackay, before returning to Sydney for some leave and refit. There I learned that we were to return to Japan to join the Occupation Force as part of the American 7th Fleet. It was a sore point with Commander-in-Chief British Commonwealth Occupation Force (at this time our Lieutenant-General Sir Horace Robertson) that RN and RAN ships were not put under his command. There was nothing to be gained by it except a larger staff.

I was to accompany *Hobart* (Captain D. H. Harries) to sample the Japanese autumn. Crossing the Equator in peacetime was a new event. Sailors seem to love dressing up and there is always someone who knows the drill. There was work to do as well since changes in personnel during the last leave required many different drills and exercises, so that life was never dull.

The USN tanker at Guam gave my sailors a chance to stock up on American cigarettes, the barter currency in Japan. Approaching Japan I said good-bye to David Harries, as I had been diverted to Sasebo in Kyushu where I was to take a turn on the Korean Patrol in the Tshushima Strait, relieving one of my flotilla, HMAS *Quickmatch*. Before arrival at Sasebo we had company — two cyclones, both of which obligingly got out of our way.

At Sasebo I reported to my senior officer, US Commander Destroyer Squadron 15. I can best describe Sasebo, the Korean Patrol, and a visit to Fukuoka from my own report:

The respite from continuous steaming was fully enjoyed. SASEBO as an operating base has much to commend it. For Officers there are innumerable delightful walks. The USN Officers Club is secluded and handy and is the general rendezvous in the dog watches. Incidentally owing to previous profits, beer and nuts are 'on' the club. Jeeps are available for local trips on atrocious roads. For the Ship's Company the bombed township of SASEBO offers attractions in an official cabaret and souvenirs. Hard work in most pleasant climatic conditions combined with novel shore attractions have been much enjoyed. Japanese working parties are available. Fuel and water are supplied by lighter. An L.C.V.P. helps the transport problem. Fleet Movie Exchange functions as usual. SASEBO with FUKUOKA is a large repatriation centre. The shipping activity is confined to the southern part of the fine natural harbour with an overflow anchorage in the approaches. Japanese merchant ships of all descriptions, Jap-manned Liberty Ships and L.S.T.'s, demilitarized destroyers, escort vessels and landing craft abound.

I made a quick visit to Nagasaki with a party, including an American lady professor, where we were allowed to climb up one of the few remaining structures. The devastation was not a happy sight.
My reports continued:

The KOREAN Patrol was organized by COMNAV-JAP. The presence of Cholera among Korean smugglers and illegal repatriates necessitated an increased effort to suppress this illegal entry into Japan. There was a danger of Cholera becoming endemic. The successful interceptions by HMIS *Sutlej* in the early stages gave rise to the present organization of 2 US and 2 RAN Destroyers, 3 US Patrol vessels and 1 RIN Escort vessel. Destroyer Patrols are of 56 hours duration. An Escort vessel anchors in TSHU SHIMA by day and patrols this intermediate stopping place by night. Interceptions at sea have not been great, but the existence of the Patrol is well known and for the present the traffic appears to have ceased. The Patrol line is from GOTO-RETTO to latitude 35 30 N avoiding minefields said to have been swept by the Japs.
Bataan proceeded [on her Patrol stint] at 0600I on Wednesday 25. Seven craft were investigated and found innocent. The passage of a depression made conditions unpleasant and not without risk to small craft. On Friday 27 made rendezvous with HMIS

Narbada to transfer mail and charts and Patrol completed proceeded to No. 4 Buoy FUKUOKA, *Bataan* being the only warship present.[35]

The Korean Patrol no doubt satisfied somebody but it was a bit of a joke. I asked one US destroyer captain how he recognized 'Koreans and illegal repatriates'. He said his boarding officer had the crew fallen in and then in English said, 'Koreans, one pace forward march'. If there was no movement, the ship was clear.

When provisions were required I proceeded to Kagoshima Wan to rendezvous with an RN Victualling Stores Issuing Ship, *Fort Constantine*. At night I had to pass through one of the famous Japanese fishing fleets. There were lights everywhere but only one in three fishing boats carried them. Without an efficient radar set, the list of ancestors would have increased dramatically.

I was to depart for Kure, in the Inland Sea, on 4 October. I had just completed my Report of Proceedings for September:

The conduct and health of the Ship's Company has been exemplary and morale could not be higher. The Ship's Company work with a will and, with a fine spirit, take prowess as the Flotilla leader, which they mean her to be in all respects.

Then a signal was received directing me to turn over my command to Lieutenant Commander Dovers and return to Melbourne by air. I was mystified by the failure to mention my next appointment.

My flight back to Australia was not without its moments. From Morotai to Darwin was a very long leg for a DC3, and there was a lot of disconcerting talk when we passed the point of 'no return', with Darwin and the Arafura Sea being the only alternative landing places. At Darwin we were required to change planes as, it seems, Customs required the wings of the aircraft to be removed to check for dutiable goods. So to another DC3 with metal bucket seats. We had gone some distance when the heating system failed and since the metal seats were too cold to sit on, a motley collection of senior soldiers, some airmen and a few sailors literally marched on the spot from Newcastle Waters to Alice Springs. Deaths from pneumonia were not reported.

It was not until my arrival home in Melbourne that I learned of my new job from my wife. The need for secrecy never became apparent. I was to serve two years in Melbourne as Deputy Chief of Naval Staff. It was a surprise indeed as the job had not entered my calculations. The heavy losses of senior officers mentioned earlier were showing their effects.

...et by my family on arrival at Port Mel-
...urne. About to pay official calls on
...vernor, Chief Justice, Premier, Lord
...ayor and Secretary Defence

The royal landing in Hobart, 1954

...ROM ... STANDARD   041026Z APRIL 54
...O ... VENGEANCE
...HANK YOU FOR A MOST ORIGINAL FORGERY'
...orting *Gothic*, Indian Ocean, SE trade wind

HMAS *Vengeance*

A 'barrier'—drama first class

9
Gaining Experience Ashore and Afloat 1947–54

The appointment as Deputy Chief of Naval Staff was pleasing from many aspects, not the least of which were the prospects of some home life combined with a responsible job in a machine in which I had already been a cog on two occasions. I relieved Captain H. J. Buchanan on 6 October 1946.

The defence forces were still demobilizing as the government deliberated upon their peacetime shapes and sizes. The pressures of war had been lifted and I was to take many 'make and mends'.[36] On Wednesdays I played tennis with four or five others, including Admiral Sir Louis Hamilton, the Chief of Naval Staff. The experiences of the Second World War fully demonstrated the need for aircraft-carriers in modern navies and his name should long be remembered as the driving force behind the introduction of the Fleet Air Arm in the RAN. My work was to understudy the Chief of Naval Staff and to control the work of the Staff; to look after the operational side of the service; to deal with problems as a member of the Joint Planning Committee; to produce briefs on Defence Committee papers for the CNS; and generally to do some advance thinking on the state of the Navy.

Sir Louis, in the absence of the Minister, presided over the Naval Board, comprising Commodore James Armstrong, Second Naval Member; Engineer Rear-Admiral Doyle, Third Member; Mr Nankervis, Secretary; and Mr Anthony, Finance Member.

The major aim of the Board was to obtain government approval for the introduction of a Fleet Air Arm. Our earlier dabbling with float planes and the advent of HMAS *Albatross*, our seaplane-carrier, has been recorded. As a Defence Public Relations paper, dated 25 February 1982, states:

In 1945 Lieutenant-Commander V. A. Smith RAN (later Admiral Sir Victor Smith, AC, KBE, CB, DSC) was asked to prepare an outline paper for the formation of a RAN Fleet Air Arm. The plan was well received by the Naval Board and with Admiralty agreement Lieut.-Commander Smith was attached to the Admiralty to develop a more detailed plan. At the end of 1946, the Naval Board requested assistance from the Royal Navy in the form of a small team of experienced officers who commenced work in early 1947 under the title of Naval Aviation Planning Staff.

At this stage I was no more than an interested spectator in the planning of the Fleet Air Arm, which was already well under way. Sir Louis, who had succeeded Admiral Royle, had the Naval Aviation Planning Staff well entrenched behind the ramparts of Victoria Barracks. The team consisted of an air expert, Captain F. W. Anstice, RN, Lieutenant-Commander (O) Victor Smith, RAN, A/Commander A. F. Turner, RN, and A/Commander B. J. J. P. Robinson, RN.

At the end of 1946 I knew little of the new Fleet Air Arm planning details, except that the general outline was that it should be a two-carrier/two-airfield organization and that the planners still had their heads down. By April 1947 the Fleet Air Arm Plan had taken shape although many items, including provision and training of personnel, had yet to be worked out in detail. Broadly, the timetable for its introduction was first to obtain the Admiralty's agreement to complete construction of a 'Majestic' class light fleet carrier which would be commissioned as HMAS *Sydney* to be ready for service in late 1948. Meanwhile arrangements would be made to acquire aircraft and trained personnel. Two naval air stations were to be established at Nowra and Schofields — both ex-RAAF bases. It was planned that a sister ship, to be known as *Melbourne*, would follow on, thus giving us two carriers by 1951. This plan passed through the Defence Committee, although a minority proposed that the RAAF run the Fleet Air Arm.

At about this time my wife and I were invited to dine with Sir Louis who lived with his two sisters. We found that the Minister and Mrs Riordan also were guests and so after dinner, when the ladies had retired, we were able to chat about the Fleet Air Arm over a glass of port. Back with the ladies, 10.30 pm arrived, the customary time to call for the barge, the car or the bicycle. Neither the Minister nor his wife seemed keen to make their adieux and time passed as my wife and I kept exchanging glances. The Admiral was looking somewhat tired and uncomfortable so my wife took courage in both hands and said to Mrs Riordan, 'And where are you staying?' She replied, 'Here' and we all had a laugh. The Burrells departed and the Admiral, no doubt like Samuel Pepys, said, 'And so to bed'.

In due course the Labor government approved the introduction of the Fleet Air Arm. The RAAF counter-plan proposal for manning the Air Arm was not accepted. Establishing the Fleet Air Arm, accepted as vital to the defence of Australia in the postwar era, was a task of great magnitude requiring a lot of work from many people who met the challenge with much enthusiasm. Recruiting of personnel for the new organization was under way in Australia, New Zealand and the United Kingdom with advertisements appearing in the press. Personnel required to operate a naval air arm were many and varied and included pilots, observers, air controllers, air engineers, air mechanics and aircraft handlers, all under the control of a commander (air) who had to be an experienced air-arm officer. Obviously we had to borrow from the Royal Navy for quite a time:

The largest single source was to be the Royal Navy which provided loan personnel or was the source of many permanent transfers to the RAN.

Another source was the RAAF. Several RAAF pilots had already transferred to the RANVR under a 1945 scheme to augment the number of pilots in the British Pacific Fleet and some of these were also available for the new air arm.

A small number of RAN officers were already in training in England in anticipation of approval to form a Fleet Air Arm.[37]

Newly recruited officers without naval experience were sent to sea for short periods to acclimatize. As preparations increased in pace, the RAAF Station at Nowra was taken over and the Admiralty, with its usual generosity, agreed to its part in the plan.

Some of my time was taken up in Defence matters. I was a member of the Joint Planning Committee. The main subject concerned the future size and shape of the defence forces. The normal routine of work kept me reasonably busy and I trust some of the work of the Joint Planning Committee of which, by attrition, I became chairman, helped in the decision-making in the more rarified atmosphere. However, I cannot recall any individual recommendations of great import. I do remember Sir Frederick Sheddon (Secretary, Department of Defence) giving us the task of writing a paper on disarmament but I felt that I had to tell him that the Committee had not a clue about originating such a paper and that it would waste our time and his. I suggested that as he had attended a Disarmament Conference in Geneva in 1930, he would be better qualified and so the task was withdrawn. Shedden's opposite number in the UK was Sir Maurice Hankey whom Shedden described as his mentor. Consequently Sir Frederick was known as the pocket hanky.

My tour of shore duty was about to expire after two pleasant years. Much postwar clearing up had been achieved and the shape of our future navy was beginning to emerge. Apart from the propitious beginning enjoyed by the Fleet Air Arm, there were many changes in the Navy. An electrical branch was established; construction was completed in Australia of two large fleet destroyers, *Tobruk* and *Anzac*; *Australia*, after making good her war damage, was re-commissioned and became the squadron flagship; and ships such as *Quadrant* and *Manoora* were paid off. Tragically, in 1947, *Warrnambool*, sweeping off Cockburn Reef in northern Queensland, struck a mine laid by our *Bungaree* during the war and sank with the loss of several lives.

There was one aspect of my time as DCNS which still concerns me and it involves the research voyages to the Antarctic made by *Labuan* (a landing ship tank) which began in November 1947. *Labuan* was not suitable as a research vessel — instead of having a fine, streamlined bow, she had a very large, blunt nose, quite unsuited to the heavy, battering seas of the higher latitudes which she had to endure. I have since wondered if I failed in my duty, after reading the letters of proceedings of the first voyage, by not recommending that the expeditions be halted until suitable vessels could be obtained. I recall the report of a medical officer which described graphically the sounds, the shuddering, the rippling of steel bulkheads, and the terrible noise and discomfort endured by all hands. In retrospect I think that I erred and believe that I have to thank the captains (Dixon, Shaw and Cartwright) during these voyages to Heard Island, for saving my reputation.

My period as DCNS also saw the Navy come of age. In January 1947 Farncomb and Collins were promoted to flag rank, the first of the RANC graduates and a landmark in the history of the college. Just a little more than a year later an even greater stride towards naval maturity was taken when Sir Louis Hamilton returned to the United Kingdom, pleased, I am sure, with his achievements. Instead of requesting the Admiralty to provide a replacement, and despite the fact that Farncomb and Collins were but junior rear-admirals, the Australian government decided that an Australian would be appointed Chief of Naval Staff. Both men had distinguished war records and the choice must have been a difficult one to make. However, the coin came down with Collins uppermost.

There had been changes in my family as well as in the Navy. My wife had paused in her activities at home and at her factory to present me with a son, Stuart, on 21 March 1947, and by the time of my departure from Navy Office, our daughter Lynne was on her way to join us.

I was able to take with me a trophy of my time as DCNS. I was honoured to be appointed for a term as an aide-de-camp to the Queen but an opportunity did not arise for me to perform my duty in that capacity and so my pair of ER II silver devices, meant for my shoulder straps, became two exclusive menu-holders.

Of course it would be Captain Gatacre to take over my office chair and I was to relieve Captain H. J. Buchanan, who had previously relieved me in *Norman*, in command of *Australia*, the flagship of Rear-Admiral Farncomb. With the ship anchored off Crib Point, adjacent to Flinders Naval Depot, in Westernport, I did not have far to go on the third day of October 1948. As seems customary in the naval service, daughter Lynne was to be born three weeks after I went to sea.

HMAS *Australia* 1949

Australia's function was to train national servicemen in nautical matters, providing classes for seamen, stokers, signal men and storemen. Being Chief Staff Officer meant additional work but, on the whole, it appeared a pleasant prospect. The Melbourne Cup was held a couple of weeks after I took command and, to maintain tradition, a visit to Port Melbourne was obligatory. After McDougal had won the honours at Flemington we returned to Sydney for leave and refit.

A royal visit had been arranged for 1949 and I was informed that my new command was to be home for the King and Queen during a week's holiday on the Barrier Reef. The King was to have the Admiral's quarters and the Queen my smaller abode. I was not happy with the toilet in my quarters and placed it on the list of items to be replaced. It was not, however, approved. Not long afterwards there was an accident when a dockyard matey dropped a large adjustable spanner and most unfortunately wrecked the unworthy object. Consequently my cabin became the owner of the quietest hush-flush known to the plumbing fraternity. I was rather flattered by the cabin arrangements whereby I was to be placed next to the ladies-in-waiting.

Sadly the tour had to be abandoned. 1949 was spent on the Australia Station giving the trainees sea experience as well as allowing them to know their continent. I was able to return to Hobart, the scene of an earlier triumph at the game of tennis. Once, when invited to have my name included in a publication, I entered under the heading of 'Recreations', with a flourish of simple snobbery: 'Tennis and Lawn Tennis'.

The routine at Hobart was to spend Monday to Friday in different anchorages, such as Port Arthur, Barnes Bay in D'Entrecasteaux Channel, and North West Bay, and to return to the city for the weekends. Soon we had to return to Western Port to change over instructional classes and made good use of the depot's recreational grounds. Before returning to Sydney, we steamed round to Port Melbourne for the weekend and opened the ship to visitors, so many of whom presented themselves that several hundred had to be turned away.

April, May, June and July passed quickly as we trained and paid many enjoyable visits to Australian ports. I remember this period also because the work I had witnessed while I was Deputy Chief of Naval Staff came to fruition and our first aircraft carrier, HMAS *Sydney*, arrived in Australia. On 6 August, *Australia* set off on an island cruise, en route fulfilling another Navy tradition which was to have a warship in Brisbane for show week. For a luncheon I gave for the Minister for the Navy and Mrs Riordan, I managed to track down Archbishop Birch, my old padre from Naval College days, who lured us into theological discussions by having a large box of chocolate biscuits handy.

The cruise was ruined by recurring cases of rubella so we remained in isolation visiting the Barrier Reef islands, Laurabada (Port Moresby) and Admiralty Islands. We returned to Sydney on 20 September with the sailors still smiling.

A little more than a month later I was relieved as the captain of *Australia* by George Oldham. Early in the new year I was required to be in London.

Imperial Defence College 1950

I had been informed that I was to attend the Imperial Defence College in 1950 and that after my course I was likely to spend a further two years in the United Kingdom. The young Burrell family, including Bridie, our housekeeper, and her husband, established itself near Sloane Square in a rented tenement house. It was a narrow building with four floors, including one below street level, and definitely not an abode for the arthritic.

However, it was handy to Belgrave Square, the site of the Imperial Defence College.

My return to London brought home to me vividly the extent of the war damage and heightened my appreciation of the stamina exhibited by the British during the blitz. Food rationing was still in force and there were long queues for rationed items, which made shopping extremely tedious. Little wonder it is that to this day Englishmen waiting for a bus automatically form a queue.

My wife was very active and not satisfied to pass the time purely in a social milieu. She had good customers in England for her mica products and her thoughts turned to setting up a branch of her Australian business in the UK. First she had to find factory space, which of course was also controlled, and the best effort by the Board of Trade was to offer her the lease of a new factory in the wilds of Scotland. This she inspected only to find no labour or accommodation in the vicinity. Eventually she was able to lease an open-sided timber mill near Oxford Road at High Wycombe, some twenty miles from London.

Having sent my wife out to work, a home was required between London and the factory at High Wycombe. An old friend had a mansion with outlying cottages at Gerrards Cross, about midway between the two, making it an ideal position. We approached the friend, dear Aunt Gladys (she was no relation), and enquired if one of her cottages might be available for letting. 'No, my dears, but you could use the old homestead if you like. Perhaps you could do up a few rooms and forget the rent.' St Huberts was a two-storey stately home of England, with butler's cottage, walled-in vegetable garden, and fruit trees, and was spread over about ten acres of ground, full of oaks and elms and scattered with white rhododendrons. In front of the house was a large, pleasant lawn with sundial and a pool full of watercress.

Inside the house it was like a scene from Nicholas Nickleby with inches of dust everywhere. Nevertheless, we decided that it was within our capabilities to make the house habitable and we were to spend nearly three very happy years there. We kept our part of the bargain in doing up rooms and Aunt Gladys was more than pleased to see her fine old homestead come back to life. I even found a tennis court completely hidden by blackberries and brought it back into commission.

I joined the Imperial Defence College in Seaford House, 37 Belgrave Square, in January 1950. To attend the course was a great privilege and I valued it beyond price. The service students were on the captain/brigadier/air commodore level. Of the fifty-six students on the course three others were from Australia — Brigadier H. G. Edgar, Air Commodore V. E. Hancock and Mr Fred Chilton from the Department of Defence. The New Zealand student was Brigadier C. E. Weir who, during the Second World War had been a major-general and accepted lower rank to continue in the service. He eventually became CGS and recovered his rank, but in the meantime many were unaware of the presence of an experienced general. One of the UK brigadiers, E. M. Bastyan, became Governor of Hong Kong in later years to be followed by governorships of South Australia and Tasmania. Our commandant was Admiral Sir Charles Daniel (of British Pacific Fleet planning days) and one of the three Senior Directing Staff was Major-General W. P. Oliver whom I was to meet again as UK High Commissioner in Canberra.

The College came into existence in 1927 as a result of a Cabinet Committee recommendation and its functions were defined as:

a. the training of a body of officers and civilian officials in the broadest aspects of Imperial Strategy, and

b. in order to ensure that the courses of study shall not become wholly academic and lose touch with realities, the occasional examination of the concrete problems of Imperial Defence which are referred to them by the Chiefs of Staff Committee.[38]

The first commandant was Admiral Sir Herbert Richmond, a naval historian of note, of whom a fellow admiral wrote: 'His general erudition, his vast knowledge of naval and military history, his power of analysis and exposition, first things first, his readiness to hear every point of view argued, won him at once the attention and respect of all those working with him'. [39] As a 'flimsy' that would make good reading. After the war the course restarted in 1947, with General Sir William Slim as commandant, when Commodore John Collins attended. Collins was followed by Captain D. H. Harries in 1948 and Captain A. J. Buchanan in 1949. Also after the war, the Charter for the College was amended and it no longer required to examine on problems referred to it by the Chiefs of Staff.

In 1950 the College routine was as arduous or as carefree as you wished to make it. One was expected to arrive about 9 am in order to be prepared for the day's lecture an hour later. The calibre of the lecturers could not be higher and included Prime Ministers, Secretaries of State, Ministers, High Commissioners, ex-Chiefs of Staff and even the Archbishop of Canterbury. These and many others were prepared to talk and be cross-questioned. Even the theory of Communism was covered academically, and by practitioners. On the Communist lecturers, Marshal of the Royal Air Force Sir John Slessor wrote:

These lectures were stopped about the end of my time; someone — I think Field Marshal Alexander . . . went to Winston and said there was a terribly subversive thing going on — actually Communist leaders lecturing at IDC! Winston I suppose had something better to think about and that edict went forth. I said I'd been brought up to believe that an important principle in strategy was to know your enemy; and if your enemy was good enough to come and lecture to you then you ought to jump at it. But no good. WSC had this extraordinary idea that Alex could not be wrong![40]

The lecture programme was divided between the lessons of the late war and future possibilities and prospects. The students were divided into syndicates of diverse composition and given a fortnight in which to solve a problem which required research and syndicate argument before a solution could be produced. Sir John Slessor (Commandant 1948–49), in a letter to Chiefs of Staff, described with great clarity the working time and effort expected from the student:

Students ... had come straight from years of hard work and responsibility and were most of them badly in need of a change from both — for that one year at IDC. As for hard work, I had no wish to discourage it but I was more interested in trying to see that the students left at the end of their year refreshed in mind by a pleasant interesting period of general discussion with their opposite numbers in other Services and with no burden of practical responsibility for grave contemporary decisions — of which they had had quite enough in previous years, and would have more when they went out into the cold hard world in Whitehall or elsewhere. I naturally expected them to take the exercises seriously — though not too seriously. I think it was Bill Slim who coined the phrase 'There are no unnecessary widows as a result of a wrong decision in an IDC Exercise'.[41]

Correctly, I was under the impression that normally Confidential Reports were not written about one's performance at the College but the marked enthusiasm of the soldiers suggested otherwise. Curiously, they would volunteer for any job and generally make a labour of the course. One could only admire their enthusiasm, but perhaps they might more profitably have heeded the advice of one commandant who quoted the Bible: 'The wisdom of a learned man cometh by opportunity of leisure and he that hath little business shall become wise' (Ecclesiastes 38:24).

Question time I found trying, especially on occasions when the lecturer or the commandant would ask the Australian view on some topic or proposition. After a painful pause, I would rise and attempt some sort of answer but there was too much guesswork about it all. Touring was a part of the course and within England we made a few short visits to service and industrial establishments of direct and indirect value. There was also a long tour which took students as far afield as Australia and Canada, but the 'far flung' types would be given a European tour which for my year included Dusseldorf, Hamburg, Berlin and Vienna. We were shown around West Berlin and attended lectures on the Allied Control Commission, but it was all very depressing and just too isolated for comfort. Naturally, we spoke with many Germans, and I wrote at the time that it was 'intensely interesting but I wouldn't trust them a yard. Of course there isn't a Nazi in the country — tripe! We sat around afterwards for a chat and didn't like the taste left on our tongues'. The visit to Berlin lacked any gaiety. The destruction meted out to the Germans was awesome, as Churchill had promised it would be. It was not a happy sight to see elderly women working in their underwear to clear rubble.

Vienna was equally depressing. We stayed at the famous Hotel Sacher, one of the few buildings intact, of which my main memory is that of being required to pay for liqueurs in the winecellar where the signature tune of the film *The Third Man* was played on a zither. I was pleased to be home from such a sordid tour — being the victor did not bring any glow of satisfaction.

Leave was due to me and as my wife needed a break from factory affairs, we decided on a car trip to Geneva and Paris. We crossed the Jura mountains and then, without warning, burst out at the top to be confronted by an amazing spectacle. The mountain dropped steeply to the plain beneath which spread out to a long sliver of a lake, with a vast white background of the Alps. It was late afternoon and the setting sun cast a pink glow over what we took to be Mont Blanc. A closer look at the lake revealed a city with a thin plume of water just visible. We passed through Customs on the Swiss border and settled in at the Beau Rivage, a popular name for Continental hotels. Not being great tourists, we preferred to stay in one place for a while and get to know it.

On the return journey we entered Paris through Versailles. Somehow I could not avoid passing round the Arc de Triomphe. Paris must be the only place in the world where the accelerators are connected to the horns. We spent two evenings at the Café de Paris and the Folies Bergere. The latter was more unusual than I had expected, with a great deal of nudity one moment, and the next the auditorium and stage would be transformed into a cathedral with nuns and priests in great chorus. I found amusing the reproduction of famous paintings using live characters in which there always seemed to be huge women with bare posteriors almost bursting out of the stage-size gilt frame. Meanwhile my wife slept in her stall, which to me was a fair reflection on the female attitude to the female form divine.

However, we were soon home to enjoy a pleasant English summer at St Huberts. The house became livable and the lawn surrounded by fine old English trees was a great delight. Slowly we were bringing the old place back to something resembling its old world grandeur and good progress was also being made with the establishment of Peerless Mica (Australia) in England.

The IDC continued on its placid way for the remainder of the year, broken by short local tours. We spent a day at sea in an aircraft carrier, visited several factories and one night watched the London *Times* being put to bed. Our final activity was a mock Commonwealth Conference with Brigadier Edgar as our Prime Minister, which brought out the areas of agreement and the reverse. Admiral Daniel gave his valedictory address, but kept his memorable opening phrase for the benefit of the 1951 course: 'Gentlemen, I am now going to cast sham pearls before real swine'.

All good things must end, and so we parted to the four corners of the earth. It had been a most absorbing year and a pleasant period without responsibility midstream in a career. As with the Staff College before the war, it brought me into contact with senior officers with whom I would have to deal in later years, and when both speak the same language, a better solution emerges in short time.

The IDC, under the new name of the Royal College of Defence Studies (RCDS), is still very much a going concern. The shape and size has been amended to keep pace with NATO and the ever-increasing numbers of Commonwealth countries. In 1970 the Charter was brought up to date and changes introduced included the writing of a thesis of great length and the initiation of confidential reports on individual officers. These resulted from talk that golf handicaps were being lowered during the year but I would vote against both changes, as it now appears that the casual atmosphere, which I found very beneficial, has evaporated.

Assistant Defence Representative London 1951–52

My next posting did not take me very far: I was appointed Assistant Defence Representative on the staff of the Australian High Commissioner. Australian representation in London was considerable and unable to be accommodated in Australia House in the Strand. The overflow was housed in a leased building in Jermyn Street, parallel to Piccadilly and a few hundred yards from Piccadilly Circus and Eros. The street had diverse reputations but I like to think that we (together with the best bespoken shirt-makers in London, of course) added a degree of respectability to it. Another profession associated with my new address had been immortalized in verse:

When Lady Jane became a tart
It nearly broke her parents' heart.
But pride is pride and race is race;
So, to preserve the family face,
She found a most exclusive beat
On the sunny side of Jermyn Street.

Naturally, my office was on the shady side.

The Defence Representative, my boss, was Major-General Rudolf Bierwirth. I was number two on his staff, with Wing Commander Ted Fyfe as number three. We had a male secretary and a typist. Our job was to liaise with the UK Ministry of Defence and to find out London views on defence topics. General Bierwirth was supposed to liaise with the UK Chiefs of Staff but we received little information at that level and I think that I was supposed to obtain views on the captain level.

That door, however, had been closed as the UK had agreed to make a desk available in the Ministry only on the commander level. Therefore Ted Fyfe was our chief informant and in touch with the Defence Planning Division Secretariat. It was the responsibility of the UK defence representatives in Australia to obtain local views on defence topics. It seemed to me that they were better informed than we on Australian defence matters.

Requests for information would come from Sir Fred Shedden in Australia and Ted Fyfe would try to find out the views on the highest possible level, returning to Jermyn Street each evening with the day's harvest, the size of which proved that his liaison ability was of a high order. My job was to draft signals and letters for the General's approval, but it soon became clear that a succinct unambiguous message would not suffice and that Sir Frederick required a letter by air mail to add the trimmings.

In a quiet room in our office sat unfortunate Jamie Armstrong who had missed out on taking command of our first aircraft-carrier because he had broken his arm as he jumped on a moving Sydney tram. He had forgotten the old adage: never run after a girl or a tram — there's always another one coming. As a commodore, he was the Interservice Technical Officer on the staff and since only two were allowed diplomatic privileges, he and the General were the two. Ted Fyfe and I were a trifle envious for, apart from missing out on cheap grog, we had to be careful to avoid parking problems and control murderous intent. The previous year, my wife had parked her car at the Navy and Army Store near Victoria Station. When the summons arrived she was conveniently in Boston. I wrote a letter informing the police that my wife was out of the country and that I was sure it was not deliberate, adding that I would reprimand her when she returned. A few days later I received a telephone call from the police:

'Sir, did you really mean that you would reprimand your wife?'

'Certainly,' I replied.

'You're a brave man — forget about the summons.'

The liaison work invariably was secret or top secret

and though important then, would be dull if recited today. The important part of my day was about four o'clock when Ted Fyfe would arrive with the crumbs that had fallen from the Ministry table. My immediate boss wanted the crumbs, now turned into a morsel (or the morsel turned into a main course), to be ciphered and transmitted to Melbourne immediately. We soon learned to select the wheat and keep the chaff under cover till the morrow. Obviously, I was seldom home early but this was compensated by a 10 am start. (Those are the hours kept at the Admiralty and they enable officers to live out in the country and to read the London *Times* in the train before work.) For me it meant that I could drop my two elder children at school on my way to London.

During my time we had one visit from Sir Frederick Shedden with a team of officers, including the CGS, Lieutenant-General Sir S. F. Rowell, for top-secret defence discussions. The Defence Representative and his staff were to make all arrangements, such as accommodation at the Savoy, cars and special arrangements for the security of classified documents. We were expected to be the type of high-class entrepreneur arranging a visit for King Farouk but without a percentage of the takings. My contribution was to provide safes at the Savoy, and sentries for which I borrowed some RAN chief petty officers who were in the UK. I even invited the dignatories out to St Huberts for a fork supper, and to our surprise all the members accepted. With daylight saving, the English summer evenings were a delight, particularly at St Huberts.

The visit appeared to be a success, but we had not allowed for the unexpected. All departure arrangements had been made and General Bierwirth and I went out to London airport to bend the knee, but as we sat in the VIP lounge ready for the last rites, rumblings were heard off-stage. The car carrying an official with all the top-secret boxes and bags had not yet arrived. The plane was delayed in the face of the demurrals of airport officials until eventually the errant car turned up. It had gone to Northolt, a domestic aerodrome, because the official had said merely 'Airport' to the driver. Our incompetence was roundly denounced in strong language, but as we had nothing to do with the official, the secret boxes, or the driver, the General and I fell into dismay.

The liaison work proceeded, but I never understood Bierwirth. He did not try hard to make opportunities to meet the Chiefs of Staff and senior officers and civilians on the high defence level, for which I chided him occasionally. He organized a lunch or two, but seldom returned with any sweetmeats worth reporting. (In truth, UK and Australian defence thinking were running on parallel lines and the period was free from emergencies.) I was amused by Bierwirth's taste for Scotch whisky. He was on the duty-free list, so this Australian would order Scotch from Holland, which is all a bit Irish. Apparently a Scotsman had been lured to Holland to do the local blending and the General's guests would have to pick the Scottish Scotch from the Dutch Scotch — a good start to a party.

Two years' liaison work found the job drawing to a close and in this time I had only one unusual assignment. A Disarmament Conference of United Nations was convened in the Palais de Chaillot in Paris, on the Seine, directly opposite the Eiffel Tower. I was required to attend as defence adviser to the Australian Delegation. At the time I doubted if it would be more than a sinecure but it was not the time to quibble about capabilities, especially since my wife was about to set off for a business appointment in Belgium and so could join me in Paris afterwards. I cannot say that I was of the slightest value to our delegation, but it was a unique opportunity to watch our diplomats at work and at play.

On the whole the liaison job had not been a very satisfying one. Admittedly we dug out and reported the answers to many questions asked by Sir Frederick Shedden and used our initiative to ferret out items of defence interest in Britain and Europe. However, we were never quite certain whether our material was put to good use, but as there were no complaints, I suppose we should have been happy in our work. The attractions of England and family life were sufficient compensation. One life-long memory was a visit to the Royal Festival Hall in the presence of the Queen. The climax of the evening came with the entire musical assembly first singing 'Rule Britannia' and then the three verses of the National Anthem with the spotlight on the Royal Box.

Having missed travelling by sea to England with my family, I was looking forward to being able to return together at the end of 1952. However, in typical service fashion, I was thwarted by the news of an appointment at sea which, as the godfather would say, was an invitation I could not refuse, and had no wish to. The press report read:

> Mr Menzies, the Prime Minister, has announced that the United Kingdom Government have agreed to lend the Royal Australian Navy the light fleet aircraft carrier *Vengeance* pending the arrival of the RAN's second carrier, HMAS *Melbourne*.
>
> About 500 RAN officers and ratings will sail from Australia in September or October to bring the *Vengeance* to Australia early in 1953. Captain H. M. Burrell, RAN, at present assistant defence representative in London, will command the ship.
>
> Mr Menzies, who was opening a new leave centre for the RAN said that the sailing of the *Melbourne*, which should have arrived in Australia this year, had been postponed while she underwent modifications. *The Commonwealth Government had asked for the loan of a carrier because it was essential that the RAN should have two carriers ready for any emergency and able to carry out the development of its air component. The RAN was being built round a core of two aircraft carriers.* [Emphasis added]
>
> Mr Menzies added that the Government and the RAN were deeply grateful to the United Kingdom Government and the Admiralty for their generosity and cooperation.[42]

This loan was required by the amended FAA plan, being a direct result of the additional time required to modernize *Melbourne*. Though not stated at the time, it was assumed that *Vengeance* would be retained until *Sydney* had undergone a similar modernization. My wife took the news well and told me that I could drop the act and wipe the disappointed look from my face.

Having been away from sea for three years, my knowledge of technical advances on naval warfare had not kept pace with tactics and hardware. To overcome this, several times a year the Royal Navy ran a short refresher course for senior officers, known as a Senior Officers Technical Course. I applied to attend the final course of 1952 and asked to spend a few days at sea in an operational carrier. The course visited the main RN schools for a few days' briefing at each, which was helpful, but three days aboard the carrier were ideal. I found most of the answers to questions that had worried me about my next job and this short experience provided all the confidence I needed.

I was disembarked by boat under the Forth Bridge at Hawes Pier — an unfortunate name. It is said that two midshipmen were returning on board, having spent the afternoon inspecting a coal mine. While waiting at Hawes Pier for their boat, two lieutenants turned over their golf bags to them and disappeared. Along came a distinguished admiral who said to the snotties, 'Where have you been this afternoon?' and the truthful reply, 'Down a coal mine, sir' was not believed. The admiral retorted, 'When you return on board, place yourselves under close arrest for insolence'.

Back in London there was much to be done to pack up the family and to leave the house in good shape. My wife felt she had the mica factory organized to work without her presence. My family sailed without me and endured a tiresome voyage during which the children went down with the measles at ten-day intervals. This was all a poor finish to three most enjoyable years which had seen my wife succeed in her business venture and our three children acquire most attractive English accents.

HMAS *Vengeance* 1953–54

One morning in December 1952 I appeared in Devonport dockyard to prepare the aircraft carrier HMAS

Vengeance for commissioning, and later to carry out trials after her refit and to take her to Australia with a load of cocooned aircraft. My heads of departments were all RAN officers with the exception of Commander (Air) A. Downes, RN. It was early days for the Fleet Air Arm and some time would elapse before we could produce an experienced senior air officer.

With great foresight, the principle of the RAN being a two-carrier navy had been accepted by the Australian government. HMAS *Sydney* had joined the Fleet in May 1949 and during the latter half of 1950 had returned to the United Kingdom to embark additional aircraft. HMAS *Melbourne* had also been taken over from the Admiralty by this time, but with the proving of the angled deck and the stabilized landing mirror, it was obligatory for *Melbourne* to be altered structurally. This would take time and meanwhile the recruiting and training of Fleet Air Arm personnel could proceed in the loaned carrier, *Vengeance*.

On her last voyage in the Royal Navy from Singapore to Devonport, *Vengeance* had been a troop carrier, the hangar full of stores and the flight deck covered with vehicles boxed or on wheels. She had paused at Malta long enough for an enthusiastic commander to paint ship, and on arrival in Plymouth, the ship looked spic, if not span. It soon became all too obvious, however, that the paint had been applied to a rusty base. It would take us twelve months progressively chipping the ship's side and flight deck to gain respectability.

The ship's company was engaged fully in general maintenance and in embarking naval, air and victualling stores which was making us unpopular with the bosun of the yard who complained that we were asking for too many railway trucks for the removal of rubbish.

The conversion of the ship back to an operational state was being made step by step in preparation for sailing on 14 January. Trials of arrester wires and barrier (all connected to hydraulic braking systems) were completed as well as light shots of the catapult. Before leaving Plymouth I invited our High Commissioner, Sir Thomas White, to visit the ship, and we, in turn, were guests of honour at a civic reception given by the Lord

Mayor, on which occasion he graciously refrained from presenting us with a replica of Drake's drum. On 7 January we moved out to a buoy in the Hamoaze to embark ammunition, aviation fuel and oil-fuel and a week later we sailed — a happy moment for us all.

We made our way up the Channel to Portland where, having a clear flight deck, it was decided to give the flight team some practice. A Firefly and Avenger were made available and went through the routine of deck-landing under ideal conditions. I think we were all pleasantly surprised that the procedure was so simple. After our three Bristol Sycamore helicopters had settled on deck, the ship sailed for the Clyde. On our run up the Irish Sea, the British turned on strike and shadowing aircraft to give our action information organization some initial training.

As we turned into King George V dock at Glasgow, I cast a lingering look across the Forth to John Brown's shipyard, where *Australia* and *Canberra* had been built, and noted the new royal yacht *Britannia* being constructed under complete cover from the elements. Our cocooned aircraft and spares were being assembled on the dock. When the hangar was full, we concentrated the remaining aircraft amidships on the flight deck to allow operating space for the helicopters forward and space for divisions, prayers and deck hockey aft. We also kept an area for 'firefly' sailing dinghies in crates and for ship's company cars, a rare opportunity in the naval service to have your motor vehicle travel home with you. In all we embarked ten Sea Fury MK XI, twenty-five Firefly Mark VI and 650 tons of free freight.

So on 21 January 1953, passing Greenoch, Gourock and the Isle of Arran, the long voyage to Australia began. The safety of the aircraft in rough weather was my prime concern for should one break loose from its moorings, it could well damage several others and jeopardize life and limb in attempts to secure it; consequently, permanent watchkeepers were placed.

The voyage was uneventful until one evening in the Mediterranean, not far from Gibraltar. Some urge took me up the ladder to the bridge where, to my consternation, I saw a merchantman about a mile and a half on our starboard bow on a collision course. There was searoom enough to order 'hard-a-starboard', which allowed us to pass safely on opposite courses, but if the other ship had been closer, the turn would have been to port and we could have collided. I was at a loss to know how this could have happened. The boatswain was the officer of the watch and possessed a full watchkeeping certificate, yet he had failed in two respects. First, to comply with my standing orders to inform me, if on sighting a ship, it was liable to pass within two miles of us; and second, as officer of the watch, to take action as required by the rule of the road. Suffice to say the boatswain was required to be re-examined for his watchkeeping certificate, and we made Gibraltar, waiting for us as solid and dramatic as ever. On Australia Day I was ordered to secure alongside the famous South Mole.

Soon we were on our way once more and the Mediterranean, almost in apology for her lack of hospitality during the Second World War, presented us with a pleasant passage to Malta, where I exchanged calls with the Commander-in-Chief Mediterranean Fleet, Earl Mountbatten of Burma. Years ago, as a snotty, I had seen and heard of Lieutenant Mountbatten at Portsmouth Barracks, where he was a communication specialist and was instructing the officers' long course in signals. There indeed, it seemed to me, was a naval officer in his prime, blessed with a key to Buckingham Palace and with the social attractions of London merely awaiting his attention. Yet he found time to rewrite the *Handbook of Wireless Telegraphy*, a textbook which remained current for many years. Furthermore, he let it be known to his students that they should feel free to drive up to his home in Hampshire on any weekend and be given a rub up on problems not understood in the lecture room.

While at Malta, three ratings who had missed the ship on sailing from the United Kingdom and who had been apprehended, were flown out to join us. Normally such men were charged with 'missing the ship on sailing', which naturally is a serious offence. Those three were charged with 'desertion' and thereby were rendered liable to pay the cost of travel to rejoin their ship.

As we continued eastward from Malta, memories of Operation 'Vigorous' could not be laid aside until our arrival at Port Said, where the commander allowed a few local dealers to set up shop. We passed through the Canal and, after fuelling at Aden, made for Colombo, the first sight of which is usually Adam's Peak, sitting serenely above the clouds. Arriving on 16 February, I made my official calls, including one to the Australian High Commissioner, Mr Roden Cutler, VC. I found the new toys, our three helicopters, were a rarity and definitely a great advance in commuting for the modern man in a hurry.

Four days later we crossed an imaginary line and entered the Australia Station, so coming under the orders of the Flag Officer Commanding HMA Fleet, Rear-Admiral Eaton. The Minister for the Navy, the Hon. William McMahon, on behalf of the Commonwealth Government and the Naval Board, sent messages of welcome. Although we were not yet operational, the aircraft-carrier potential of the Navy had been doubled according to plan.

Melbourne was our first port of call, but the Navy kept me busy in Sydney for some time, and so it was not until the end of March that I could spend time with my family. We were now pleasantly housed in Melbourne and were happy to think that when I came to retire, probably as a captain aged fifty-five, there would be comfort in my so-called declining years.

At the end of the voyage my order to 'finish with the main engines' seemed to have a ring of finality about it, but soon we were to realize that our work was just beginning. In April, while *Vengeance* was refitting, I visited the Naval Air Station at Nowra where for some time *Vengeance*'s air component had been preparing for embarkation. Pilots, observers, air control personnel, air engineers, mechanics and aircraft handlers had all been going through their paces, simulating as far as possible conditions on a carrier. I watched the 'touch-and-go' practices and soon realized that many important factors influencing the landing on deck are in the initial approach. With the carrier head to wind, the 'groove' (flight path) starts on the port bow. The aircraft should be on an opposite course to the carrier and at the correct height and lateral distance the pilot commences a 180-degree turn to port and begins losing height at a set rate. This should put him on the final approach when he receives guidance from a landing signals officer (or 'bat' man) to correct minor errors or, if beyond correction, to wave him away. The pilots allocated to us were a mixed bag, ranging from experienced to novice. My senior officers also were at Nowra getting to know the air personnel, and vice versa. We all were aware that without mutual confidence and co-operation the entire venture could not succeed. Nevertheless, I was in no doubt that there were to be some tense moments ahead.

Meanwhile, the ship's air equipment was being modernized as far as finances would permit, and the other members of the company brought themselves up to date in their respective fields. The medicos became familiar with air medicine and the usual damage control courses at Balmoral were attended by officers and ratings.

On 10 June, with refit and leave over and the ship fully stored, we made for an anchorage off the Naval College at Jervis Bay. The next stage in our preparations was thoroughly to check and calibrate the ship's direction-finding equipment. This was a slow but vital operation, for the safety of air-crew and satisfactory air direction depend upon its accuracy. We then proceeded to sea to carry out further radio and radar trials and to exercise flight deck drills with a Sea Fury and a Firefly.

Before long we were ready to embark the Fireflies in Jervis Bay and begin flying training. The first test for us all was their arrival from their shore base. Eight of the nine landed on the first leg and the ninth, which had been delayed ashore, landed an hour later. It was a good start and it seemed that the pilots' advance training had paid off. After embarking the ground personnel, we put to sea to practice further deck landings, travelling north to find weather conditions suitable for inexperienced pilots.

After less than a week's practice the Sea Furies of 805 and 850 Squadrons could land without causing a marked rise in the blood pressure of the bridge personnel.

However, it was just as much a time of learning for me as for my pilots. Although I had been watching operations from the carrier screen for many years, I was still new to this particular game. I had had only a week's experience as a guest in a sister ship operating in the North Sea. The pilot of an aircraft expected that when he was about to land, the ship would be steering a steady course with the wind a few degrees on the starboard bow, that the wind-speed over the deck would be within the required limits, and that if he found himself in trouble every effort would be made to save him. My pilots knew that I was not a Fleet Air Arm type and that as a consequence I did not know too much of the finer details of naval aviation. However, they knew me to be an experienced seaman familiar with the foibles of the deep, which I hope proved of some comfort to them.

In *Vengeance*, a straight-deck carrier, an aircraft landing down the centre line of the ship would be arrested by the athwartship wires; then it would be unhooked, and it would fold its wings and park in the forepart of the flight deck. To ensure that a following aircraft making a bad landing did not crash into the aircraft park, a hydraulically controlled wire barrier was raised, which would bring the miscreant to an undignified, but safe halt. There was always concern for the pilot in these circumstances, but strapped in his seat the likelihood that he would be seriously injured was remote. Surprisingly, the damage to a machine that hit the barrier usually could be repaired on board. Propellers were the main sufferers, and so we kept ample spares on board.

The primary advantage of an angled-deck carrier equipped with a stabilized landing mirror is that aircraft are parked in the eyes of the ship, to one side of the flight deck. There they are no longer in the direct path of incoming aircraft, and so if the arrester hook below the aircraft fails to catch an arrester wire, the pilot can accelerate the aircraft and gain flying speed to go around again. It was accepted generally, in the Navy at least, that *Sydney* would be converted to an angled-deck carrier later in her career. In the meantime we set about acquiring the basic skills with the straight-decked *Vengeance*.

We continued northwards with the object of reaching the stage where taking off and landing were just routine, so that we might then concern ourselves with the air mission rather than the aircraft. However, we still had to make some progress with landings in adverse weather conditions. We knew that there were times in war when the need to attack the enemy would justify certain damage to the aircraft on their return. By this time we had reached Hervey Bay near Bundaberg and had been allocated eleven days' training there. It was ideal for our purposes, but as night flying was not a practical proposition in those days, we had to make the best use of daylight. The ideal day was to weigh at sunrise, steam downwind to give ample searoom for the day's flying, then to find a suitable anchorage with two hours of daylight remaining for physical jerks, deck hockey and fishing. Many evenings I would take a party — a different one each night, but with emphasis on the pilots — in a motor cutter to fish. Usually there were sufficient fish to flatter even the most rudimentary angler. Farmers may complain about daylight saving, but for our purposes it was perfect. The pilots could fish while the aircraft they had bent during the day were repaired.

We found that the variable strength of the wind caused us trouble. It was essential for landing that there be a wind-speed of twenty-six knots over the deck, but as our full speed was only twenty-three knots, a three-knot breeze was required. Without those three knots there would be unacceptable strain on the hooks and the arrester wires. Obviously, once the wind started to fade it would be essential to recall all aircraft. As soon as the smoke from the burning sugar cane on shore tended to the vertical, we knew that flying time was running out. During one afternoon's flying I simply could not find a three-knot breeze and so had to send three Fireflies and two Furies to Bundaberg for the night. Soon we began to feel masters of the rudiments of naval flying and turned our attention to the real purpose of our aircraft: tactical reconnaissance, interceptions and ground support. We required shore targets to practice rocket firings at land objects, and nearby Fairfax Island was allocated for the task and the targets established. *Bataan*, the attendant destroyer, would carry out the bombardments of shore targets also, and we carried two Army officers to ensure that a call for gun support from ashore could be translated into a language understood by sailors. At this time it confidently was expected that later in the year *Vengeance* would be sent to Korea and so the prospect of active service added zest to the training programme.

After a weekend in Brisbane I was given a further eleven days at Hervey Bay to complete the 'working-up' programme. During that period I sent a plane to Brisbane to bring out Captain G. C. Oldham, captain designate of *Sydney*. He had had carrier experience as an observer some years earlier and wanted to get the 'feel' once more. The culmination of this second phase of training was a long-range strike on *Australia*. Despite cloud and heavy rain, the aircraft, flying at 100 feet, sighted her and a rocket attack was launched against her splash target. The strike had avoided detection until it was within nine miles. It was a pleasing performance indeed. Soon a larger exercise designed to co-ordinate our many capabilities was devised. Saumarez Reef, about 150 miles to the north-east of Hervey Bay, had embedded in it a wrecked Liberty ship. For the purposes of the exercise, the reef was assumed to be an enemy defended anchorage containing an important supply ship. A photographic flight of Sea Furies first reconnoitred the area and the resultant photographs were used to plan a strike. To achieve surprise, the strike was divided into two sections, which were to proceed towards the target on separate headings before joining for the attack. Then they were to climb to a position up sun of the target and press home the attack with rockets and 20 mm ball ammunition. Another section was allocated the task of carrier protection (the defence against an enemy counter-strike), an anti-submarine patrol was maintained, and a section of the strike aircraft was required to take damage assessment photographs. With *Vengeance* 150 miles south of the target, the performance took three hours. The results left no doubt

209

in my mind that we were well on the way to being a proficient team. We could not rest on what few laurels we possessed, however, and so flying continued, punctuated with fishing when possible. Nevertheless, it could be said that *Vengeance*, the second carrier, was fully operational and ready to take her place in the fleet.

With a war being waged to our north, to take our place in the fleet is what we expected, but we were to be disappointed. I was told that *Sydney*, not *Vengeance*, had been earmarked to proceed to Korea later in the year, and furthermore that she would take my three squadrons with her. Reasons were not given and while I have no doubt that it was the right decision, my ship's company was most disappointed. Perhaps *Sydney*'s air control equipment was more modern than mine or possibly it was considered preferable for a vessel on loan not to be risked in a war zone. We were sad at bidding farewell to our squadrons but as they had been selected for the Korean excursion in *Sydney* they felt differently and we understood. They performed with great efficiency and distinction in Korea and I think *Vengeance* can take some small credit for that.

After some leave in Sydney, we were back on board at the end of August and carrying out a self-refit. The task now before me was to bring the partly new ship's company (for I had lost 200 seamen to *Sydney* as well) to an efficient state, and, having embarked the Sea Furies and Fireflies of 808 and 817 Squadrons, to bring the air component to fighting fitness. In mid-September *Vengeance* sailed for Jervis Bay with *Quadrant* for attendant destroyer duties. It was back to the grind but we were old hands now and knew when not to worry. As we made our way northwards, favourable winds allowed full flying programmes as well as radar and direction-finding calibrations. Our previous experience in the area suggested a ground party to be established at Bundaberg and so I despatched a lieutenant and three maintenance ratings to act as postmaster, receptionist and mechanics for aircraft which might not be able to land on the ship owing to unfavourable winds.

As before, '*Vengeance* daylight saving' was brought into operation. With so many fishing enthusiasts, I decided to give a prize for the heaviest fish landed and hurriedly wrote to my wife to send up some beer tankards. As far as more serious matters were concerned, I had been given until the first day in October to bring everything into shape. It was a tight schedule, but the elements were kind.

Sydney, on her way to Korea, had orders to join me and exercise as time would allow before taking a short break in Brisbane and then heading for the distant conflict. While still 200 miles to the south, she sent off a force to attack *Vengeance*. We picked up the aircraft from *Sydney* 'on the deck' when they were still twenty-five miles away, thus proving there was nothing wrong with our radar equipment. During the days which followed I formed the combined force into a two-carrier task force and named it the 10th Carrier Division. At the time, the future of the RAN as a two-carrier service seemed assured and appropriate for the task of defending our island continent. Of course we three captains could not know then that we had participated in a unique exercise. The third four-striper, Captain S. H. Beatty, VC, was in command of *Quadrant*. He was well known for his daring action in ramming the dock gates at Saint-Nazaire. More recently, when an engine-room telegraph defect almost involved him in a serious disaster to graving dock gates, a knowledgeable observer remarked loudly that Beatty was attempting to get a bar to his Victoria Cross.

The first day of October was our final day of flying training. As we found ourselves close to Lady Elliot Island lighthouse, I sent a helicopter ashore with some reading material, but, to our surprise, it returned with the keeper who had some unpleasant carbuncles, which we were able to treat for him. It reminded me of an occasion where one of Her Majesty's smaller craft sent a signal: 'Have hand with sore foot. Request medical assistance'.

Heading for Brisbane at midnight we met *Sydney* bound for Korean waters. After some short leave in Brisbane we were again at sea, this time as a fully worked-up carrier. My new orders were to position *Vengeance* in mid-Tasman so that I would be able to assist in the London–Christchurch air race. I was to track the competitors and to give them their geographical position if required. We followed the race by spasmodic reports from commercial radio stations until at midnight the competitors had passed and we could return to Jervis Bay.

We had been watching the movement of an intense cyclonic depression to the south-west which unfortunately appeared to have a magnetic attraction for us. A strong gale and rising seas were soon upon us. The only choice seemed to be to ride it out by steaming at seven knots to maintain steerage way, but without making any ground, and keeping the wind and sea at about twenty-five degrees on the port bow. This was a compromise between being head-on to the heavy sea and swell, which was a great strain on the ship's structure, and beam on, which risked heavy rolling and was to be avoided at all costs. By a careful watch on the veering and backing of the gale we were able to maintain a comfortable position, but *Bataan*, which had accompanied us as plane-guard, had comparatively low freeboard and was soon in considerable trouble. She had shipped some heavy seas on the upper deck and had taken in water through the engine-room fan inlets which put out of action her turbo-generators, resulting in a complete power blackout. The ship was steered by varying the revolutions on the two main shafts, a dangerous method in the conditions. By sunset the fury of the storm had subsided and speed could be increased and so I detached *Bataan* to proceed to Sydney as early dockyard assistance was imperative. This encounter was yet another reminder to a mere mariner that the sea is a dictator who requires much humouring.

After a short anti-submarine course at the joint Air Force and Navy school at Nowra, I was back in Sydney for Trafalgar Day on 21 October when the fleet was open to visitors. *Vengeance* was one of the main attractions with its large variety of equipment, of which the still novel helicopters drew the most interest. The Navy was always anxious for the public to see and understand the necessity for Australia to have a modern navy, particularly one which had as its core carrier-borne aircraft. Perhaps more time should have been spent educating the politicians.

The remainder of the year was taken up with exercises and early in the new year we had to be ready to join part of the fleet required to meet Her Majesty Queen Elizabeth in mid-Tasman. Once again the Tasman Sea seemed to resent our presence. A depression formed south of Lord Howe Island with low visibility, driving rain, gale-force winds and a heavy swell. As we approached the regal rendezvous, we first had to find the royal yacht, SS *Gothic*, and her escort, HMNZS *Black Prince*. Neither unit would be sure of its geographical position in the weather prevailing, but we picked up *Gothic* on radar in good time.

Sydney Harbour on 3 February 1954 was resplendent. The royal landing was in Farm Cove which was crammed on both sides of the approach lane with yachts and craft of every type. Everybody had 'dressed ship'. It was a memorable spectacle on an historic occasion when, for the first time, a reigning monarch of the British Commonwealth had set foot in Australia. For my wife and me it was an exhausting round of official functions following the wake of a much-loved monarch. After the Tasmanian visit, *Australia* and *Vengeance* were positioned in Bass Strait to cover the Queen's flight to Melbourne. After the Royal flight had passed overhead, we took the opportunity to exercise flying. There followed escort duty with the Royal Tour. I had been introduced to the Queen at Hobart, and met her again on several occasions. I felt greatly honoured.

Our royal duties were interrupted by providing some sea experience for trainees. One of the cutters ferrying recruits to us in Port Phillip bay foundered and two lives were lost. A subsequent board of inquiry found that the cutter had been travelling too fast in a short, steep sea. After this tragic interlude we rejoined the royal party in Perth. There, to my surprise, the Queen presented me with an autographed photograph of herself and the Duke. It had been a carrier custom over the years to form words on the flight deck with lines of sailors, and so after we put to sea once more as escort to *Gothic*, en route to Colombo, my thoughts turned to reproducing the royal signature. Having just received one, it did not take long to copy it on to graph paper, which would permit its accurate formation on the flight deck. Although each square on the deck would be ten feet by ten feet, it would have only one line across it, so massive magnification was simple. The flight deck was divided into the requisite squares and the signature chalked in, square by square. The ship's company duly stood on the white marks and a helicopter took photographs from which we deemed it was a success. A print was sent across to the Queen in *Gothic*, from whom we received the reply, 'Thank you for a most original forgery'.

Soon afterwards our escort duties ended, by which time *Anzac* and *Bataan* had barely enough fuel to reach Darwin. When refuelling *Bataan* the wind and sea conditions were difficult indeed. With a carrier into the wind (in fact a few degrees on the port bow) and doing twelve knots, *Bataan* came up on the starboard side and maintained a steady station by small alterations of course and speed. The latitude for error in this operation was not great. If she came in too close, the forces of interaction would tend to bring the ships dangerously near. If too far out, the oil hose would part, although in that case the only harm would be a broken length of hose and a ship smothered in oil-fuel. Unfortunately *Bataan*, after half an hour, came in too close with serious results. The forecastle port side, 'B' gun deck and the bridge structure were badly bent, and the difficulty was to extricate without further damage, which we eventually accomplished. It was not a cheerful moment to see a ship I had once commanded being so battered. At the subsequent board of inquiry in Darwin, it was established that the trouble started with a changeover of quartermasters, I think without the captain's knowledge. It proved that, especially in bad conditions, a momentary lack of concentration can prove disastrous.

After fuelling at Darwin we travelled to New Guinea and the surrounding islands before returning to Jervis Bay in early May. I was informed that I was, after leave, to proceed to Navy Office for special duty. I had

ecorated by the Governor-General, Field
arshal Sir William Slim, to become a
ommander of the Most Honourable
rder of the Bath, recognising many
ars of undetected crime! The order dates
ck to Letters Patent by King George I,
May 1675. It is fast becoming rare in
ustralia.

FOCAF with his two carrier
captains—W. H. Harrington
(left) and G. G. O. Gatacre
(centre)

sit of Admiral Lord Louis Mountbatten to HMA Fleet and East Australia Naval Command.
cending to inspect representatives assembled on the flight deck *(left to right):* Captain A. N.
her, Mr J. Scholtens (Government Ceremonial Officer), Henry Burrell, Flag Captain W. H.
rrington, Vice-Admiral Sir Roy Dowling (CNS), Captain F. N. Cook, Rear-Admiral H. J.
chanan (FOICEA) and the guest of honour.

A short-lived two-carrier Navy—HMA ships *Melbourne* and *Sydney*

Field Marshal Sir William Slim with my wife at my farewell cocktail party. The photographer is reputed to have said to His Excellency, 'Smile, please, sir' and HE to have replied, 'Damn you, man, I *am* smiling.' (*John Fairfax and Sons*)

enjoyed my time in *Vengeance* and left with great admiration for the bravery of her air-crew.

At this time, *Melbourne* was being modernized in the United Kingdom and was not due to be commissioned until late 1955. As related earlier, it was taken for granted that *Sydney* would be modernized, *Vengeance* being retained meanwhile. Australia would be protected by two modern carriers, supported by two airfields. Politicians, influenced no doubt by armchair strategists, and the RAAF in particular, had other ideas.

On 10 April 1954, the Minister for Defence, Sir Philip McBride, issued an interim defence policy statement which contained a body blow not only to the new enthusiastic Fleet Air Arm, but to all naval officers and those who understood 'Sea Power'. The Minister stated:

> In view of the probable nature and scale of attack laid down by the Defence Committee, it has been decided that priority should be given by the Navy to surface anti-submarine vessels and that the responsibility for air protection at sea *within the range of land-based aircraft* should be assigned to the Air Force. [Emphasis added]

This responsibility, in my view, cannot be met. For example, the warning of an air attack on ships or an escorted convoy is only a matter of minutes. Fighters from a shore base just could not arrive in time, so a combat air patrol is required. The numbers of fighters and airfields required to maintain this, even for forty-eight hours, makes it impractical. Further, in the policy statement, protection of shipping beyond the range of land-based aircraft does not rate a mention. In-flight refuelling is no answer to this problem.

The outcome of the new government policy was that the two-carrier/two naval air station Fleet Air Arm was to be halved. Such a decision can only be accepted on financial grounds. Strangely, it was not debated in Parliament and a diligent search failed to reveal even a bleat from Mr W. J. F. Riordan, the Minister for the Navy, when the Fleet Air Arm was established.

Despite this body blow to the Fleet Air Arm (and

Australia), my *Vengeance* commission was not entirely wasted. We provided the opportunity for FAA personnel, particularly pilots, to gain valuable experience, which was put to good use, and I too had gained knowledge from my time in command.

10
Years of High Responsibility
1955–58

After a brief and uneventful posting as Deputy Chief of the Naval Staff (temporary), I was appointed Flag Officer Commanding HMA Fleet. For me, 23 February 1955 was quite a day. That morning my flag (as an Acting Rear-Admiral) was hoisted in the Port Melbourne shore establishment, HMAS *Lonsdale*, immediately prior to my assumption of duty as the Flag Officer Commanding the Australian Fleet. My predecessor, Rear-Admiral Dowling, relieved Vice-Admiral Sir John Collins as Chief of Naval Staff. For John Collins it marked the premature end of a career of great distinction. He belonged to the first entry to the Royal Australian Naval College, justly enjoyed the reputation of a man with a brilliant war career, and, at the age of fifty-five, had just completed almost seven years as Chief of Naval Staff.

My flagship was HMAS *Sydney* commanded by Captain George Oldham. The fleet under my command consisted of my old *Vengeance* in Tasmanian waters in a training role, the 10th Destroyer Flotilla, the 1st Frigate Squadron, and three rather old frigates.

It is a requirement for the FOCAF to call officially on his Commander-in-Chief, the Governor-General, who in my case was Field-Marshal Sir William Slim. His numerous and distinguished decorations reflected the unusual life of one of Britain's great men who had risen from private to field-marshal. Accordingly, my wife and I proceeded to Canberra. I made my report, was invested with the CBE for thirty-seven years of undiscovered crime, and we both were entertained at lunch. It would be tedious to mention all the other official calls made by me during my time as FOCAF. At each capital city I was required to call on the Governor, the Chief

Justice, the state Premier, the Lord Mayor and senior officers of the three services, if they were senior to me. Calls were required to be returned with full honours and it was my custom to have the local naval officer-in-charge arrange the timing of the return calls so that the callers could stay for lunch.

Leaving Melbourne and my family astern, *Sydney* and *Anzac* sailed for Fremantle. I happened to be accommodated in the former as she was fitted with the desirable accommodation and command communication facilities. Once the unit was under way, I would order *Sydney* to assume tactical command and then I would retire to my sea or day-cabin to get on with my fleet thoughts and correspondence. *Sydney* would order courses and speeds as required for navigational and flying training reasons.

I was to find over the years that, although it is fine to be a flag officer, it is dull compared with being in command of a ship. Admittedly I commanded the men of the fleet, but it was from afar. The pleasures of handling and berthing ships were denied to me and I could only look on and possibly hoist 'manoeuvre well executed' or precede it with a negative flag. It became my habit to stand aft on the flight deck while the carrier berthed where I could tell the engine movements through the soles of my shoes. I was to have a few opportunities to control reasonably sized forces which at least put a modicum of exhilaration back into a spoilt, but pleasant, existence.

In April, I managed to collect enough ships to stage major exercises off the New South Wales coast using two merchant ships to act the part of a convoy. Generally our exercises at sea were concerned with anti-submarine work. The Royal Navy had been lending us two submarines to keep efficient in the art and we drew in the RAAF maritime squadrons whenever possible. During the exercises I was invited to initiate the ten thousandth 'takeoff' from *Sydney*'s flight deck.

Mid-April brought full realization of the government decision to halve the size of the Fleet Air Arm after so much effort had been expended in its introduction. On 22 April I carried out a brief inspection of *Vengeance* prior to her leaving my command and returning to the Royal Navy. I could not resist noting in my report of proceedings: 'I am hopeful that [Sydney] may yet be modernized and may once more become a powerful fighting unit of the Fleet.' A faint voice crying in the wilderness! *Vengeance* was sold to Brazil, where she was modernized with an angled deck, and is still in commission as *Minas Gerias*.

By this time the personnel of the fleet were beginning to get to know me. I had talked to most ships' companies and my captains had had discussions with me after exercises and had dined with me at opportune times. I made sure that my requirements for alertness and efficiency were well known and hope that my enthusiasm was contagious.

I was required to make an official visit to New Zealand. The programme allowed for a few days at the famous Bay of Islands, where my flagship had to endure an Admiral's Inspection. This can be a rather daunting affair for everybody except the admiral. First I inspected the entire ship's company at divisions in their No. 1 suits. Then followed the internal inspection of the ship so often portrayed by caricaturists as a long procession headed by the master-at-arms, the last body being a forlorn ordinary seaman kicking the cat. I frightened both the captain and commander a couple of times by a rapid alteration of course, but a call of 'This way, sir' prevented me from seeing half-naked sailors with arms full of kerosene tins and sullage hiding just out of sight. In such a tour there is always more vertical ladder work than horizontal walking, but I was fit and soon had the cavalcade well strung out. A welcome pause came when the traditional halt was called to allow the admiral to drink a 'goffer' with the canteen manager, who had the unlikely name of Jesus Zammit.

In the afternoon my staff inspected kits of those men who at divisions had looked on the scrubby side. The story still persists that one such man had only an empty kitbag to show, his standard answer to all questions being 'One on and one in the wash, Sir' (even for footwear). Meanwhile, my secretary had been going through the array of ship's books. I made it a practice to glance at a few at least, particularly the officers' wine book, to ensure that the rules were in operation. The following day an hour was spent at general drill. All in all, the results were very pleasing. On arrival at Wellington, my wife (who had flown there to join me) and I were invited to dine at Government House. After dinner we retired to the ballroom, its walls hung with old masters, to play mixed cricket, with a soft ball of course. I must say it all seemed a bit odd, but we played the game, though evening gowns were not designed for such frolics. Although some dresses may resemble a full-rigged ship with staysails and studding sails set, they are without forestay, backstay or martingale to keep the 'sails' in full trim.

We toured many centres, and at Christchurch, as it was Navy Week, I allowed myself to be talked into allowing a march past of 250 sailors. The leading article of the *Christchurch Star-Sun* on Tuesday, 24 May, read:

Citizens of Christchurch, most of them getting their first view of a helicopter, may have concluded that the traditional term of 'silent service' no longer attaches to the Navy. The arrival of this machine, to bring Rear-Admiral H. M. Burrell from the deck of HMAS *Sydney* direct to Hagley Park, gave a modern and dramatic touch to the opening in Christchurch of Navy Week — the first Navy Week this city has ever had. It was a wise decision to use the occasion of the arrival of the aircraft carrier from the Australian Navy to impress on the people the importance of the Royal New Zealand Navy and the claims it has on the support of all.

Perhaps not surprisingly the Canterbury Trotting Club invited me to their meeting with a request that I arrive by helicopter and the latter's versatility was not lost on a local pressman, who wrote:

In New Zealand, only the helicopter can deal with the conditions that so frequently obtain when alpine accidents demand the dispatching of quick relief. The Christchurch public have seen enough to know that there can be hardly a mountain peak or an alpine situation anywhere that is inaccessible to such a machine. Even in searching the helicopter has unique advantages, for, by it alone, can there be made the close and detailed inspection that is so often called for when difficult country had to be looked over. So far as its accidents and emergency services are concerned New Zealand lags a long way behind the rest of the civilized world, all because officialdom has looked at the costs and not at the service that can be given.

Having entertained the New Zealanders with my rotary-winged activities, we soon were homeward bound, pausing en route to take part in a fleet exercise in mid-Tasman. Back in Sydney I had to undergo minor surgery for skin cancer caused by the effect of excessive tropical sunshine on my head and face during the war, after which I took midwinter leave. At the end of June, while still on leave, I was confirmed in the rank of rear-admiral. This fulfilled a secret ambition which, for a long time, seemed well below my horizon. Perhaps the satisfactory operations in *Vengeance* had at least put me 'on the blocks'. Certainly it was not as a result of my time in *Norman*, since, as I mentioned earlier, my 'flimsy' and confidential report for that period never reached Australia. Unkind friends might have sung that well-known hymn — 'God moves in a mysterious way His wonders to perform'.

There were three incidents in my career which could have jeopardized my chances of reaching flag rank. The first was the incident in *Norman* when she could have been grounded by the navigator had I not paid attention to channel buoys. The second incident was also in *Norman*, in the Mozambique Channel where the current deceived me and there was just a chance of grounding the ship on an island in fog. The last was the near-collision in *Vengeance* when the boatswain had been officer of the watch. Good luck could not be denied a part in my success.

After a hectic round of activities in the latter half of 1955, I took my Christmas leave, returning to my duties in time to attend a senior officer's study period at the Australian Joint Anti-Submarine School at our air station at Nowra. It was staffed by RAN and RAAF officers, and the commandant alternated between our two services. For reasons which will be seen later, I want to emphasize that the submarine was, and will remain, a major threat to Australia and that our two services realized this and worked together with the utmost harmony in trying to find solutions to anti-submarine problems. The School performed a valuable role in providing courses for air-crew and senior officers of both services.

The visit of the First Sea Lord, Admiral The Earl Mountbatten of Burma, dominated the early part of April. I flew down to Melbourne to be present at three functions in his honour and had to organize one of his five Sydney appearances. I met him on a number of occasions and that he was a great man there is no doubt. As a senior officer, he had the great knack of flattering everyone he met by knowing a great deal about them, and he spent much time considering how the lot of sailors and their wives might be improved. It goes without saying that more than a palace connection is required of a captain if he is to be selected as a Supreme Commander and later Viceroy of India. Yet I was more impressed with his handling of the latter than the former. I am left with the impression that when he pressed for more resources to be allocated to his command he was not concerned only with shortening the war. For much of the squabbling during the last years of the war over the correct strategy in South-East Asia he enjoyed Churchill's support. However, this was a time when Churchill's finest hour was running out, at least in the views of his chiefs of staff, and only a rapid American advance against Japan from the south and the east removed the need for any of the conflicting strategies in which he had become embroiled.

In late April 1956, as my time in command was drawing to a close, *Melbourne* came under my command after returning from undergoing modernization in the United Kingdom. My activities while in command may appear to have been mainly social, but without an operational carrier for most of the time, with two ships in the strategic reserve, one in Korean waters during

1955, and one on fishery patrol duties, I could not give the fleet extensive operational experience. Much had to be left to my destroyer and frigate commanders if the Navy was to remain efficient in the anti-submarine, gunnery, torpedo and communication areas. Nevertheless, all ships saw a lot of activity outside Australian waters and for my part I tried to show the flag to the people of Australia and, by speeches and discussions, to justify the need for a Navy commensurate with our wealth and geographical position. I would have liked more opportunities to talk with the politicians, especially regarding the decision to cut the Fleet Air Arm from two carriers to one.

New Officer Structure 1956

After winter leave 1956, I was appointed to Navy Office to investigate and make proposals regarding a new officer structure. Early in 1956 the Admiralty distributed Admiralty Fleet Order (AFO) 1/56 which covered their intended changes and the Naval Board had to decide whether to follow suit. The Admiralty alterations covered many facets of the service and each required detailed consideration, for which task I was given to assist me Commander Alan McIntosh as a staff officer.[42] Since then, the results of my proposals have produced endless discussions and much heart-burning in officer circles. The preamble to the decisions made three points: first that there was a tendency for the executive officer to be more technical and for the technical officers to increase in numbers and to assume more executive duties. Second, full use was not being made of the experience and knowledge of the senior officers in the technical branches and that they could play a more important part in the administration of the Navy. Third, there was a need for better prospects of promotion to the rank of commander to attract into the Navy young men required for future officers.

Under the new scheme the principle remained that only seaman officers would command ships, but for other commands all officers of the four main specializations (seaman, engineer, electrical, and supply and secretariat) would be placed on one general list. Other

223

specializations (inspector of naval ordnance, instructor, surgeon, dental surgeon and chaplain) would be placed on a miscellaneous list. Seaman officers were to be divided into post (seagoing) general lists in the proportion of 7:4 to ensure that officers who would ultimately exercise higher operational responsibilities would have the full measure of sea experience in command. Also, the number of junior officers entering the Navy should be such that each entrant would have not less than six chances out of ten of being promoted to commander. Further, the broadening of the role of instructor officers was to continue and warrant officers were to be incorporated into a new special duties list, making them ward-room officers with the consequent closing of warrant officers' messes.

With my personal views on non-executive (non-seaman) officers being given added authority, I found I was not the appropriate person to work on bringing one of these major changes into operation. I was opposed to the new RN structure under which such officers could command shore establishments and schools. In cases where ships were included in such commands, an executive chief of staff would be appointed to advise his senior officer of the correct actions to take. This new system has allowed a non-executive officer to be a defence representative overseas.

Perhaps I was, and remain, old-fashioned but this abrogation of the powers of command and punishment from the executive side of the officer structure still seems unwarranted to me. I remember well the 1920s when a curl on an officer's stripes indicated the command authority of the seaman branch. A paymaster, for example, wore straight stripes with white between them. Apparently, this absence of a curl was considered offensive in that it advertised a lower status, and so the uniform regulations were amended to give everyone a curl. At the time this annoyed me as it seemed to be the start of a levelling process at the end of which everyone would come together as equals. Over the years the loquacious, when discussing command, have talked about 'all to be of one company' and similar handy, but inept phrases. If this trend in these circumstances continues, the captain of a ship will be a non-executive officer with a staff of technical advisers to counsel him on how best to command and fight his ship! This tendency to arrive at the lowest common denominator can only be a recipe for mediocrity. I like the word 'admiral' to mean someone who commands ships. I would prefer a surgeon rear-admiral to be called a fleet surgeon or a rear-admiral (E) to be called the engineer-in-chief and so on. Before long, I expect to learn of a WRAN rear-admiral.

To be blunt, I like to think that with my skill and experience I could, for instance, fight a naval battle or rescue a disabled 300,000-ton tanker in dangerous waters. These are things which a non-executive officer could not do. After all, he chose to specialize in such fields as engineering, electrical, and supply and secretariat, and, in so doing, knowingly sacrificed the pleasures and responsibilities of executive command.

With my strongly held views in favour of conforming, in general, to the Admiralty practice, I was in a dilemma. Much as I disliked the new structure, I felt it would damage seriously our relations with the Royal Navy if we did not follow suit. We have the privilege of ranking and commanding (according to seniority) with officers and men of the RN. I have served under RN officers and many of them have served under me and the continuance of that arrangement would be in jeopardy if we had differing command rules. It was this aspect alone which influenced me to recommend, without enthusiasm, that this part of the Admiralty scheme be introduced, and the Naval Board agreed with my recommendations. I think that my decision was correct, but I remain convinced that the Admiralty erred in the first instance in adopting such a scheme.

Another problem I had to deal with was the need to give adequate sea experience to executive officers, particularly those who could be expected to command ships and the fleet. The problem arose due to a shortage of ships which meant that if equal sea service was given to all executive officers, all would lack the essential experience to some degree. Until then this was overcome by not promoting officers who were not successful at sea, but who otherwise were very bright which, to my mind, was a waste of good men. I proposed we agree with the Admiralty scheme which would place officers on to either a 'wet' or a 'dry' list. The 'wet list' officers would be given ample experience at sea and the 'dry list' could rise in the administrative field and become admirals via that avenue. It made sense to me and the Naval Board accepted it, with the proviso that in exceptional cases changes between the lists could be made.

One crucial point which arose, however, was whether officers should be informed which list they were on. The arguments for and against could be advanced indefinitely; for example, there might arise the case of an officer on the 'dry list' who thought he was a good seaman and handler of men, but did not know that the Navy held different views. On the other hand, there would be some who knew they were not cut out for command at sea and would be delighted at the new possibility of joining in the flag rank stakes. Was there a need to tell anybody? After a few years the answer would be obvious anyway. On balance, I felt it was preferable not to let officers know. However, the rules were not inflexible and I understand that one 'dry list' officer commanded the fleet in later years.

The whole 'New Officer Structure' required a great deal of paperwork but I was in my home port and was able to enjoy home life. This was extended in early January 1957 when I was appointed Second Naval Member and given the task of establishing the New Officer Structure in the RAN.

Second Naval Member 1957

I only had to move along the corridor from my office to sit in the chair of Commodore Copper Morrow and deal with Personnel and Stores. With the exception of the New Officer Structure, I was in new territory. However, I knew Stores (Naval and Victualling) would cause me little trouble as I had Mr J. L. Flynn and Mr T. F. Daniel as respective directors, both of whom I had known from my earlier activities in Navy Office. On the personnel naval side, I had Commander W. K. Tapp as Naval Assistant and Commander R. G. Craft as my secretary and was fortunate to have Mr W. J. Kenny as civilian head of naval personnel branch. Also in the building was Captain (S) Bernard Foley who had three jobs: Director-General of the Supply and Secretariat Department, Chief Naval Judge Advocate, and Director of Administrative Planning. He was a most likeable, knowledgeable and efficient officer and had been the secretary to a long succession of First Naval Members. No doubt he remained in that job too long, but I am sure that each incoming CNS was told to hang on to Bernard because of his depth of knowledge. He had critics in high places but he certainly deserved flag rank.

In April the Prime Minister announced that consultation had commenced between the Ministers for Defence and the Interior regarding an intended move to Canberra of officers of the Defence Department and the three services associated with the operation of the Defence Committee and the Chiefs of Staff Committee. The plan was for 500 people to move at the beginning of 1959, and they to be followed later in the year by a further 600 from the Service Departments. With the centre of government in Canberra, the need for this move had been obvious for a long time. Cabinet, Prime Minister's Department, Treasury, External Affairs and Defence needed to be cheek by jowl for policy and decision-making in highly important spheres, but in the meantime we remained in Melbourne.

My work on personnel was not the raw material for an Edgar Wallace thriller. I was dealing with numbers and bodies; that is, providing the personnel to man the ships, checking court martial and punishment returns, and dealing with a host of matters concerning individuals. Promotions and advancements of officers and ratings was particularly important. I put into operation the New Officer Structure and instituted a form of career planning. Previously, appointments had been made on an ad hoc basis — a poor way to get the best out of the talent available. I was aloof from interests of the Naval Staff concerning the fleet and policy matters such as our standing in SEATO, ANZUS, and ANZAM and instead busied myself with such things as the reintroduction of the RAN Nursing Service, which was an urgent matter because of the acute shortage of sick-berth attendants. I achieved a remission of the remaining portion of one man's term of imprisonment. Being discharged from HM's service with disgrace is a tough punishment in itself.

In May the half-yearly officer promotions were on my plate. A confidential report was made of every officer by his captain when any appointment exceeded three months. The reports were in two parts: the first listed the characteristics required of an officer, for which marks from one to nine were awarded, and the second part expressed in writing the qualities of the officer. The Second Naval Member produced a summary of the officers in the zone for promotion and this, together with all the confidential reports, was circulated to each Board member. If, for example, there were vacancies for two officers to be promoted, a member of the Board was requested to list four selections in order of merit. Finally, the lists were given to the Second Naval Member to correlate them and discussion with the First Naval Member followed. Normally the answer was clear-cut, but if not, the matter was discussed with the member of the Board whose recommendation had caused the close finish until unanimity was achieved. Personal favouritism did not stand a chance and I am convinced that our system was as fair as it could be.

Under this procedure all the confidential reports of each officer over the years from the rank of lieutenant are produced for inspection. A question often asked, and one which cannot be fully answered, is whether a blot as a junior lieutenant affects promotion to commander ten years later. From my experience the answer is that it does not. Another question sometimes asked concerns the effect that officers' wives might have on their husbands' promotion. I did not know the views of other Board members, but to me it was not a factor.

On 19 June I placed a paper before the Naval Board on the manning situation in which I recommended an early review of the pay code and conditions of service. [43] We needed an incentive to increase recruiting and to encourage re-engagement. The Board agreed and directed that I discuss the matter with the other two services. Our minister attended this meeting and asked for a brief to discuss the matter with the Minister for Defence. The outcome of this, later in the year, was the setting up of the Allison Committee, named after the Chairman, Sir John Allison (Chairman and Managing Director of Permewan Wright), a public-spirited Australian who found time to be president of many boards in many areas.

About Cup time, scarcely a year in my present job, Admiral Dowling told me he wanted me to command the fleet in 1958. In my wildest dreams I could not have expected a second turn and was astounded. No one could refuse a job such as that described in Gilbertian style in an RN magazine years ago:

> The Admiral is a demi-god
> From whom a passing kindly nod
> In answer to one's awed salute
> Is calculated to transmute
> Us common men to nothing less
> Than pampered darlings of success.
>
> I like the Flagship's ample bridge
> Whereon the great man's privilege
> Is to manipulate his Fleet
> In such formations as are meet;
> For instance, at a word, a sign,
> The heavy ships swing into line,
> The cruisers dart ahead to scout
> And, as fresh flag-hoists flutter out,
> Far off destroyers hurry back
> To screen against a flank attack.

The reason for this surprise appointment I cannot fathom to this day.

As I made to depart, the Allison Committee was getting on with its job. I was called before it several times, but the Committee had not completed its task before I took some leave prior to assuming my command. Being relieved halfway through a normal appointment I did not feel particularly satisfied with my efforts. My hope was that the Allison Committee's report would make life in the Navy a more attractive career to the adventurous as well as the technically minded young men of Australia. I left envying the Pied Piper of Hamelin who solved juvenile delinquency as well as environmental pollution in one act.

Flag Officer Commanding HMA Fleet (HMAS *Melbourne*) 1958

On 7 January 1958 my flag was hoisted in HMAS *Melbourne* once again as Flag Officer Commanding the Australian Fleet. Captain Humphrey Becher was in command of *Melbourne* and also served as Chief Staff Officer. My year was divided into three segments: the annual visit to Hobart; a cruise of over four months taking in Fremantle, Singapore, Hong Kong, Yokosuka, Pearl Harbor and Suva; and then, after leave and a long refit, a visit to Melbourne over the Cup period. The most important period was, of course, the overseas tour during which I had many opportunities to operate ships tactically and to play a part in the diplomatic field of naval co-operation with our allies.

Before beginning the year's activities I took the flagship to Jervis Bay in February to embark aircraft and exercise all concerned in order to regain operational efficiency. It was my first experience of the latest aircraft operating from a modern angled–deck carrier. No longer would I be worried about the menacing wire barrier waiting to enmesh a plane making a faulty landing. The carrier air component was eight Sea Venom fighters, twelve anti-submarine Gannets and two Sycamore helicopters for rescue work. The Sea Venoms and Gannets were a marked advance on the earlier Sea Furies and Fireflies.

After the Hobart visit there remained little time in which to prepare for the long cruise ahead. Then on 6 March I sailed in *Melbourne*, with *Quiberon* in company, on the second segment of the year's programme. By 1958 the chair of the Fourth Naval Member (the Member for Air) was occupied for the first time by an RAN officer, Commodore George Oldham, which was a sign that at last we were growing up. He took passage with me in the early part of the voyage to watch flying

pleasing gesture on supersession—the modern alternative to being pulled ashore to Man of War
ps in the Admiral's galley—brass-hatted galley-slaves galore!

Robert Black (Governor of Hong Kong) arrives by helicopter to witness flying
rcises. Following Henry Burrell is Commander B. S. Murray (later Governor of
:toria). Note the arrestor wires in the raised position ready to be caught by the arrestor
ok of the landing aircraft.

Welcome to Pearl Harbor
(US Navy)

Inspecting a US Navy submarine

operations before we flew him back to his desk by Gannet.

After visiting Fremantle and Singapore, early April saw our arrival in Hong Kong to begin the usual round of official calls. There I was introduced to William Holden who related some interesting incidents which had occurred during the filming of *The Bridge Over the River Kwai*, including a train being stranded on the bridge, where the ashes from the engine set the bridge on fire. The script required the bridge, train and other sundry items to be blown sky-high. When this scene was finally shot, the explosion terrified a large flock of birds, much to the personal discomfort of William Holden who happened to be beneath them at the time.

In listening to his stories the time had slipped away unnoticed. I had missed the last ferry, and was forced therefore to cross the harbour by sampan, as were other miscreants from the flagship. On the admiral's bridge are heavy bullet-proof glass ports with counter-balance weights. As we were leaving Hong Kong harbour, one of these collapsed, knocking off my right thumbnail and ruining the flag lieutenant's tropical uniform. It was an unpleasant end to an enjoyable visit and I am reminded of it every time I have to use a plumber's spanner to open a bottle of champagne.

Voyager, *Warramunga* and *Quiberon* accompanied us south through the China Sea to Singapore. There on 28 April we began three days of preparation for the large-scale SEATO exercises, known as 'Ocean Link', in which ships from the navies of the United States, Britain, New Zealand, Pakistan and Australia participated.

The first part of the exercises occupied four days in the waters to the east of Singapore. The force was divided into several groups exercising anti-submarine tactics and the final day saw the entire force in a 'replenishment at sea' formation under attack by three submarines after which we all retired to an anchorage near the Johore Shoal. On the following day the force weighed and carried out a series of exercises on passage to Manila. The exercises were not complex, but showed the need for improved communications.

231

Approaching Manila on 13 May, HMS *Bulwark* fired a twenty-one gun salute to the flag of the Republic of the Philippines on behalf of the force. A large programme of SEATO calls had been arranged and included a wreath-laying ceremony at the Rizal Monument. In the dogwatches Admiral Loomis, USN, turned on a reception at the local Naval Officers Club. Afterwards the Australian chargé d'affaires, Mr Scott, and his wife entertained me and my captains to dinner. The following day was occupied with the exercise post-mortem and an official luncheon. I gave the fleet 'at home' on board *Voyager*. Manila harbour had been completely rebuilt after the war. I remembered it as I had seen it on VJ-Day, when all the wharves had been wrecked and the waters alongside were lined with sunken ships.

On returning to Hong Kong with *Voyager*, *Melbourne* was given a berth in midstream. I used the three days there to carry out my annual inspection of *Voyager* and late in May sailed without escort for a diplomatic visit to Japan. Before departing I received a small brass flagstaff bearing a flag with the upper half blue and lower red. Engraved on it was:

24th March–23rd May 1958
Presented by the Captain and Officers of HMAS *Voyager* in direct contravention of QR and AI Article 1831.[44]

The red and blue flag was hoisted by the admiral to indicate that difficult manoeuvres will not be ordered while the flag is flying. Its signal-book meaning is 'Flag and Commanding Officer will have time for the next meal'. Obviously I should have used it more frequently.

After leaving Japan we sailed with an American escort for Pearl Harbor, where we took part in further exercises. That visit, apart from generating goodwill, was of particular value to *Melbourne*, because it enabled her to take part in large-scale exercises, something which would not have been possible without the co-operation of a powerful ally. I was privileged to be given operational control of USN and RAN combined forces.

Pearl Harbor is the headquarters of six commanders-in-chief (or equivalent) and nine other commanders on the rear-admiral level. Consequently, official calls and exchanges of hospitality seemed to fill the waking hours. During the twenty-day visit only nine days were spent at sea. My report on the social aspects covered eight pages. Great kindness was shown to all in the flagship, from the admiral down to the youngest ordinary seaman.

Two four-day exercises were organized with a night in harbour separating them. As mentioned above, I was in command of the 'Blueland' forces in both exercises. One of my problems was to keep the enemy submarines submerged in order to reduce their mobility. During the first night of the exercise *Melbourne* was using a radio frequency which disrupted the inter-island radio telephone system, and we were politely asked to switch to another frequency. The capabilities of *Melbourne*'s Gannets by night as well as by day surprised and hampered the enemy. Altogether, the exercises were realistic and very good value indeed.

Although I was privileged to be shown over the world's first nuclear submarine, *Nautilus*, I must be one of the few visitors to Hawaii who missed seeing Honolulu and swimming at Waikiki beach.

At the conclusion of our visit Admiral Stump signalled Vice-Admiral Dowling:

Visit of the *Melbourne* at Pearl Harbor which included operations with the United States Navy has been most profitable to the Pacific Fleet. The splendid appearance, impeccable conduct and unending friendliness of the officers and men of the *Melbourne* is being favourably commented upon in both civilian and military circles in Honolulu to the great credit of the Royal Australian Navy.

This adds another chapter to the firm and lasting friendship between our services and our people with warm regards *Felix Stump*.

We made our farewells at Pearl Harbor and sailed for Suva. En route I received a signal informing me that Vice-Admiral Sir Roy Dowling would be leaving the post of Chief of Naval Staff in February the following year and that I had been chosen to succeed him. I was stunned by the news. On arrival in Sydney on 22 July I was met by my wife who had travelled up from Melbourne. A great welcome awaited the sailor home from the sea, but the CNS designate affair seemed illogical to me. I was only fifty-four and full of the joy of spring. It was too soon to become CNS. Also, although professionally I had been delighted to command the fleet for a second time, in the light of events, I am not sure that it was in my best interests. I lacked administrative experience in a shore job, with all its dealings with civil servants, finance and works programmes. Domestically, however, all appeared ideal initially. I would be able to spend a great deal more time with my wife and children, I would enjoy a comfortable home, Norge, in Balwyn, Melbourne, ideal for entertaining, a cottage at Somers with a view of Phillip Island and Bass Strait, and it was convenient for a working wife with a factory in Malvern. The conditions were perfect for my retirement in due course. However, a very large fly was about to land in the ointment.

Since the opening of Parliament in Canberra in 1927 it had been the intention of every government to bring to Canberra the numerous Commonwealth departments divided between Melbourne and Sydney. Such moves had been considered from time to time, but always, it seemed, abandoned. Eventually Sir Robert Menzies decided that the dithering would cease. A National Capital Development Commission with Sir John Overall as head was set up to plan for the expansion of Canberra on the assumption that government departments would transfer there on a timetable regulated by the construction of offices and houses. Until 1958 the Parliamentary Triangle, with Capital Hill as its apex and Commonwealth Avenue and Kings Avenue as its two sides, had within it only Parliament House, an administrative building and East and West Blocks of offices. From Parliament House on the central axis could be seen the Australian War Memorial in the distance at the end of Anzac Parade and through the base of the triangle meandered the Molonglo River. Commonwealth Avenue crossed the river by a long wooden trestle bridge while Kings Avenue was but a narrow road to Duntroon and the airport with a small weir at the river crossing.

I had not taken particular notice of the determination to develop Canberra until it was rumoured that the operational side of the Defence Department and the three fighting services would be part of the initial move. I was soon to find out that the rumour was soundly based.

I and my flagship were in Melbourne for the first ten days in November. I took the opportunity to discuss affairs with Sir Roy Dowling and Mr E. W. Hicks, the Secretary for Defence, and my successor, none other than Rear-Admiral Gatacre, called to check the lie of the land. Even before I had taken up my chair in the office of the CNS the job began to make demands. On Melbourne Show Day our three children were competing in riding events with some success. About four o'clock I was bidden by the ground broadcast to repair to the secretary's office where a message awaited me requesting my presence at Government House. Without thinking, I took the car and at Government House found the First Lord of the Admiralty, Lord Selkirk, anxious to learn my views (as CNS designate) on future plans. This was a bit sudden and I was unaware of the state of the plans divisions and the drawing board. I talked about looking into Fleet Air Arm trends and the rumours that the Admiralty would have difficulties in helping us out in the submarine field. I expect I talked about the RN guided missile *Sea Slug* soon to be tested at Woomera and undoubtedly I expressed concern at our lack of minesweepers. The First Lord seemed satisfied, but I remained surprised that there was a need to cross-question me. It was obvious that the CNS and defence personnel at Victoria Barracks had not briefed him adequately. Meanwhile, I was in great trouble, my family had to find their way home by tram with buckets and scrubbers and gear for tizzying up horse and pony.

Nevertheless, there was time for my wife and me to visit the architects designing the chiefs of staff houses which were then under construction in Canberra. We inspected the plans and found that, to our eyes, the sizes of the bedrooms and the dining-room were incredibly small, but the responsibility for the mean dimensions, as will be seen later, did not lie with the architects. I took a flight in a Gannet to the capital to inspect the house being prepared for me in Hamlin Crescent, Narrabundah. The actual brick veneer cottage was no better than my wife and I had feared, but I appreciated that some sacrifices had to be made in such a major movement.

The Christmas leave period was absorbed by activities concerned with the move to Canberra. On return to the flagship I took leave of my captains and fleet staff officers and, on 20 January 1959 with due ceremony, welcomed my successor. No conductor can make good music without a good orchestra, and for that reason my captains and their ships' companies deserve my grateful thanks. Having turned over my command in few words, I took my departure with the usual formality. Then my captains and senior officers manned the tow-ropes of the flagship's jeep in a kind gesture of farewell and my flag was struck at sunset. 'The curfew tolls the knell of parting day.'

11
Chief of Naval Staff
1959–62

I assumed responsibility as Chief of Naval Staff in
Canberra on 20 January 1959 after my predecessor, Sir
Roy Dowling, had become Chairman of the Chiefs of
Staff Committee. [45] We all had offices in the administrative block in the Parliamentary Triangle and it was to be
almost three years before we moved across the Molonglo River to the new Defence complex at Russell.

Shortly before taking over the tiller, my wife and I
took up residence in No. 4 Hamlin Crescent, Narrabundah. The reservations we felt after seeing the plans were
justified — everything about No. 4 seemed Lilliputian.
The backyard was barely big enough for a rotary
clothesline. My thoughts turned to the days when the
Commander-in-Chief Australia Station had Admiralty
House, Kirribilli, as his official residence. I did not feel
that I should have been given anything comparable with
such an imposing residence on the best site in one of the
finest harbours in the world. But No. 4 Hamlin Crescent!

My wife and I were still recovering from the shock of
such inappropriate quarters when we learned that Sir
Roy Dowling had walked out of his accommodation in
Red Hill and had bought a private house. I was given
the option of moving into the house he had vacated,
which, although identical in design, was in an acre of
ground in open country with sheep enjoying the surrounding pasture. We made the change from Hamlin
Crescent and I erected a sign bearing the words 'Admiralty House' and my flag was flown over the front lawn.
It was my intention that this opportunity of establishing
the presence of the Navy in the blossoming capital of
Australia should be taken at the outset and in this I had

the support of my minister, Senator John Gorton. However, this was not to be easy. Senator Kendall made a reference to 'Admiralty House' when speaking on an Appropriation Bill in the Upper House:

I have had a long association with the Navy. I have, also, a great admiration for the work that is proceeding in Canberra. Indeed, these days I think of Canberra as my second home. Accordingly, I am always interested in going around and seeing what is being done. When I heard that an Admiralty House had been built, I made tracks in that direction, in order to have a look at it. I found my way all right to the end of Mugga Way but then encountered what could only be called a sea of mud. In fact, I felt like calling, 'Away, sea boat's crew', when I saw it. I proceeded for about 300 yards and then saw what looked like a fibro residence of about ten squares with a flagstaff in front and a notice stating that it was Admiralty House. I could not believe my eyes. It was almost unbelievable that a senior officer — the Chief of Naval Staff of this country — should be put into a poky little place like that, surrounded by a sea of mud.

From inquiries that I made afterwards — though not from Admiral Burrell — I learned that it was so small inside that around the wall of the dining room there was what, at sea, we would call a rubbing piece, so that when guests put their chairs back after finishing their dinner they would not push them through the plaster of the wall. I bring this matter to the notice of the Minister for the Navy [Senator Gorton], although perhaps it has something to do with the Minister for the Interior [Mr Freeth] also. I consider it disgraceful that the senior naval officer in Canberra, indeed, in Australia, should be housed in such a place as that. There are, just being finished, plenty of homes where he could have been placed until at least the road to his residence was sealed. I had great difficulty in even turning my car around to get back to Mugga Way. I make these few remarks in the hope that something will be done.

Senator Gorton, in reply to a question in the Senate regarding the size of the chiefs of staff 'official' residences, commented:

The Chiefs of Staff were asked what kind of houses they wanted (in Canberra), the amount of rent they were prepared to pay and they settled for houses of this kind. It was a matter, of course, entirely for the Department of the Interior and for the Chiefs of Staff. (*Hansard*, 1959, p. 1360)

I can but blame my predecessors in 1958 for 'settling' for such poor residences. 'The amount of rent they were prepared to pay' seems to have been the criterion for size, not the services' reputations at the seat of government and the heart of the diplomatic corps. I wondered if the millions spent on our embassy in Paris bear any relation to the rent paid by our ambassador. I did not have delusions of three years' grandeur, but I had visions of the Royal Australian Navy being represented in Canberra in the future in a manner which even an able-seaman would expect to see.

Later in the year a sub-committee of Cabinet considered the question of official entertaining by the chiefs of staff. It transpired that accommodating the visiting service VIPs was not required and that entertainment could be carried out in the local hostelry and the entertainment allowance was raised from £50 to £100 a year. To my mind this approach violated the most basic standards of naval hospitality.

The government did, however, clear the air, and my wife and I felt no longer obliged to live in a poky house. A splendid house, 54 Mugga Way, was approaching completion by a Mr Schlager and, with the help of the bank, we bought the house and gave notice to cancel the lease of No. 50. Thus the visible signs of an admiral in Canberra disappeared and we thoroughly enjoyed the type of home which should have been provided in the first place. The powers-that-be unwittingly forced me into the best investment available in real estate.

The problems of accommodation, however, could be attended to only as my new appointment permitted. My working week did not leave as much time for purely naval matters as I would have wished. Two mornings were taken up with Chiefs of Staff and Defence Committee matters. My staff would produce briefs on the numerous and varied items and all too frequently agenda with urgent tags would arrive with insufficient time for close study. The Naval Board met only three or four times a month. It had been the accepted practice for the Minister to preside at these meetings when a major item was up for decision. Our Minister, however, wished to attend all meetings, as was his right, but in so exercising it he slowed down many routine matters. Perhaps it assisted him to answer 'questions without notice' in the Senate. I was to have discussions with the Minister over our separate roles. Eventually he accepted that his job was to use his influence to obtain funds to be spent on new ships and equipment as desired by me. At the time it did not occur to me that I was dealing with a future Prime Minister.

Routine work and vital planning left little time to visit our ships and establishments, but, in any case, it was my desire to keep such tours to a minimum. I had experienced and reliable admirals and captains to run the Navy, most of whom I knew personally. They all looked to me to plan the Navy of the future.

To summarize our naval strength, the fleet now consisted of the carrier *Melbourne*; three 'Daring' class destroyers (built between 1951 and 1956) *Vampire*, *Vendetta*, *Voyager*; two 'Battle' class destroyers (1946–47) *Tobruk* and *Anzac*; and three war-built 'Q' class anti-submarine frigates (1940) *Quiberon, Queenborough* and *Quickmatch*. The latter had been converted from destroyers earlier in the decade.

Surveying, including oceanography (with CSIRO), was being carried out by three 'River' class frigates (1943–45), *Barcoo, Diamantina* and *Gascoyne*. Our new fleet tanker, *Tide Austral*, was on loan to the Admiralty for financial reasons. Of the ships in the reserve fleet, *Sydney* alone was of any real value.

The only ships under construction were two modern 'Type 12' destroyer escorts, *Parramatta* and *Yarra*, which later were to become known as anti-submarine frigates.

They had been laid down in 1957 but were not due to be completed until mid-1961. Plans were well in hand to lay the keels of two further frigates, *Stuart* and *Derwent*, in March, although they were not expected to join the fleet for over four years.

The personnel of the Navy consisted of 1,350 officers (including nine admirals) and 9,326 ratings. With these men and the ships at our disposal I was to guide the Navy in its strategic role which was to secure the defence of sea communications and to assist the Army and Air Force, and our allies, in general war operations. It would not be an easy task and there were several problems to overcome.

To my surprise, there was an immediate carrier problem. *Melbourne*'s aircraft, Sea Venom fighters and Gannet turbo-prop anti-submarine aircraft, would be worn out in about four years. My information was that the replacements being considered would need a bigger carrier from which to operate. Another problem was that we had loaned our new, and only, oil tanker, *Tide Austral*, to the Royal Navy for financial reasons. Nevertheless, to my mind she was needed now in Australia to increase the mobility of the fleet. She could carry stocks of oil-fuel, aviation fuel, gasoline, lubricating oil and fresh water. Proficiency at fuelling at sea was important and required practice. I decided to inform the Admiralty that we would require the ship to be returned at the end of the lease in September 1962.

The absence of any minesweeping capability was more than disturbing and it appeared that we would shortly face a problem with submarines. The Royal Navy generously maintained three in Sydney to assist in our anti-submarine training requirement. However, the Admiralty had informed us that there was difficulty in continuing this essential assistance. Without practice targets we would have the alternatives of sending our forces to Pearl Harbor to exercise with the USN, or, for the fourth time, to develop our own submarine service.

The Three-Year Programme
Being the last year of a three-year defence programme, 1959 would require a new programme to be drawn up

by the spring. This would be my first task as CNS, and perhaps the most important. Unfortunately the plans division of the Naval Staff had little prepared to offer me on the 'way ahead'. I had the impression that ad hoc arrangements had been the order of the day, though I expect all new brooms feel the same.

As a start there seemed an immediate need to have prepared a paper covering the strategic role of the Navy for the next twenty years as a basis for the 1959/60–1961/62 defence programme required later in the year. It was a valuable exercise and gave rise, for example, to establishing the expected working lives of all ships and the need to allow for major alterations and additions at half-life periods.

Thus it was that a start was made on a means of arriving at the three-year programme. Broadly, we established the tasks of the Navy to meet its strategic role and so arrived at the naval forces required to meet them. The deficiencies in the fleet, allowing for the reserve fleet and new construction, showed up clearly. Obviously, all such deficiencies could not be included within the broad financial limits of the naval vote, nor could many be made good in a three-year time scale. Priorities had to be established, recognizing that long-term commitments should not become a financial embarrassment in later years and that the Treasury would be awake to having its hand forced.

On 3 April the Naval Board approved the background paper 'The Three-Year Defence Programme 1959/60–1961/62 — Narrative Statement of Plans', of which the following are extracts:

The Strategic Role of the Navy
The Revised 'Strategic Basis of Australian Defence Policy' (January 1959) gives rise to significant changes in the role of the Australian Navy. Whereas previous emphasis lay in providing an appropriate contribution to regional arrangements, these contributions were not necessarily self-contained.
2.   Australia's strategic situation is now seen as one demanding the ability of its defence forces to be able to act independently in certain circumstances. This

concept in no way removes or reduces the desirability of acting in concert with allies. The ability of Australian forces to act independently will in fact increase the effectiveness of an Australian contribution to an allied force ...

4.   To meet the requirements of the Strategic Basis the Royal Australian Navy must:–

(a)   Have forces in peace which are highly mobile and which are ready for immediate independent action with Allies.

(b)   Have forces capable of offensive as well as defensive action, designed for operating under tropical conditions.

(c)   Have forces which are compatible with United States forces ...

[paragraph deleted]

Tasks of the Navy to Meet the Strategic Role

6.   The Strategic Basis suggests that the following conflicts are possible for Australia —

(a)   Cold War activities in South-East Asia

(b)   Aggression in the Formosa area

(c)   Viet-minh aggression

(d)   Communist China and Viet-minh aggression

(e)   Global war aftermath.

7.   In order to meet the strategic role the Navy must be capable of the following tasks —

Limited War

(a)   Anti-submarine operations (using the most advanced techniques for hunting and killing submarines) to protect sea borne operations and trade.

(b)   Surface and air operations to destroy enemy surface forces.

(c)   Amphibious operations with the capability of transporting and landing a battalion group against light opposition. Landing forces will require air defence and air and naval gunfire support.

(d)   Air defence of Naval forces and mercantile convoys outside the range of shore based fighter cover.

(e)   Mine counter measure operations including the ability to sweep mines embodying the latest known techniques.

(f)   Anti-shipping and blockade operations.

(g)   Logistic afloat support for Naval operations and in the early stage for amphibious operations.

(h)   Defence of defended ports.

(i)   Hydrographic surveying.

Peace (Including Cold War)

(j)   Contribution to the British Commonwealth Strategic Reserve in South East Asia.

(k)   Search and rescue operations.

(l)   Flag showing in support of foreign policy.

(m)   Support of LRWE Woomera trials and British Commonwealth Atomic tests.

(n)   Hydrographic surveying.

[paragraphs deleted]

Deficiencies in the Present Composition of the Fleet and Reserve Fleet and in Logistics

22.   Examination of the naval forces required to meet the Strategic Basis and the composition of the fleet, reserve fleet and logistics in the three year programme, reveals the following —

(a)   By 1963 the Gannets and Sea Venoms will no longer be serviceable and the Fleet Air Arm will be run right down.

(b)   *Melbourne* will not be capable of operating replacement aircraft.

(c)   The age of the Reserve Fleet makes it ineffective.

(d)   The Navy is without missile defence against attack by modern aircraft.

(e)   The Navy is short of modern surface ships.

(f)   There is a complete lack of minesweeping capability against modern mines.

(g)   There is a complete lack of amphibious capability.

(h)   There is no submarine force.

(i)   With the exception of the Fleet Tanker there is no Fleet Train.

(j)   The surveying ships are reaching the end of their useful times.

244

(k) A deficiency in logistic support ...[46]

The references to the Fleet Air Arm, paragraph 22(a) and (b) were very disturbing. I have recently discovered that this had been raised by the Fourth Naval Member in 1955, shortly after *Melbourne* was first commissioned. My advisers were firm in the view that *Melbourne* would not be capable of operating the replacement aircraft which would be available in 1963 and I had no option but to take serious notice of this information. I was not prepared to accept, however, that the Gannets and Sea Venoms would no longer be serviceable in 1963 or that *Melbourne* would not be capable of operating replacement aircraft. Much could happen over a four-year period and I needed time in which to review overseas drawing boards before being prepared to make firm recommendations. It was also becoming increasingly clear that we should take the plunge once again and develop a submarine service. The need for a modern survey ship was high but that would have to wait until decisions were made in the fighting area. It was time to start shaping the submission to the Minister and Cabinet.

As we worked on the programme, close collaboration was maintained with defence scientists concerning a possible breakthrough in anti-submarine warfare. By 1952 missile research at Salisbury in South Australia had progressed to the point where a wire-guided anti-tank missile promised to be a feasible proposition. Strangely, the Army decided it had no requirement for such a weapon as it would be valueless in tropical jungle conditions where tanks would not be visible at long range. However, the United Kingdom saved the day by requesting us to develop a weapon with a large warhead which would destroy any type of tank, and so the 'Malkara' project went ahead. By 1958 evaluation trials in Britain had commenced. With the help of British specialists, we had available in Australia a scientific team which could carry a new project from the design stage through to the delivery of the hardware. Follow-on work (with follow-up money) was essential if this expertise was not to be lost. It transpired that an impressive naval anti-submarine weapon, 'Ikara' (the Aboriginal word for 'throwing-stick'), was to provide this.

On becoming CNS I was not aware of any such details concerning our scientific capability. It was a pleasant surprise to learn that as far back as 1952 an operational research group had made a feasibility study of providing our destroyers and frigates with a means of attacking submarines at ranges well in excess of those of existing weapons using a guided missile. Technical reasons, such as the short range of sonar and the lack of a homing torpedo, had caused the project to be shelved, but the problem was known in some detail. In early 1958 we knew that the Royal Navy had developed a homing torpedo. If such a weapon could be carried by the Malkara type missile, the moment had arrived for the dust to be removed from the file on the shelf. A demonstration was arranged, but reluctantly it was agreed that the RN homing torpedo was both too large and too slow to meet our need. Then, most opportunely, there arrived a report from the USN research station at China Lake that a smaller, faster and much lighter 'Type 48' homing torpedo was showing great potential. Mr Ward, a naval scientist on loan from the Royal Navy, was able to confirm that a new sonar, designed in the UK for fitting in the new 'Type 12' frigates, would provide the second facility to make possible the scientific concept of a missile carrying a homing torpedo being guided in flight to the last known position of a submarine. With the enthusiastic support of Rear-Admiral Becher (DCNS), it had been agreed before my arrival that a request for an authorization of a feasibility study be prepared.

Now I was fully briefed to usher the project through the Defence Committee. With the existing anti-submarine armaments in ships the advantage lay with the submarine, but if this new project proved successful a major breakthrough in anti-submarine warfare would be achieved, perhaps even turning the tables completely. The available evidence suggested that the project was within the scope of the scientific talent available and I felt that I could approach the subject enthusiastically, confident that there would be little chance of failure.

While a preliminary study (leading up to a feasibility study) was being carried out, a fortuitous ad hoc meeting was held at Parliament House. The project had been mentioned to the Minister for Supply, Mr Hulme, who called upon Senator Gorton, the DCNS and myself to present our views. Naturally the argument that the project should proceed without delay in light of the great benefits which could accrue to the Western world was expounded.

Even so, the project still had to weather the Defence Policy and Research Committee (DPRC) and the Defence Committee. By August 1959 the feasibility study was concluded and the project put before the DPRC, outlining the reasons for the rejection of US and RN systems. The DPRC supported the submissions of the Departments of the Navy and Supply and recommended that the development proceed as fast as possible and progress be reported once a year.

The Defence Committee considered the subject on 16 September. The financial aspects were complicated and Mr Hewitt, the Treasury Member of the Defence Committee, made it quite clear that he and his seniors were not prepared to recommend financial support unless I could guarantee that the Ikara project would succeed. This naive approach annoyed me. All the evidence placed before the Committee showed that the prospects of success were very good indeed and since success would strengthen the anti-submarine capability of our potential allies, and correspondingly decrease the offensive power of the submarine, the very small risk of failure, as in all such projects, should have been quite acceptable. The Chief of Air Staff, Sir Frederick Scherger, was far from enthusiastic and I suspect he thought that any spare money should go to his service. To avoid an impasse I invited the Committee to a demonstration to explain the project visually, with scientific advisers in attendance to answer questions and confirm that I had not gilded the lily.

On 15 October the Defence Committee reconsidered Ikara. It was a tiresome meeting. My nickname for Len Hewitt was Mr No, a name which no doubt would have endeared him to his superiors. To me, withholding funds for the good of Australian finance to the detriment of the defence of Australia did not seem to be the role of the Treasury. However, in spite of the opposition the Minister for Defence formally approved the project on 2 November. The development of a most valuable weapon had commenced at last. I felt that things were beginning to move.

The attempt to prepare the naval three-year programme made it painfully obvious that there were too many unknown factors to make positive recommendations. Although our naval liaison officer in London and our naval attaché in Washington were doing their best to keep up to date, it was obvious that talks on the highest level were required. I requested some time to consider further the programme and put forward the 'composition of the (naval) forces' submission — in brief a request for six months' grace before making solid proposals. This was to have strong repercussions. Gorton wrote to the Minister for Defence, Mr Townley, on 20 October 1959:

1.   Below are given the requirements of the Navy for the present three year programme. On the basis of the figures sent to you by me on 29 September, these requirements can be met and the present Navy can be run on a vote of 45.6 million in 1960/61 and 46 million in 1961/2.

2. Sure requirements for the Navy are —
   (1)   Continuation of the approved Frigate building programme.
   (2)   Introduction of a submarine service with construction in Australia of the first pair of submarines beginning 1960/61.
   (3)   Continuation of the Fleet Air Arm with its present equipment not longer than the duration of the present programme and probably discontinuing before that programme ends because of personnel difficulties.
   (4)   Provision of a safer level of stores, particularly ordnance stores.
   (5)   Close examination overseas of SAGW (Sur-

face to Air Guided Weapon) capacity for existing escorts.

3. There are other requirements of the Navy which cannot be stated with precision until —

(a) Investigations abroad as to availability, cost, and suitability have been made on the highest service levels.

(b) Final decision has been made on whether the Fleet Air Arm is to be re-equipped.

4. The Naval Board, CNS, and I would like a decision on (b) above deferred until a final approach overseas has been made to make final checks on the aircraft recommended and to see once and for all whether a suitable carrier can be made available at an acceptable cost. Even if it can be made available it will not be possible to re-equip the Fleet Air Arm in a vote of the magnitude mentioned in paragraph 1. But deferment would enable Cabinet to have before it final data on the possibilities of re-equipping the Navy with an attack carrier, and would enable Cabinet to examine an alternative possibility of equipping *Melbourne* as an anti-submarine, commando carrier. This last possibility is not favoured by the Naval Staff but is one Cabinet should, I feel examine. I would suggest an announcement could be made that within six months a final decision will be given as to whether the Fleet Air Arm is to be re-equipped or replaced by alternative equipment. [Paragraphs 5–15 excluded][47]

The day arrived for Cabinet to consider the submission and I was required to sit outside the Cabinet Room in case my presence was required inside. I realized that, in general, Cabinet papers were considered on the written word and that it was the exception rather than the rule to call in advisers and as time passed I realized that this occasion was to be no exception. Eventually my Minister came out and said to me, 'Sorry, Henry, Cabinet agreed with your paper but due to lack of funds the Fleet Air Arm is to go'. I was astounded by such an incredible decision, all the more so because it came upon me much sooner than anticipated. Perhaps the Naval

Programme letter from Gorton could have been phrased differently but at least it stated the position of affairs honestly. I did not dream that advantage could be taken of our suggestion to wait six months before making a decision.

The decision was confirmed in a ministerial statement by Mr Townley on 26 November, just before the Christmas recess, which meant that it could not be debated until April 1960. The crux of the whole matter rested with the falsity of the assertion that the RAAF could maintain the security of our sea communications, particularly from bomber attack, while ships and convoys are within range of land-based aircraft. The decision caused barely a ruffle in the press, which indicated just how much the Australian public needed to be educated in defence matters. There was considerably more concern in UK and US defence circles.

It seemed to me that I had fallen at the first high hurdle. Of course I was aware that there were influential and vocal detractors of the Fleet Air Arm, but I had misjudged their influence. Neither the Minister for Defence, his Secretary, nor the Chairman of the Chiefs of Staff Committee gave me a clue as to their recommendations on the Navy proposals. Perhaps they supported the Navy, but probably they did not. I wondered what Menzies' stand had been on the issue. I knew that he enjoyed thoroughly the occasional cruise in one of HMA ships, but from my admittedly slight personal experience, he seemed to lack interest in defence. At the few Cabinet meetings I attended, he appeared to leave it to others to do the talking and to Jack Bunting, the Cabinet Secretary, to deduce some conclusion for the minutes. Nevertheless, I am surprised he acquiesced in the matter and thereby permitted such a premature decision to be made.

I knew that the Navy, particularly the Fleet Air Arm personnel, would be shocked at such a peremptory and ill-considered decision. I did not seriously consider resigning for that would have been a twenty-four-hour wonder and would have achieved nothing. In any case, I still considered myself to be the best qualified to find a way ahead in the changed circumstances.

My request for high-level talks, however, had been favourably considered. I was given permission to take a team to visit the Admiralty and the US Navy Department to bring us up to date. A major change in our plans automatically followed from the Cabinet decision. After 1963, with the RAAF able to give continuous fighter cover for short periods only in limited focal areas and quite unable to answer a call for fighter cover in time in other waters (I was then and still am tired of pointing this out), the need for surface-to-air guided missiles in the fleet would be imperative. Consequently, this item moved up the shopping list.

By this time both my wife and I were feeling the pressure of our respective occupations, and in addition the social obligations of the service chief and his wife. Naturally, I was prepared to give up some time to the social round, and quite enjoyed it. Seated alongside the beautiful wife of the Italian Ambassador at a dinner party with our only means of communication being French could be hilarious. But my wife and I realized that to survive work and play we would need to be incommunicado at weekends. Our escape began at a cocktail party where my wife was talking to Joe Gullet. Jokingly she told him that we could not stand the racket and would have to either buy the Canberra Brick Works or a farm. Joe knew of a farm for sale on the Shoalhaven River near Braidwood and in no time an agent carted us off to look at a square mile of land on the southern side of the Kings Highway, which leads to Batemans Bay, forty miles from Canberra. After entering the first 200 yards there stretched below us a beautiful river flat partly covered by tussocks. Closer inspection showed a second smaller river flat ringed with tree-covered hills forming a giant amphitheatre. Further back were wooded areas, suitable for use after being cleared. The price was right so Illogan Park came into being. This development would give me a job in my retirement, as well as ensuring that I was fresh and alert every Monday morning. In due course, builders started to work on the two houses, a garage/workshop and a shearing shed. On weekends we became for some time arsonists of the highest order: at any one time we might have a dozen

251

fires going to clear away ringbarked timber and centuries of debris. It was a great antidote to the high-tension life in Canberra.

1960

My first year as Chief of Naval Staff had ended with a severe blow to the service. I hoped that 1960, and my investigations abroad, might bring it some recompense. The grounds for the exploratory visits to the UK and USA had been prepared through our naval liaison officer in London, Captain N. A. McKinnon, and our naval attaché in Washington, Captain J. H. Dowson. Rear-Admiral (E) K. Urquhart and Captain D. H. Wells (Director of Plans) were to accompany me. Before departing I received a most extraordinary personal letter from the Secretary of the Department of Defence directing me to refrain from investigating the question of a replacement carrier for HMAS *Melbourne*. My mental convolutions regarding the need for such a directive still leave me with the feeling that the ill-considered and rash decision of November, which failed to take cognizance of history, could only come from quarters determined to eradicate the Fleet Air Arm.

In mid-January 1960 we flew direct to London and were billeted at the Hyde Park Hotel. I sat down in my room at afternoon tea time with the London *Evening News* and awoke with a stiff neck in time for breakfast. Then I was off to Australia House circling Trafalgar Square to pay my respects to the great lord en route. Staff meetings were held and a programme mapped out to provide for official calls on our High Commissioner, Sir Eric Harrison, the Chief of Defence Staff, Admiral of the Fleet Earl Mountbatten of Burma, and the First Sea Lord, Admiral Sir Kaspar John.

My visit with Mountbatten was not a happy one. From what he said to me, he was under the impression that I had recommended the closing down of the Fleet Air Arm. When he had finished his harangue, he left immediately for some important engagement, discourteously not offering me the opportunity of reply to rectify his misconceptions. I was not amused and put the facts of life to his chief of staff who I trust passed on the message.

Later I was invited to lunch by the First Lord, Lord Carrington, and my Lords Commissioners of the Admiralty. This was one of the great moments in my life. In 1923 a scrubby midshipman from HMS *Caledon*, wearing an ill-cut monkeyjacket with worn lapels, would not have believed it possible. Throughout my career I, and the RAN, had received the greatest help and consideration from the Royal Navy. There were a few signs in the twenties that help to the RAN was to be discouraged, but they enjoyed a deservedly brief existence. I had no idea if any Australian naval officer had ever expressed the gratitude of our navy to the Royal Navy, but at that lunch I did just that. This story of my life should reek with the opportunity, experience and friendship given to me by the Royal Navy. If it does not the fault is mine.

Further staff discussions were held at Australia House so that the relevant information could be collected and appropriate meetings arranged. Apart from getting up to date with naval thinking in general, I had particular interests to pursue. With the demise of the Fleet Air Arm in 1963, the fleet would now need to be fitted with surface-to-air guided missiles; minesweepers were high on my list because of our complete lack of minesweeping capability; Cabinet had directed me to find a solution to the provision of submarines to act as anti-submarine targets; and I wanted to investigate the progress being made in the use of helicopters in anti-submarine warfare.

The simple answer to the provision of the surface-to-air guided-missile problem was to acquire ships of the 'County' class, then under construction. Ships of this class would be of 5,200 tons with four 4.5-inch guns, a Twin Sea Slug guided-missile launcher and a helicopter pad. The main engines were to be novel — steam and gas turbines geared to the same propeller shafts and producing 60,000 horsepower. The gas turbines were to be of sufficient power to get the ship out of harbour while steam was being raised and could supplement steam power at high speeds.

The initial fly in the ointment was Sea Slug. It was an embarrassment to have to say to the Admiralty that our authorities were not impressed with the weapon then undergoing trials at our testing station at Woomera. I knew that I had no hope of obtaining approval to acquire 'County' class ships with the weapon fitted, nor would I have made such a recommendation.

I was aware that there existed a well-tried and proven US guided missile, Tartar, which was about to be fitted to a new DDG class destroyer. The range was fifteen to twenty miles and control would be by two separate radar systems for tracking and attacking two aircraft in the one raid. Sea Slug was not capable of this and therefore Tartar was providing two at the price of one. Accordingly I invited the Admiralty to consider making design changes to install Tartar which, admittedly, was asking a lot. Our doubts about Sea Slug would cause a flutter in the dovecotes. On the other hand, naval shipbuilding firms would benefit greatly as the Sea Slug magazine and loading arrangements were extravagant of space whereas the Tartar system, by comparison, was a neat package.

To complicate the picture further, my engineer specialist, Admiral Urquhart, was not happy with the novel propulsion system in the 'County' class vessels. I felt bound to take note of his views although I could not imagine the RN making a major mistake in their modern propulsion arrangement. Mention of this to the officials in the Admiralty cast further gloom and it was not surprising that I was informed politely that the drawing office effort was not available to make the desired changes to the design. Nevertheless I was disappointed and was not anxious to look elsewhere for guided-missile ships. The entire life of the RAN had been built around RN classes of ship, their armaments and store items — everything except Royal Marines and rum.

I proceeded to work through the shopping list while I pondered this turn of events. My next port of call was HMS *Vernon*, the torpedo and anti-submarine school in Portsmouth, where as a sub-lieutenant I had been unable to master the circuitry of a telephone exchange. The object of my visit this time was to discuss coastal minesweepers and inspect those held there on reserve. The prospects of making a purchase seemed good. I also

AS *Derwent* which was launched by Lady Burrell *(Department of Defence)*

arles F. Adams' class guided missile destroyer (DDG)—HMAS *Hobart (Department of ence)*

'Bird' class mine warf
vessel—HMAS *Teal (Departn*
of Defence)

Anti-submarine guided weap
Ikara, firing from DDG *(Dep*
ment of Defence)

had a chance to talk to the Flag Officer Submarines at Haslar on the other side of Portsmouth harbour. He had no difficulty in convincing me that the Royal Navy 'Oberon' class submarine was the best conventional submarine in the world. I had not realized until then that the US Navy, with the advent of their nuclear-powered submarines, had almost ceased research and development of the conventional type. The RAN problem was well understood by British submariners who had been operating from Australia for many years.

In the midst of all this high-powered activity, I was invited to the RN College at Dartmouth for a weekend to meet our midshipmen completing their training there. I travelled down with Captain McKinnon by train. Just as the train was leaving Euston, into our carriage sidled a most beautiful creature — obviously a film star of the highest order. Putting on the required English reserve, we refrained from starting a conversation until she eventually commented upon the green fields and we talked on. She even talked about the time she had spent in Australia making *The Sundowners*, but neither of us could recall her name until after she had left the train at Taunton, and the name Deborah Kerr flashed into our minds. Once at Dartmouth I realized that there were no problems with our midshipmen. There was an RAN lieutenant on the staff who seemed happy with his job and his charges.

I took the opportunity to visit the shipbuilding firm of Vickers at Barrow on Furness in Lancashire. Submarine construction was discussed and I saw the hull of Britain's first atomic submarine being welded in the yard. On the quiet, I was told that they could handle the drawing office side of the 'County' class destroyer proposal, but I was not prepared to consider circumventing the Admiralty by those means.

Soon my time in England had run out. What had been achieved? I had failed to solve the guided-missile problem, but I had learned that good progress was being made in research and development on the use of sonar equipment by helicopters. I do not think I appreciated at the time the relevance of this work to the RAN in the not-too-distant future. The cloud, which followed me from England, was the prospect of introducing US Navy ships to the RAN. It was not the ships and equipment that worried me but the practicability of dealing with logistics, problems resulting from different types, sizes and nomenclature of equipment.

We arrived in New York on Sunday, 31 January for a nine-day official visit to the US Navy. A four-engined navy plane was made available for the tour and the programme was designed to meet my particular interests and to allow me to meet their Chief of Naval Operations, Admiral Arleigh Burke, who ordered that I be given salutes of seventeen guns, rather than the fifteen to which I was entitled, because I was Chief of Naval Staff. Admiral Burke had been a tough destroyer captain during the Second World War and, despite not having fleet command experience as an admiral, in 1955 was chosen as Chief of Naval Operations over ninety-two admirals. He risked his career at hearings before the House Service Committee when he criticized the cancellation of a large aircraft carrier, shooting down once again the age-old arguments that carriers were no longer required.

So on the first day of February I landed at the naval air station at Anacostia, Washington, DC, to be greeted by Admiral Burke with full military honours. It was a great compliment to the Royal Australian Navy as were similar events in the next nineteen days. The welcoming party included Mr Loveday, the counsellor to our embassy, Rear-Admiral Gatacre, our defence representative, and Captain Dowson.

I then left for a long chat with Admiral Burke at the Pentagon. Discussions covered a wide field and I was at pains to point out the benefit to us of joint exercises whether in Australia, Hawaii or South-East Asia. Our liaison with the USN has always been happy at all levels and there really was no need to make an effort to keep the friendship alive. It would have been unnatural if the announcement regarding the future of our Fleet Air Arm was not brought up by Admiral Burke. However, my instructions not to raise the subject did not prevent me being offered a straight-decked 'Essex' class carrier, with the proviso that any alterations, such as the angled deck, landing mirror and catapult, be paid for by Australia. I could only express my appreciation for the offer and change the subject to surface-to-air guided missiles.

The next day was used to show me a modern conventional submarine at the New York Shipbuilding Company at Camden, New Jersey, in the Philadelphia area. The details of USS *Bonefish*, recently commissioned, were proudly displayed for us by her captain. Two days later we flew south over the Potomac and down Chesapeake Bay to Norfolk, Virginia, to meet Admiral Jerauld Wright, Commander-in-Chief of the Atlantic Fleet at his headquarters. There was the usual convivial chat and exchange of views and this time a press interview was included. It was clear that, to reporters, Australia was a long long way from Norfolk.

In the afternoon the team was to be flown out to the anti-submarine carrier, *Wasp*, the flagship of Rear-Admiral Shinn. The aircraft was specially fitted for passengers and equipped with an arrester hook. This was to be the first and only deck landing in my career. It was a miserable day with varying visibility and, being more valuable dead than alive, my insurance company had cause to be worried. But neither the brokers nor I need have been concerned, for the hook caught the arrester wire and we were down. Before I had time to relax after my historic flight, Admiral Shinn asked if I would like to call on the captain of a destroyer fuelling alongside at a speed of about sixteen knots. I was soon suspended in mid-air between the carrier and destroyer with the disturbed waters of the Atlantic close below. I was back in the seaman's element.

After crossing back to *Wasp*, we had an interesting discussion on anti-submarine tactics. This was the procedure at each port of call, and I really had to be alert as my views were required on most subjects. I had Captain Wells playing in the slips for answers to the curly ones. After spending the night on board there was enough wind for a deck take-off to return to Norfolk, and then to Washington for the weekend.

After visiting USS *Dewey* in Boston and the Naval War College in Newport, Rhode Island, on Monday, the next day found us at the Naval Base at Newport where the object was to learn about surface-to-air guided missiles. Discussion centred on the Tartar missile and the new generation of destroyers, the 'Charles F. Adams' class, in which it was to be fitted. My earlier reports of the missile were now confirmed. Guided-missile destroyers were becoming increasingly interesting to me.

Soon we had completed our east coast tour and set off in our plane for an overnight flight to the west for visits within the Eleventh Naval District. I noted that the programme showed that after two days in San Diego and Los Angeles, the next weekend included a visit to Disneyland. I suggested to Commander Jack Miller, the liaison officer for my visit and the future naval attaché in Canberra, that perhaps we could substitute a visit to Las Vegas instead of Disneyland. It was apparent that to the entire crew this was an inspired thought and so Jack Miller sent off a proposed amendment to the agenda which was approved with the rider that the cost of accommodation at Las Vegas would be a personal matter.

Being a great naval base, San Diego was full of admirals so my first day was to be one comprising many visits, a press conference, and a visit to the Mayor, who presented me with a key to the city. The afternoon found us in a conference room where we were given a set piece intelligence briefing using modern instructional aids which was so professional that it was quite clear that many people had taken a lot of trouble.

A day after, we travelled to Los Angeles where a similar round of visits ensued. I made time to visit a good family friend, Mary Hughes, in Hollywood. Her brother was an engineer and inventor who worked for the New England Mica Company in Boston and who had come to Australia to help establish my wife's mica machinery in Melbourne, and who later went to England for similar work in her English branch at High Wycombe.

The Saturday flight to Las Vegas was short. We had booked in at the Sands Hotel and each member of the party and the crew went his own way. I am not a great

258

gambler by nature, but I must admit that I would enjoy Las Vegas for three or four days every couple of years. I could not follow craps, but roulette, at the lowest price table, I thoroughly enjoyed. The atmosphere was not comparable with the quiet and cool of Nice and Cannes; it was not quite pandemonium, but the sounds from bands, singers and poker machines filled the air. Time simply did not seem to exist there.

Back to work at San Francisco the next Tuesday, Rear-Admiral Ferrall, Commander of the Pacific Fleet submarine force, briefed us on new equipment, and particularly that found in a modernized conventional submarine, USS *Tiru*. This was my last visit and the time had arrived to extend thanks and to take leave of Commander Miller and the aircraft crew. A lot had been achieved in a short time in continental America. With the lights of the Golden Gate fading away astern, course was set for Hawaii where I was to visit the Commander-in-Chief of the Pacific Fleet, Admiral Herbert G. Hopwood.

Admiral Hopwood's staff put on a special briefing of US views on Pacific affairs, and in turn quizzed me on Australian affairs connected with waters to our north. The briefing was probably a standard type of affair, but again much care had been put into the preparation. I was able to examine the facilities required at a submarine base and witness a few submarines going through their escape-hatch routine. It was clear that the costs connected with such a base would be heavy. Then I was shown a ship about to sail north for a long stretch on a radar 'early warning' line. The ship was fitted with a vast array of radar sets. In the operations room were numerous wall displays interspersed with equally numerous photographs of well-proportioned nudes.

The Pearl Harbor visit, although short, was extremely valuable as well as enjoyable. Now it was time to get back to Canberra and set the ball rolling for the future. I returned to Australia in a better position to carry out my job. Not only had I been able to investigate problems of immediate concern but had acquired some of the 1960 feeling on nautical trends in the Royal Navy and US Navy. I was now better able to tell my minister which direction should be taken in the naval programme awaited by the Minister for Defence, and there was no time to waste. Detailed investigations had to be made into the projects envisaged in the naval blueprint covering the next two years, but I knew that the items would have to be spaced to conform with availability of finance. These were the early acquisition of minesweepers and destroyers fitted with surface-to-air guided missiles, and the introduction of a submarine service, while a close watch was kept on the anti-submarine helicopter progress in the United Kingdom. Further, I was determined to squeeze into the programme a new survey ship. Throughout my service I had watched the survey service go about their vital work unheralded and unsung in venerable ships taken from the scran bag. Our fine hydrographers and cartographers deserved better treatment and what better way to express appreciation than to direct them to write their own 'staff requirements' to fit into a ship of about 2,000 tons standard displacement.

It would be late in the year before the naval programme had developed to a stage where some items could be put through the defence machinery and government decisions made public. Then it would be my responsibility in the Defence Committee to see that the Navy slice was commensurate with its war function. It was also in my interest to see that the RAAF was allocated appropriate money to play its part in the defence of sea communications.

In the meantime, as detailed negotiations with the RN, USN and local shipbuilding authorities continued and the naval programme began to take shape in preparation for an October deadline, the normal running of the Navy and the fleet continued. We kept our usual two destroyers or frigates serving constantly in the Malayan area with the British Commonwealth Far East Strategic Reserve and there was that year another large-scale SEATO exercise in which we played our part.

Events during the year included the Navy being represented at North Borneo liberation celebrations and at the unveiling of a memorial to the *Sydney–Emden* action off the Cocos Islands. There was also an extraordinary incident during a gunnery exercise when a shell from *Anzac* hit *Tobruk* amidships. In the absence of a floating target a 'throw off' procedure was adopted, using a friendly ship as a target. The fire control instruments were supposed to be adjusted so that the guns were 'thrown off' ten degrees and after each round the target ship signalled the fall of shot. By an odd misunderstanding the 'throw off' was subtracted and the last safety measure, a sentry at each gun whose job it was to see that his gun was kept pointing in a safe direction, failed. This incident caused some indignation and a lot of parliamentary comments and jibes which was fair criticism, but no one pointed out the accuracy of the range finder. No one was hurt in this encounter but we were not so lucky when *Woomera*, engaged in dumping ammunition at sea, caught fire and exploded, killing two of the crew.

There were also many official visits throughout the year. The First Sea Lord, Admiral Sir Charles Lamb, arrived to discuss general naval problems, and also the peculiar difficulties of South-East Asia. Shortly after he returned he fell ill and from hospital he sent a message warning me not to 'overdo it as I have done'. He was promoted Admiral of the Fleet on his deathbed.

Other VIPs to visit included Admiral of the Fleet Lord Louis Mountbatten and Rear-Admiral Phipps, the Chief of New Zealand Naval Staff. At one Defence Committee meeting we could not agree with quite a few of Mountbatten's proposals, yet at dinner that night at Government House, he assured the Governor-General that there was unanimity on the day's discussions. Such flexible interpretations were not endearing.

There were also less demanding duties to be attended to, such as a mannequin parade to raise funds for the Navy League's sea cadets. Lady Dunrossil had accepted an invitation to attend and so I felt that I should be present on her arrival at the Netherlands Embassy. My duty over, I was standing well removed from the scene of action when an unknown lady started a conversation with me, saying that it was a shame a particular admiral had not got the job of CNS because the present incumbent obviously was not suitable. When I mentioned who I was the conversation ended rather abruptly. Despite the misgivings of some, the naval service was honoured on 8 August when I was promoted a Knight Commander of the British Empire and dubbed by Lord Dunrossil.

By October the naval programme was ready to go before the Defence Committee. There were still problems to be discussed and I was prepared for some hard bargaining to obtain the equipment I wanted for the Navy. I envisaged little difficulty as far as the surveying vessel was concerned and the Admiralty was prepared to sell to us six 'Ton' class mine warfare vessels, one of which I had inspected at HMS *Vernon*. Detailed investigations showed a need to fit new engines and to add stabilizers and air conditioning. Most of the cost of modifications would be the replacement of the main engines with more modern ones, constructed of non-magnetic metals, which were manufactured only in England. Apart from their minesweeping capabilities, these craft could be very useful in coastal patrol work in peacetime and provide experience in command for lieutenants.

I had decided to ask for anti-submarine helicopters. The trials of the 'Wessex' 31A had, in April, been most successful and proved the arrival of a valuable addition to the search and destroy aspect of the war against submarines. The Admiralty was placing orders so that 'Wessex' could enter front line service in July of the following year. Of course helicopters required helicopter platforms and therefore it was decided to add to our October proposals that *Melbourne* continue after 1963 as an anti-submarine helicopter carrier. She could be valuable in this role in maintaining my aim to keep the Fleet Air Arm in existence. The prospect brought some colour back to my cheeks.

As far as new destroyers were concerned, I proposed a major break with tradition. The Royal Navy had turned down my proposed alterations to its 'County' class, which were a trifle impertinent. Under pressure I would have accepted the steam/gas turbine combination in the British ships. However, there was not the slightest doubt that the 'Charles F. Adams' (CFA) class filled the bill exactly. It was a new class using war and post-war experience and to have two of these ships within a few years would give the fleet the most modern ships in western navies.

I had no misgivings about the fighting capabilities of the 'Charles F. Adams' class. In addition to the dual Tartar missile system, she would carry modern anti-submarine systems and two rapid-firing 5-inch guns, all of which would be controlled by radar and computer. The normal boiler-turbine main machinery would produce 70,000 horsepower and a maximum speed of thirty-five knots. All this would be in a hull with a displacement of 4,500 tons — altogether a pleasing package.

There were a number of factors which had influenced my recommendations. The two most important reservations I had experienced concerned the government's readiness to pay a considerable US bill and the training of our personnel to master the operation of equipment and logistics. On the financial side, I believed I could show that the need would justify the means and I was not unduly worried about the adaptability of our sailors, even though every department except communications would be foreign. My nagging worry concerned the handling of two differing types of stores ashore. The US stores ledgers would list thousands of items with foreign names and strange pattern numbers — even simple screws had differing threads. The logistics side would have to be made to work, that was all. Meanwhile, all departments had lengthy investigations to carry out, not the least being the training facilities for the varied new equipment. There seemed little doubt that the US Navy would welcome an order, but it would have to be fitted in to their new construction programme which included twenty-three of the destroyers for its own use.

The submarine problem, too, was sorting itself out. The US investigations showed that the minor alterations made to their conventional submarines did not measure up to the RN 'Oberon' class, so our direction was clear. Unfortunately, expertise gained by our three earlier attempts at establishing a submarine service was lost, but at least Cockatoo Island Dockyard could cope with major submarine refits, which removed one headache. Arrangements were under way with the Royal Navy to train a number of our officers and ratings in submarine warfare and when this was completed it might be possible for the trained men to serve in RN submarines on the Australia Station. The Royal Navy understood our predicament and did not force the pace by pressing for the return of their ships. The major constraint would be that perennial — finance. On 11 October, in introducing the Defence Estimates, the Minister for Defence could only say he expected to announce government decisions on proposed new naval projects in the very near future. He mentioned that the RAAF order for the twelve Neptune maritime reconnaissance aircraft had been placed in the United States. These would greatly improve our ability to control our sea communications.

After approval by the Naval Board, the programme to be placed before the Defence Committee contained the firm recommendations to acquire six modern minesweepers from the United Kingdom and to construct a specialized survey vessel in Australia. It was proposed, subject to financial considerations, that twenty-seven anti-submarine helicopters be purchased in England and that, as a consequence, *Melbourne* would remain in commission after 1963 as an anti-submarine helicopter-carrier. The Defence Department was to be asked to note that consideration was under way to order two guided-missile destroyers from the US Navy.

To my surprise and annoyance, these proposals met with much opposition in the Defence Committee, in part owing to the general ignorance of naval technical details. Also, the other members wanted to know more than I thought they needed to know. Regarding minesweepers, the Chief of Air Staff, Scherger, would only support the acquisition of two minesweepers and would not listen to reason. To deal with the array of modern mines in our harbours with only two minesweepers was the height of absurdity, but at least the proposed survey vessel caused no trouble.

The capabilities of the Westland Wessex helicopters were given in the Defence Committee submission, but again members wanted greater detail. Perhaps the simple concept of a 'dunking sonar' was hard to comprehend. The proposal to acquire guided-missile destroyers was received in comparative silence. With the government having decided to remove the fighter protection from the fleet in 1963, no one would dare to speak against the provision of some form of anti-aircraft protection. To clear the air on the minesweeping and helicopter items, I suggested to the chairman that the committee reconvene the following morning when I would provide greater detail on the contentious matters.

I then rallied Captain Wells, Director of Plans, and told him we had a night's work at my house and needed two stenographers early in the morning. We wrote and rewrote late into the night, and into the early hours of the next day. At the Defence Committee meeting later in the morning the proposals whistled through, which was as it should have been. I do not think it is the concern of the other chiefs of staff to attempt to veto particular naval projects on technical grounds. For my part, I might have asked questions for my personal information regarding a new type of tank or aircraft, but for me to have attempted to influence a decision on a technical matter relating to another service would have been an impertinence, as indeed was the interference I met.

On 9 November Senator Gorton was able to report to the Upper House:

Cabinet has had preliminary discussions on the shape of the new naval programme. A firm decision has been taken that the Royal Australian Navy should acquire six modern minesweepers equipped to hunt for, and dispose of, modern types of acoustic, pressure, and magnetic mines. The minesweepers selected are the 'Ton' class at present in use in North Atlantic Treaty Organization navies. Four will be bought 'off the shelf' in the United Kingdom but modified and altered to suit Australian climatic and other conditions. Inquiries will be made to see if the other two can be built in Australian shipyards at a comparable price and with a comparable delivery date. These ships are of specialist nature constructed of wood and aluminium, with engines designed of materials specially selected not to activate a sensitive mine and equipped with the latest devices for locating and disposing of mines. A firm decision has also been taken to build in Australia a new survey ship of approximately 2,000 tons and construction, which will take place in a civil yard, is to begin as soon as possible.

It has also been decided that, subject to a firm price being obtained for an anti-submarine helicopter which meets all the Navy's military requirements, *Melbourne* will continue in commission after 1963 as an anti-submarine helicopter carrier. Other items under consideration in the naval programme are to be the subject of detailed investigation as to price, the firmness of that price, the method of payment, and availability before a final decision is made. Such investigations, though they delay the announcement of a full programme, will not delay the planned date of acquisition of these items should it be eventually firmly decided that they will be acquired. (*Hansard*, 9 November, 1960, p. 1426)

The other items included the 'Charles F. Adams' proposals.

Naturally, these decisions pleased me greatly, especially *Melbourne*'s survival, and so it was with a much lightened load that I attended to a less demanding duty before returning to more pressing matters.

Illness had prevented the Governor-General from attending the graduation parade at the Royal Australian Naval College, and so I was pleased to deputize. I found that I could not remember the name of the officiating officer at my 'passing out' or even one word of good advice that I was supposed to act upon throughout my career.

Earlier in the year there had been mild criticism that the Minister for Defence, while meeting his senior ministers, saw little of the chiefs of staff. To remedy this it was ordained that at 6 pm on Tuesdays, when the House and Senate were sitting, there should be a get-together in the Minister's suite to discuss current matters. I duly attended the first three or four and then stopped. The mood of the party was not conducive to serious service talk. I had better ways to spend my time and my absence was not noticed.

So ended my second year as CNS. At least the dawn was beginning to break. God had taken only four days to produce light in the firmament of heaven, but he was omnipotent and to the best of my knowledge was not opposed by vested interests, as I was. Such opposition is inevitable when the defence finance cake is too small to feed three hungry services.

January 1961 – February 1962

My third year as CNS brought with it no slackening of pace although there were new faces in the Defence Committee. Roy Dowling was relieved by Fred Scherger as Chairman of the Chiefs of Staff Committee. His seat was taken by the physical fitness fanatic, Val Hancock. He had a much broader tri-service outlook than his predecessor. Ragnor Garrett was relieved by Reg Pollard, both war-experienced people.

With every reason to expect that the helicopter programme would move ahead, the timing of deliveries and training of crews and ground staff would require careful monitoring. Moreover, the guided-missile destroyer items had to be ready for the next estimates which required a great deal of attention to ammunition supplies and missiles, provision of base spares, and US dollar schemes for payment. Fortunately our USN liaison wheels were well oiled and things began to run smoothly. Equally, the Royal Navy was happy to prepare the minesweepers to our requirements. Turning away from Britain for our guided-missile destroyers produced little reaction in the UK, although in later years I was told that the Admiralty regretted the loss of income for the shipbuilding industry.

After Christmas with my wife and children on the farm, I returned to face the new year, which, although it was to be busy, put no undue pressure on me and enabled me to carry out a few visits to commands. In Western Australia I had to walk around our Junior Ratings Training School and took the salute at the first passing-out parade. The state of the school buildings and particularly the ablution blocks shocked me and I gave instructions that the priorities in the works programme were to be more closely supervised. I spoke at the Perth United Services Institute in the evening, but I did not notice the Hon. Frederick Chaney in the audience till late in the piece. He was to relieve John Gorton as Minister for the Navy in 1963 and later became Administrator of the Northern Territory. Perhaps some of my words fell on fertile soil.

Meanwhile the ships of the Navy continued the usual round of foreign tours and exercises. Rear-Admiral Gatacre took his flagship, *Melbourne*, and other fleet units to the Far East for the annual SEATO exercises and afterwards visited Bombay, Karachi and Trincomalee. In the preceding four years we had shown the flag over a wide area of the Pacific and Indian Oceans and I am sure that our ships and men bolstered our prestige, influence and reputation which, of course, is an important peacetime function of any navy. On its return, the flagship was to lead the fleet in a ceremonial entry into Port Jackson on 15 June to mark the RAN's 50th anniversary. The celebrations began on 11 March with the parades by servicemen in the capital cities, naval balls and the issue of an appropriate message by the Chief of Naval Staff.

About this time a small alarm sounded when an edict from the Defence Department required the standardization of helicopters in the three services. Of course this would have been ideal but was thoroughly impracticable; for example our new survey vessel was designed to carry only a small type helicopter. It all caused unnecessary paperwork and came to nothing.

In the office, plans already in the machine kept the wheels spinning. The highest priority was to ensure that the 'Charles F. Adams' project was ready in all respects to be put to the Defence Committee later in the year. It was a big financial commitment for us, although perhaps minor to the Americans, but the ready co-operation of the US Navy smoothed the path many times.

Two important 'Type 12' frigate launchings occurred in April. *Stuart* was to be launched on the 8th by Her Excellency Lady Dunrossil at Cockatoo Dockyard in Sydney, and *Derwent* on the 17th by Mrs John Gorton at Williamstown Dockyard. However, the unfortunate death of Lord Dunrossil required that Mrs Gorton cut the ribbon for *Stuart*, and my wife was delighted to be invited to officiate for *Derwent*. The Cockatoo Docks and Engineering Company had the happy custom of presenting a piece of valuable jewellery to their female guest, but in the sad circumstances the company sent the original gift to Lady Dunrossil who had returned to England, and presented another gift to Mrs Gorton, who had carried out her task to perfection on an occasion which ever makes my blood stir.

The following weekend at Williamstown my wife felt honoured when, by cutting the ribbon, smashing the champagne bottle and naming HMAS *Derwent*, she too added to the strength of the Navy. At the reception she made an appropriate speech with the Mayor of Hobart present (and later was asked if she would stand for a seat in the Senate). She was presented with a fine diamond and sapphire spray with earrings to match as a present from the Naval Board. Public funds would only cover a silver salver but by devious means and a cheque from me, the substitute was arranged. The steel scissors used in the ribbon cutting also were presented to my wife, but later Senator Gorton, who was taken aback at the sight of the instrument, had substituted a pair of gold ones.

In July 1961, Roy Dowling's long career ended and he was relieved by Air Marshal Sir Frederick Scherger who was to be in that job for the next five years. The position was upgraded in 1965 and he became Australia's first Air Chief Marshal since the war. It would have been difficult for any chairman to wear a tri-corn hat comfortably, but it would have required a major effort by Fred to list in the slightest towards the Navy. The bright spot of the month was the addition to the fleet of *Parramatta* and *Yarra*.

On 3 August, General Sir Dallas Brooks handed over the administration of our Commonwealth to our new Governor-General and Commander-in-Chief, Viscount De L'Isle, VC. He was a man with close business connections in the city of London, chairman of the Winston Churchill Memorial Trust Council, and a trustee of the National Portrait Gallery and Royal Air Force Museum. As a conservative MP for Chelsea he was Secretary of State for Air 1951–55; altogether a brave and public-spirited and, to me, young man. As protocol required, Senator Gorton took his complete Naval Board to Government House to call officially.

By mid-August the extensive groundwork for the purchase of two Charles F. Adams guided missile destroyers had been completed and only required processing through official channels, and no further obstructions were expected. It was the best solution to the problem resulting from the decision of 26 November 1959 to disband the Fleet Air Arm. The fighter protection to our fleet and shipping convoys was to be erased in 1963 and some substitute was essential; it could not be shore-based aircraft. The passage of the proposal was unimpeded, and so on 29 August the government formally announced its intention to order two Charles F. Adams destroyers which for a time afterwards were known as the 'Charlie Burrells'.

The contract was given to the Defoe Shipbuilding Company of Bay City, Michigan, an unexpected site for a shipyard as it is 600 feet above sea-level. To make the open sea, the completed ships would have to traverse Lakes Huron, Erie and Ontario, pass through sixteen sets of locks and then steam down the St Lawrence River passing Montreal and the Heights of Abraham at Quebec. The cost of these ships is hard to determine. The best information suggests $40,000,000 each, and that includes a complete set of guided missiles and base spares. The ship carried a vast array of radar and other equipment to control the numerous weapons in its computerised system. The captain would now fight his battle from the operations room. This in turn ushered in a new type of specialist, the principal warfare officer, who was capable of getting on with the battle in

Surveying vessel—HMAS *Moresby (Department of Defence)*

'Oberon' class submarine, HMAS *Ovens*—all hands inspecting the Sydney Opera House
Department of Defence)

Wessex helicopter *(Department of Defence)*

Viscount W. F. S. de L'Isle, Commander-in-Chief *(centre)*, and Senator the Hon. J. G. Gorton, Minister for the Navy, with Vice-Admiral Sir Henry Burrell, Chief of Naval Staff and First Naval Member.

the absence of the captain. There would always be one PWO on watch. We were to have two modern good-looking destroyers in the first flush of life. That would be great for morale.

On 17 October the Minister for the Navy was called upon to explain why these ships were not to be built in Australia. He replied:

> My responsibility as Minister for the Navy is to get for the fighting men of Australia who join the Royal Australian Navy the greatest amount of the most modern equipment in the shortest time and at the lowest cost, so that they will be able to do their work with the greatest of safety to themselves and with the greatest benefits to the country they serve. That is a responsibility which, I believe, has been discharged by ordering the ships to which Senator Dittmer has referred. In that way we are getting for Australian sailors in the shortest time and at the lowest cost the most modern ships of this class that are available. (*Hansard*, 17 October 1961, p. 1174)

The first destroyer was scheduled for delivery in September 1965 and the second in March 1966.

I had my only major disagreement with my Minister during my term of office when preparing for the 1961/2 estimates. It had been decided earlier that *Sydney*, which had been in reserve since May 1958, should be refitted (without alterations) for service as a fast transport for the movement of army personnel, stores and equipment to an operational area in the event of an emergency. I had finished my work for the estimates and taken a fortnight's leave to recuperate, not only from the paper-work but a slight ailment which later developed into appendicitis. I returned to find that Gorton had added to the naval estimates the commissioning of *Sydney* in 1962. I told him that I could not see how we could afford it and that to have her actually in commission was not a high priority. He replied that he would find the money and that the item was to remain in the estimates. I had expressed my opinion, and that was all I could do.

I was never quite sure how he found the money, but

then I was not *au fait* with Treasury rules. I believe the Secretary of the Navy and the Secretary of Defence could permit minor transfers of funds, but parliamentary approval is required for a major transfer. I am not sure, but in the case quoted I have a suspicion that the payment of an Admiralty bill for ammunition might have been deferred. However, despite the rush, it was not until May 1964 that *Sydney* was put to any real use.

Included in the estimates were the Seacat surface-to-air guided-missile systems for the four new frigates. They were to replace close-range anti-aircraft guns whose efficiency was founded on guesswork and divine intervention. Guessing had a dismal record and God retained his miracles for other purposes. The naval estimates enjoyed a calm passage through the seas of bureaucracy.

It was not until 5 October during the debate in the Lower house on the Defence estimates 1961/2 that the Minister for Defence, Mr Townley, drew together all the threads of my naval defence projects during my time as CNS. He mentioned that the Charles F. Adams destroyers were to be delivered in 1965 and 1966; the purchase of twenty-seven Westland Wessex helicopters and the conversion in 1963 of *Melbourne* to a helicopter-carrier; the construction of the second pair of 'Type 12' anti-submarine frigates fitted with Seacat; the beginning of the RAN submarine service; the provision of a minesweeping force; the construction of a specialized survey vessel; and the appointment of an RAN officer, Captain W. J. Dovers, DSC, to command the Royal Malayan Navy. I was also pleased with my decision to recall our fleet tanker when her lease to the Royal Navy expired and the progress made with the anti-submarine weapon, Ikara. However, on the debit side I had lost the Fleet Air Arm, but I counted myself lucky to have been able to save *Melbourne* as a helicopter carrier.

My final year was almost over, but I was still kept occupied with routine visits and other matters. During a visit to Government House, Lord De L'Isle, amongst other things, wished to discuss the senior officers of the Navy, some of whom he had already met. Before I left he asked me to let him have a list of them, indicating their prospects; for example, who might be chiefs of staff in the future. I objected strongly and said it would be quite unfair to all concerned if my views were found floating around or discussed other than in the greatest confidence. Strangely, he insisted and I could not object further. I marked the list 'Personal' and 'Top Secret' and so complied with an unfair instruction.

Over the previous two years work had been under way on the Russell Hill Defence complex of buildings on the north side of Lake Burley Griffin. By the end of the year office accommodation for Navy, Army and Air departments was ready for occupation. We had a small ceremony transferring the flag of the Naval Board to its new quarters and the fine administrative block was taken over by the Department of External Affairs.

Christmas was once more with us and I was delighted to receive a beautiful coloured photograph of the 'Charles F. Adams' at speed with the inscription: 'A promise of things to come'. It was a kind thought from Rear-Admiral R. K. James of the USN Chief Bureau of Ships.

My three-year appointment was to expire on 22 February 1962. Although I was still more than two years short of the retiring age for a vice-admiral, I had no wish for my appointment to be extended. There were prospective successors waiting in the wings and a change of headman after three years is better for the service. In any case, I was not offered the chance to remain. I wonder if that was because the defence vote could not afford any more of my proposals.

The Cabinet had appointed Admiral Harrington to relieve me and I felt that I could leave knowing that the Navy was in good hands. However, it happened that an edict arrived requiring the services proposals for the next three-year programme to be forwarded before my departure date. This was hardly fair to my successor, but he would have every justification to make any changes he desired.

Obviously the introduction of a submarine service had to be the main additional item in the ensuing three years. It was proposed that four 'Oberon' class be ordered in 1963 and that our fleet tanker RFA *Tide*

Austral be commissioned and join the fleet when her lease to the RN expired on 7 September 1962. With all the other commitments, the finance team had plenty of work compiling naval expenditure for each of the next three years.

During my last few weeks I visited the flagship, the naval establishments in Sydney, the Royal Australian Naval College at Jervis Bay, the Naval Air Station at Nowra and Flinders Naval Depot at Westernport. After expressing my thanks to ships' companies, I assured them that the Navy of the future would be in good hands and that an efficient naval service was essential for the security of Australia. At the Royal Edward Victualling Yard at Pyrmont in Sydney I was amused when I was invited to leave my uniforms to the uniform museum, and I was not even half dead.

There is some profit in looking back, and I should mention that during the 1959–62 period I knew that I was well equipped to handle the naval aspect of my job. On the other side, however, I was at a disadvantage. I had had experience in the lower levels of defence organization, but at higher levels I found that I was kept in ignorance of all defence matters after they left the Defence Committee. Apart from the Chairman of the Chiefs of Staff Committee, which was in any case only a sinecure, matters were handled by civil servants, the Secretary of the Department and the Minister for Defence. The chiefs of staff remained ignorant of the fate of their views and recommendations on current problems. That some reorganization of the Defence Department was needed was clear to me but with my meagre knowledge of the Public Service I did not have the answer, nor the time to find it.

A study of Hansard during my time as CNS shows that politicians of all persuasions were not students of military history and I hope, unrealistically I think, that Cabinet discussions reached a higher level than that displayed on the floor of both Houses. Perhaps it is trite to say that failure to study the lessons of history imperils our nation, but it is true nevertheless.

12
Epilogue

When I retired, very few hardware projects initiated in my time had come to fruition. I will cover their completion briefly and add comments on a few items of general naval interest over the last twenty years, which I feel in some way are linked with my career.

After my departure as Chief of Naval Staff, twenty-seven Westland Wessex helicopters for HMAS *Melbourne* (approved in November 1960) arrived in good time to allow pilots, crew and ground staff to be ready for service. In 1963 a squadron of helicopters replaced half of *Melbourne*'s complement of Gannets, which (with the Sea Venoms) were still going strong despite dire forecasts. No doubt thanks to Admiral Harrington's supplications, government action was not taken to carry out its 1960 decisions which would have had *Melbourne* revert to an anti-submarine helicopter platform in 1963. The Sea Venoms and Gannets still had good life left in them.

Then in 1967, due to Admiral McNicoll's influence, *Melbourne* replaced these aircraft with Skyhawk fighter bombers and Grumman Tracker anti-submarine aircraft. Such developments confirm my earlier remarks about the unwarranted decision to scrap the Fleet Air Arm. That Fred Scherger retired as Chairman of the Chiefs of Staff Committee in 1966 might have had something to do with this change of policy.

The existence of an Australian operational carrier (it might well have been two) in my view has increased Australia's standing in the world for thirty-three years, from 1949 (HMAS *Sydney*) to 1982 (HMAS *Melbourne*). The possession of a fleet, backed by such a powerful fighting unit, gives enviable prestige to any country. I have no doubt that the presence of our carrier added

275

strength to the voice of Australia in world forums, whether it be in the United Nations or organizations in South-East Asia. There can be no denying that Australia's international policies have benefited by the existence of our aircraft-carrier.

On a lower level, the value of 'showing the flag', in earlier days, increased with the number of funnels. I mentioned my visit to Colombo in *Vengeance*, during the short period when we had two carriers. There is no doubt that our High Commissioner, Sir Roden Cutler, used that visit to the great diplomatic advantage of Australia.

On 7 March 1962 *Sydney* was commissioned (without conversion) as a fast transport. I have already recorded my view that this should have had a low priority. A job was not found for her until May 1964 when she transported Army and RAAF personnel and equipment to Malaysia, but a year later a real job arose in troop-carrying to Vietnam. Up to 1972 she had made twenty-three voyages in that capacity and was up for disposal a year later — a pathetic end to our two-carrier Navy concept. There were encouraging developments in the Navy nevertheless.

I mentioned progress towards the reintroduction of a submarine service and the ordering of 'Oberon' class boats from the United Kingdom. My successor continued with the proposals and eventually the die was cast — the government approved the proposals, the Royal Navy retained their boats here for our training until we were able to help ourselves and at the same time continued turning out submarine-trained RAN personnel. Our First Submarine Squadron, based on HMAS *Platypus* — a shore establishment in Neutral Bay, was built up during the years 1967–70.

The Royal Navy returned the fleet tanker RFA *Tide Austral* on time. She was commissioned at Portsmouth with an RAN crew on 7 September 1962 and her name was changed immediately to HMAS *Supply* by Val Becher, the wife of the Head of the Joint Service Staff in London, Rear-Admiral Humphrey Becher. The desired alterations to the six minesweepers purchased by us had been completed. On the first day of October *Supply* sailed as escort to them — HMA ships *Curlew*, *Gull*, *Hawk*, *Ibis*, *Snipe* and *Teal*.

The minesweepers had commissioned with sixty per cent RANR ships' companies and had carried out a 'working up' programme in Scottish waters. A base had been prepared for them at Waverton, on the north side of Sydney harbour upstream from the Bridge, where they arrived on 7 December. Australian harbours at last had a minesweeping capacity available in war. Their peacetime uses were many and varied. They even served in the Far East Inshore Flotilla in the mid-1960s on anti-infiltration patrols in the Malaysia–Borneo area. *Snipe*, *Curlew* and *Ibis* form the 1st Australian Mine Counter-Measures Squadron. Altogether they were a good buy and with *Supply* in Australian waters, the mobility of the fleet had been increased greatly.

My *pièce de résistance*, a modern survey vessel, was launched at the State Government Dockyard at Newcastle on 7 September 1963 and named *Moresby* by Wendy Gatacre, the wife of Admiral Gatacre, then Flag Officer Commanding East Australia Area. I understand *Moresby* has been a great success (as she jolly well should be) and generally has sped the process of mapping from field work to fair chart.

The two 'Charles F. Adams' class ships, on completion, were fitted with only single-range launcher for 'Tartar' missiles. However, a single-launcher can fire two missiles at a short interval, the second one being given settings by a second radar system and so achieve the same result as a twin-launcher, which had attracted me initially. HMAS *Perth* was named at launching by Lady Beale on 26 September 1963 and commissioned on 17 July 1965 with Captain Ian Cartwright in command. Ikara was installed after her arrival in Australia on 11 March 1966. *Hobart* was launched by Mrs David Hay, commanded by Captain Guy Griffiths and arrived in Sydney on 7 September 1966. To my delight, my successor was given approval to add a third ship; she was ordered in January 1963 but not laid down in Bay City until February 1965. Mrs Chaney, wife of the Navy Minister, carried out the honours on 5 May 1966 and named her HMAS *Brisbane*. After the usual 'working-up' period with the US Navy, she arrived in Sydney on 22 October 1968.

I am responsible for a destroyer success story not quite by accident, but because the Royal Navy was unable, perhaps for understandable reasons already mentioned, to alter the design of their guided-missile destroyers to meet what I considered were RAN requirements. Then, being forced to turn to the US Navy, the timing was opportune in that the 'Charles F. Adams' class guided-missile destroyers had just been created after postwar consideration and experimentation. Every component of the ship's structure machinery and armament had been evaluated in detail. It was not luck that produced such ships of great quality. Over the years, when I ask questions about individual characteristics of these ships, the replies are superlatives.

The 'Charles F. Adams' class is now over twenty years old. I quote from the *Canberra Times* of 19 December 1981:

> More than $220 million will be spent modernizing the Royal Australian Navy's three DDG-class destroyers.
>
> The program, announced yesterday by the Minister for Defence, Mr Killen, is expected to keep the ships in service until about the turn of the century, by which time the oldest of them will be nearly 40 years.
>
> The modernization will include better gun and air-defence missile systems, modern radar and communications, improved accommodation and overhaul of the ship's machinery.
>
> Part of the proposed expenditure will be on the Australian-designed Ikara anti-submarine weapon system to improve its accuracy.

Earlier I stated my concern as to whether the naval and civilian stores organization could cope with the complexity of two logistic systems (RAN and USN) meeting head-on with the arrival of the new destroyers. I believe that although initially the settling down process was considerable, the arrangement eventually proved to be a workable proposition.

After my departure, Ikara progressed satisfactorily, despite its detractors and financial complications. Progress was in phases approved by Cabinet in 1962 and by mid-1963 Ikara had shown itself to be a practical proposition at sea. By the end of 1964, a fully engineered system had to be produced for sea trials. During this period, my successor, in brave anticipation, obtained approval for our two (and later three) DDGs being built in America to be fitted with Ikara after their return to Australia. This approval was a pleasing change of heart in the higher firmament.

The UK authorities had been taking a keen interest in the project since its inception. In 1965 it was agreed that we should develop the flight vehicle and various ship-guidance elements while the UK worked on the ship's stowage and other ship systems such as computer-predicter. The combined effort produced a finished product that was a weapon of great value and capable of further development. This was proven by comprehensive trials in a fully instrumented sea range in the Bahamas in 1969.

In addition to our three 'Charles F. Adams' class destroyers, Ikara was fitted in our 'Type 12' frigates, our destroyer-escorts, seven ships of the Royal Navy and four ships of the Brazilian Navy. The latter were built in the United Kingdom, the Ikara outfits being provided by our Department of Supply.

The US Department of Defence, while putting money into our project to take advantage of our experimental results, had proceeded too far, in capital investment, with their 'Asroc' to make a change.

Compared with earlier means of delivery of depth charges (dropping over the side and abeam-throwing followed by ahead-throwing weapons), the long range of Ikara gives greater scope for harrying enemy submarines. Furthermore, the homing torpedo overcomes the problem of guessing correctly the depth of the submarine. One way to use this increased capability is to increase the range of ship-borne sonars. A big advance has resulted from the 'dunking' sonar, carried by helicopters. Such machines can collect the desired

279

information (position and possibly course and speed of a submarine contact) and pass it through a computer to an Ikara-fitted ship for action.

Ikara's advent is directly due to outstanding technical ability and drive from a small band of dedicated personnel from the Aeronautical Research Laboratories, the Weapons Research Establishment, Government Aircraft Factories, the Munitions Department and last, but not least, Australian private industry. I am sure, when the full story is told, that the rapid increase in defence scientific knowledge will be seen to have carried Australia well forward. In the past twenty-three years it has attained heights which would not have been possible if Ikara had been cancelled through a paucity of funds and a lack of enthusiasm on the part of senior defence authorities.

An assessment is now being made to update Ikara and introduce the Illaroo tracking and display system. It seems likely that Ikara will play its part as a first-class weapon until the end of the century. There is no doubt that the introduction of Ikara has been a notable Australian defence weapon-development success story. I am pleased that the RAN has played a part in it. Senator Gorton and I played only a small role, but in 1959 we did appreciate that the economic survival of the team of scientists connected with Malkara was of national importance, and so it proved. We can claim some credit also for an additional bonus — £180 million in export earnings. I often wonder whether these aspects of the maintenance of our defence and research capabilities are understood more clearly today.

There is the story of a destroyer nudging a cruiser flagship during a night exercise. Both ships were stopped some distance apart to survey the damage when the admiral signalled to the captain of the destroyer: 'What are you doing now?' Came the reply: 'Am about to buy a farm!' Although not for the same reason as the hapless destroyer captain, I decided on the same course of action in my retirement. My retirement benefits from the Navy were meagre, but thanks to my wife's business acumen I did not have to look for a job and instead was able to become a farmer whose only agricultural attribute was an ability to read. I devoted my time to Illogan Park and by great good fortune enjoyed the services of a father-and-son team, Lieutenant-Commander John Dent and his son Tony, to manage the property. To say that they were a fine, reliable and tireless pair would be an understatement.

The family ship glided smoothly through unruffled waters for the first thirteen years of my retirement. With great delight Terry and I watched our family grow up, marry and have children of their own. Terry and I had an ideal existence. We lived in Canberra and occupied ourselves by attending to the farm, the mica factories in Melbourne and in England, and visiting our children and their families which were at various times scattered between Australia and the United Kingdom. My wife and her brother, Sam Weller, inveigled me into a horse-racing syndicate. In theory, for a sailor this would be a poor investment — the slow horses, fast women syndrome. We were not gamblers, however, and relied on the winning purses to keep funds in the kitty. Although we have had failures it has never required topping up in twenty years.

In 1975 Terry's health gave us a great scare, but skilful surgery kept us together for several more years. I, too, let the side down in 1980 when my heart, which had faltered earlier, decided to misbehave seriously (thankfully while my specialist was standing at the foot of the bed). Such troubles are the familiar companions of advancing years, but a great tragedy befell us at about that time. Our daughter Fayne's husband, Paul Mench, a lieutenant-colonel in the army, was killed in a freak accident on Mount Tamborine near the Land Warfare Centre at Canungra, where he was attending a course.

The joy occasioned by the 'safe and timely arrival' of grandchild number eight in 1981 was offset by deterioration in Terry's condition. She cracked hardy for a time, but it was obvious that cancer had been working surreptitiously. Despite the best care in the world, she died peacefully on 14 August 1981. I had not realized in 1944 that I was proposing to such a remarkable woman. She had triumphed over great adversity in her formative years and deserved all the joy she received in abundance from family and friends. She was a wonderful mother, a woman of the world, a great business woman, and one who could, and did, 'speak with kings nor lose the common touch'. She could cope with being the wife of an itinerant naval officer and, perhaps to her even greater credit, put up with one in his retirement.

Although I was determined that I would not loiter around harbours, as many retired admirals do, I did not lose interest in naval affairs during my retirement. I have watched with interest the fate of naval aviation in this country. Before the Battle of the Falkland Islands, the United Kingdom government, to assist government finances, offered to sell us one of her jump–jet carriers, HMS *Invincible*. After close investigation, Australia accepted the offer. However, during the Falklands affair, our Prime Minister graciously offered to let the UK off the hook if she so desired. In August 1982 the UK decided to retain *Invincible*. The government was then in a quandary due to the very heavy cost of building a new carrier. The Joint Committee on Foreign Affairs and Defence set up a sub-committee, before the Falklands war, to investigate the carrier problem and I was invited to make a written submission in which I made several suggestions designed to safeguard the fixed–wing element of the Fleet Air Arm, if only in embryonic form. (See Appendix II.)

By mid-1982 *Melbourne*, whose keel had been laid in 1943, came to the end of her tether. With a change of government in March 1983, the new Minister for Defence, Mr Scholes, announced the immediate demise of the Fleet Air Arm and, a short time thereafter, the disposal of fixed–wing aircraft. HMAS *Albatross* was to become a helicopter station. Although Scholes had been Shadow Minister, he would not have been aware of the arguments contained in secret defence papers on this highly controversial subject. To me, it was like ordering the death sentence without considering the evidence. However, I must admit that a decision should have been made many years before. Not to have done so was quite unfair to Fleet Air Arm personnel who found them-selves redundant with little warning.

282

I have with difficulty kept my story brief. If it has given some fresh insight into one arm of our defence process and given people cause to think about defending their good luck in being Australians, I will be satisfied.

Under the Official Secrets Act, not only is it an offence to disclose classified information, it is an offence to let anyone know that a secret exists on a sensitive subject and so draw attention to it. I do possess a secret which I have kept to myself for the last half century and which I am now prepared to divulge. It is based only on circumstantial evidence, which the law has been known to accept. My secret is of a whimsical nature — and I did not drink at sea. I, like many other seamen, would lean over the bridge of many ships and watch the dolphins frolic in the bow wave but, on dark nights in the tropics in calm seas, I have moved quietly to the wing of the bridge to listen to the murmur and swish as the phosphorescent waters appear to glide astern. Within these low-key sounds, I would be prepared to swear in a court of law that on many occasions I have heard a female voice whisper a seductive 'hello'. Mermaids do exist.

Appendix I
Joint UK–USA Staff Conversations
Telegraphic Reports by Australian
Naval Attaché
February/March 1941

Summary of United Kingdom Delegation's Instructions
From: First Secretary in Washington
To: Department of External Affairs
Cablegram No. 98
For Chief of Naval Staff from Naval Attache
  With reference to your telegram No. 336.
(1) Summary of United Kingdom delegation's instructions. Begins.
  (a) Conversations to be based on hypothesis of war between Germany, Italy, Japan and British Empire, present allies, United States. Hypothesis is without prejudice to any developments in the political situation and implies no political commitments.
  (b) Conversation[s] to be conducted in spirit of complete frankness.
  (c) Object to co-ordinate on broad lines plan for employment of forces of associated powers in above hypothesis.
  (d) Discussion will be within framework of general strategic policy of Chiefs of Staff. Any agreement reached will not have any binding effect until confirmed by His Majesty's Government.
  (e) His Majesty's Government advocated following strategic policy:—
    (a) European theatre of war vital theatre where decision must first be sought.
    (b) General policy should therefore be to defeat the Germans and Italians first and then deal with Japan.

(c)   Security of Far Eastern position includ-
        ing Australia and New Zealand is essen-
        tial to our strategy. Retention of Singa-
        pore as a key to the defence of these
        interests must be assured. End of sum-
        mary.
Please repeat to Chief New Zealand Naval Staff.
(2)   Appreciate the desirability of the results of staff
       conversations here being available prior to the
       Singapore conversations beginning February 22nd
       and every endeavour will be made to give as much
       information regarding progress as is possible. I
       should make it clear however that it is most
       unlikely that discussions will have reached definite
       conclusions in time.
(3)   Your remarks as to the importance of the bases to
       north and east of Australian possessions noted
       especially by United Kingdom delegation, and this
       question will be raised with United States commit-
       tee.
Commander H. M. Burrell.

It appears that copies of this and the following cablegram from Burrell (Document 279) were not shown to
the Acting Prime Minister, A. W. Fadden, until he
asked to see them on 13 February. In a teleprinter
message to the Minister for External Affairs, Sir
Frederick Stewart, on 13 February the Secretary of the
External Affairs Department, Lieutenant Colonel W. R.
Hodgson, explained that these cablegrams had been sent
by Burrell 'direct to his Chief only. In such cases as
these operational and strategical messages, we regard
ourselves as channel of communication only, the responsibility for showing them to the Minister or the
Acting Prime Minister being the Chief of Naval Staffs'.
See file AA:A1608, Y27/1/1. Subsequent progress reports on the conversations (Documents 294, 316, 318,
365 and 380) were teleprinted to Fadden on receipt.

First Progress Report
From: First Secretary in Washington
To: Department of External Affairs

Cablegram No. 99   Sent: 7 February 1941
                       Received: 8 February 1941
My Telegram 98. For Chief of Naval Staff from Naval Attache

(1)   First progress report. Discussion has been opened on major lines of strategy and co-operation in all theatres of war. Present position is as follows.

(2)   United States Pacific Fleet proposed to be somewhat weaker than that shown in dispositions vide my most secret safe hand message to you and Chief of Naval Staff New Zealand and Naval Board only. *No* reinforcement of the present United States Asiatic Fleet.

(3)   Forces thus made available are destined for the Atlantic and the Mediterranean areas where the majority of the United Kingdom Chiefs of Staffs' desires will be fulfilled.

(4)   Pacific Fleet will remain based on Hawaii and its intended operations do not appear to the United Kingdom delegation sufficient to threaten Japan.

(5)   United Kingdom delegation will return to the attack on the lines of their instructions. Present indications are that it is improbable that Delegation will succeed in moving the Pacific Fleet westward. Delegation thinks any reinforcement of Asiatic Fleet would only be agreed upon at the expense of Atlantic and Mediterranean.

Second Progress Report
From: Mr Watt
To: External Affairs
Cablegram No. 117   Sent: 12 February 1941
For Chief of Naval Staff from Naval Attache

(1)   Conversations are proceeding and have reached the following stage.

   (a)   In their view the main U.S. contribution should be in the Atlantic and Mediterranean. With this U.K. Delegation has agreed but the U.S. representatives are most reluctant to recognise that the position in the Far East must be held with minimum force and that the security of Singapore is an essential element in our joint strategy for the prosecution of the war against Germany and Italy. U.S. representatives would contemplate in the last resort abandoning the Far East in order to ensure the maximum concentration in the Atlantic and Mediterranean.

(b) U.S. representatives intend that the U.S. Pacific Fleet should operate from Hawaii with the object of protecting the West Coast of America and at the same time containing Japanese from conducting major operations against Malay. U.K. delegation have yet to examine the precise operations which are envisaged but they will press for an active and forward policy.

(c) U.S. representatives maintain that any reinforcement of their Asiatic Fleet, the present strength of which is 1 heavy cruiser, 1 light cruiser, 13 destroyers and 17 submarines, would serve no useful purpose in the event of war.

(2) At request of U.S. representatives, U.K. delegation have submitted an appreciation elaborating the views of the Chiefs of Staff on the strategic importance of the Far East position in relation to the main object, the defeat of Germany and Italy. Needless to say the U.K. delegation have presented the strongest possible case and it is just possible that this may yet influence them to appreciate our point of view and agree at least to some reinforcement of their Asiatic Fleet, but U.K. delegation must discard finally any hope of this reinforcement including a U.S. capital ship force to operate from Singapore.

(3) With regard to present critical situation in the Far East the U.S. representatives agree that everything possible should be done to keep Japan from coming into the war and also that there is now no advantage to be obtained from a policy of appeasement. U.K. delegation tentatively suggested that a temporary reinforcement of their Asiatic Fleet with forces of the order of one carrier, four heavy

cruisers and auxiliary craft in proportion would have a salutary effect but U.S. representatives hold that this would serve no useful purpose and would in fact be provocative.

Third Progress Report

From: Australian Minister
To: External Affairs
Cablegram No. 132   Sent: 18 February 1941
                        Received: 19 February 1941
For Chief of Naval Staff from Naval Attache

Third progressive report.

Second progressive report was contained in my telegram No. 117.

Further consideration of Pacific problem has been deferred until receipt of written reply from United States Staff Committee on Far Eastern appreciation. Vide my telegram No. 117.

Meanwhile most satisfactory progress is being made in Atlantic and Western Mediterranean theatres.

Casey

Teleprinted to Chief of Naval Staff Melbourne, also copy to Acting Prime Minister and Minister External Affairs. 19.2.41

Fourth Progress Report

From: Australian Legation
To: External Affairs
Cablegram No. 151   Sent: 21 February 1941
Following is summary of U.K. Delegation appreciation vide para. 2 of my telegram No. 117. Begins.

(1)   Maintenance of fleet base at Singapore cardinal point in British strategy. Conception based not only on purely strategic but political, economic and sentimental considerations, which even if not vital on strictly academic view are of such fundamental importance to Empire that must be taken into serious account. Compare United States' attitude to defence of western seaboard. We are Maritime Empire, various Dominions and Colonies held together by communications and trade routes across the oceans. Home population dependent

288

imported food and overseas trade. Security and prosperity of India our trust and responsibility. Defence of all these interests, vital to maintenance of associated war effort, depends on capacity to hold Singapore, and in last resort to base battle fleet there.

(2) Until recently, consistent policy of H.M.G. to despatch fleet to Far East on outbreak of war. This now impracticable. If U.S.A. do not come in we would hope to hold out in Malaya long time, though air forces there far below strength required. But if Singapore in serious danger of capture and U.S. still withheld aid, we should be prepared to send a fleet to the Far East, even if this would compromise or sacrifice position in Mediterranean.

(3) Active intervention of U.S.A. would profoundly modify situation. If U.S. Navy were active in the Pacific, invasion of Australia New Zealand precluded. These Dominions would only withhold their collaboration in war effort in last resort, and with U.S.A. active allies proportion of their trade and military contribution could be transported eastwards across the Pacific provided U.S. Navy could ensure reasonably safe passage.

(4) In reply to arguments put forward by U.S. representatives in discussion, we agreed that Japanese with hostile U.S. fleet on their flank would not base main fleet on a captured Singapore; that even if we retained Singapore, Japanese operating from Kamranh Bay or Batavia would threaten seriously our Indian Ocean communications, and that we could afford some measure protection to those in Western Indian Ocean from COLOMBO but not as much as if we can use Singapore.

(5) If the United States intervene we might thus still hope maintain cohesion and war effort British Commonwealth without abandoning position in Mediterranean. We still consider issues at stake so fundamental that loss of Singapore would be disaster first magnitude, second only to loss British Isles.

(6) Then stressed importance Singapore card of re-

entry, so that if threat in Indian Ocean and Western Pacific became intolerable we could still accept risks elsewhere and send fleet. Failure to do so would mean Japan becoming undisputed master of East Asia, East Indies and Western Pacific. Empire and U.S. would lose resources in food and vital irreplaceable war materials. Japan would become self-supporting and U.S. economic weapon useless. Our morale and prestige would suffer resounding blow with grave consequences during and after war. All hope of Chinese resistance would end, and Russia might throw in her lot with the Axis. India and Burma would become a liability. Unless we retain this foothold, even if Italy eliminated and Germany defeated, highly problematical, whether we could ever undertake huge combined operation necessary to restore position in FAR EAST after exhaustive and desperate struggle.

(7)   We then went on to give views of Japanese courses of action, suggesting that Japanese plan was to avoid implicating United States and possibly Dutch and to attack Malaya. In reply to question how long Malaya could hold out, we pointed out imponderable factors; namely, stage at which U.S. might intervene; whether or not Dutch would fight; effect of present deficiencies in our forces in FAR EAST and ability of joint Asiatic forces to neutralize Japanese forces in South China Seas; and extent to which operations of U.S. Pacific Fleet would contain Japanese forces in the North. We stressed need for Pacific Fleet to undertake active repeat active operations against Japan and finally pressed home point that the Asiatic fleet required reinforcement if it was to constitute real menace to Japanese advanced sea communications.

(8)   In reply to further U.S. arguments put forward in discussion we went on to discuss the meaning of their phrase QUOTE holding the Malay barrier UNQUOTE and the minimum forces required. No question of sustaining the whole of our position in the Far East. For instance, no hope of

retaining HONG KONG, PHILIPPINES or BORNEO indefinitely. Irreducible minimum which must be held was Singapore, and to do this must deny Japanese uninterrupted freedom of action to carry out sustained operations in water and from territories surrounding Singapore. Japanese attack on Malay would involve sustained operations with large land and air forces and establishment of naval control in South China Seas. Such operations could not be carried out satisfactorily without cover of capital ships in South China Seas if affective associated naval forces were operating from Singapore and any possibility remained of capital ships appearing in those seas.

(9)   Strength of Asiatic forces must be determined to some extent by strength of forces that may not be contained by operations of U.S. Pacific Fleet. Only real solution capital ship force at Singapore. Realising, however, that there were initially many real difficulties we pointed out that in view of weakness of British and Dutch forces the essential was that we should be able to gain time to move land and air reinforcements to Malay[a] when emergency arises, or in last resort re-distribute and concentrate necessary naval forces.

(10) We should therefore be in a position to dispute Japanese control of sea communications in South China Seas. In absence of capital ship force this can only be done if U.S. or British Asiatic naval forces are reinforced to an extent which would constitute a real threat to Japanese advanced seas communications, and enable us at least to interrupt them. Naval reinforcements of the order of one carrier, a division of heavy cruisers and auxiliary craft in proportion would be minimum required to fulfil this role in early stages.

(11) In view of the fact that main theatre will be Atlantic and Mediterranean obviously desirable that naval reinforcement of Asiatic forces should not be at expense of those areas, which means that it should be found from U.S. Pacific Fleet. That Fleet must be strong enough to fulfil its strategic

function, i.e., containing really important enemy forces away from South China Seas; but distances involved are immense, and if Japanese are to conduct serious operations in South China Seas they will be compelled to make substantial detachments from their main fleet, including capital ships. It is suggested, therefore, that small reduction in strength of Pacific Fleet proposed above could be accepted without weakening capacity of main fleet to fulfil its offensive role, exposing U.S. interests to attack or exposing U.S. naval forces to defeat in detail (this in reply to points made in discussion).

(12) We then expressed our conviction that if the U.S. Pacific Fleet was to draw off the Japanese from sustained operations against Malaya it was essential that it should be extremely active in Japanese waters and against Japanese mainland.

(13) Finally, we invited US representatives to agree with the contention of His Majesty's Government that the security of the Far Eastern position, including Australia and New Zealand, is essential to the maintenance of the war effort of the associated Powers. Singapore is the key to the defence of these interests, and its retention must be assured. UNQUOTE. Appreciation ends.

Summary of US Staff Committee written reply will be telegraphed shortly.

Fifth Progress Report
From: Australian Legation
To: External Affairs
Cablegram No. 159   Sent February 23, 1941
For Chief of Naval Staff from Naval Attache. Fifth Progress Report.

(1)   Following is summary vide last paragraph of my telegram No. 151. The views expressed have received approval of US Chiefs of Staff but have not repeat have not, as far as is known, been discussed with State Department. Begins.

(2)   *General*. United States representatives find them-

selves unable to subscribe to the view expressed in paragraph 6 of my Telegram No. 151. They consider that retention of Singapore is 'very desirable' and that its loss would be 'unfortunate' but they hold that its loss 'would not have a decisive effect upon the issue of the war'.

(3) In support of this view, they argue:
  (a) Invasion of Australia, New Zealand or India beyond the present resources of Japan.
  (b) Distances make serious Japanese attack on sea communication in Indian Ocean unlikely, and United States could ensure security of communications from Australia and New Zealand to the Western Hemisphere and thence to the United Kingdom.
  (c) Proportion of material support to war effort which is now provided by Australia and New Zealand might repeat might be replaced by further supplies from Western Hemisphere.
  (d) Loss of raw materials now drawn from Malaya and East Indies would not be fatal. Replacements could in time be found from elsewhere.

Despatch of US Capital force to Singapore
(4) US representatives finally rule our possibility of despatch of US capital ship force to Singapore arguing:
  (a) Such a deployment would be inconsistent with the fundamental principle of US policy that Western Hemisphere must remain secure. In event of British defeat United States must have immediately available for use in the Atlantic and Pacific Naval forces capable of withstanding attack from overseas.
  (b) Associated Far Eastern bases are incapable of protecting and supporting a battle fleet, and in view of the needs of the British Isles it would be impossible to collect enough shipping to maintain a large fleet in that region.
  (c) Associated naval strength in the Atlantic requires the maximum possible augmentation

in order to ensure the defeat of Germany.

(5)   They suggest that if, in spite of these arguments, we still maintain that it is essential to send reinforcements to the Far East, the necessary naval forces should be British and should be released from the Atlantic or Mediterranean in the light of the substantial US naval reinforcement proposed for these theatres. This suggestion, which at first sight would appear quite illogical in view of paragraph (4)(c) above, is put forward reluctantly and is based on the contention that it is preferable for the armed forces of each nation to operate in the areas in which its own interests are primarily involved.

Reinforcement of the Asiatic Fleet

(6)   United States representatives refuse to contemplate any reinforcement of their Asiatic Fleet, either now or on the outbreak of war. In support of this they argue:

(a)   It would be strategically unsound to detach any forces from the Pacific Fleet which would then have difficulty in taking offensive action to divert Japanese naval strength away from Malaya. Any reinforcement of the Asiatic fleet could therefore only be at the expense of the United States naval effort in the Atlantic, which effort they are not prepared to reduce.

(b)   It would be strategically unsound to locate any additional surface forces in the Philippines during peace-time. Far from being a deterrent, such forces would invite attack if their strength were considerable, because they would be far from support by the Pacific fleet. It would be politically impossible to locate any such forces at British or Dutch bases in advance of war.

(c)   Any additional submarines would have to come from the Pacific fleet, whose submarine strength is already now for 'effective diverting action', or alternatively from the Atlantic contribution.

(d)   The despatch of additional aircraft might act as a deterrent, but could not long delay the loss of the Philippines. Any such contribution, however, would be at the expense of the Atlantic theatre.

Political Background
(7)   The United States representatives consider it would be a serious mistake for the United Kingdom, in making their strategic dispositions to withstand a Japanese attack against Singapore, to count upon prompt military support by the United States. In support of this they argue:
(a)   It is most unlikely that the United States would declare war against Japan solely because that country had occupied Indo-China or Thailand.
(b)   There is serious doubt that the United States would immediately declare war against Japan were she to move against Malaya, British Borneo or the Netherlands East Indies, unless the United States were previously also at war with Germany and Italy. Congress, before deciding whether or not to declare war against Japan for attacking Malaysia, almost certainly would require a considerable period for debate.

SUMMARY ENDS
(8)   Discussions on this subject will be resumed on Tuesday 25th.
(9)   It is essential at this stage that no repetition of effort be made to bring any political pressure to bear in respect of subject matter of above message.
Grateful therefore if no reference be made to contents of this telegram. Minister fully concurs.

Sixth Progress Report
From: Australian Legation
To: External Affairs
Cablegram No. 199   Sent 14 March 1941
                                                   Received 15 March 1941
From Naval Attache to Chief of Naval Staff

With reference to my telegram No. 159. Progress report 6.

(1)   Probable date of completion of conversations, March 25th.

(2)   United States have accepted the responsibility for strategical direction in the Pacific area defined as follows:

    (a)   Area North of Equator to the East of longitude 140 degrees East.

    (b)   Area North of latitude 30 degrees North [to] the West of longitude 140 degrees East.

    (c)   Area South of Equator to East of longitude 180 degrees.

(3)   They have refused responsibility for strategical direction in the Far East area and they have refused to place the Commander-in-Chief of the United States Asiatic Fleet under British direction until after the fate of the Philippine Islands has been settled.

(4)   United Kingdom delegation have agreed as follows:

    (a)   The commanders of Associated and Allied Military Forces will collaborate in formulation of strategic plans for operations in that area.

    (b)   Defence of Territories of Associated and Allied Powers will be the responsibility of the respective commanders of the Military Forces concerned. These commanders will make such arrangements for mutual support as may be practicable and appropriate.

    (c)   Responsibility for strategical direction of Associated and Allied Naval Forces, except of Naval Forces engaged in supporting the defence of the Philippines, will be assumed by the British Commander-in-Chief China. Commander-in-Chief of the United States Asiatic Fleet will be responsible for the direction of Naval Forces engaged in supporting the defence of the Philippines.

    (d)   For the above purposes the Far Eastern Area

is defined as the area between latitude 30 degrees North and 11 degrees South and between longitude 140 degrees East and 92 degrees East. Northern boundary of area is a line from a position 020 degrees North, 092 degrees East to boundary between India and Burma.★

(e) British Commander-in-Chief China is also charged with the responsibility for the strategical direction of Associated and Allied Forces which may operate in Australia and New Zealand stations west of longitude 180 degrees.

(5) This is the best the [UK] delegation can get in the way of an agreed solution to the problem of [unified strategic] control in the Pacific and Far East and appears acceptable.

(6) Group Captain Isitt has been in close touch with the United Kingdom delegation for a short period during the last week and will return to Washington before the conversations end.

Casey

★ In the final report this sub-paragraph was recast and read: 'For the above purposes (cruiser area) is defined as area from coast of China in latitude 30 degrees north, east to longitude 140 degrees east, thence south to equator, thence east to longitude 141 degrees east, thence south to boundary of Dutch New Guinea on south coast, thence westward to latitude 11 degrees south, longitude 120 degrees east, thence south to latitude 13 degrees south, thence west to longitude 92 degrees east, thence north to latitude 20 degrees north, thence to boundary between India and Burma'. See Casey's cablegram 260 of 5 April.

Seventh Progress Report
From: Australian Legation
To: External Affairs
Cablegram No. 277   Sent: 25 March 1941
                                   Received: 26 March 1941

For Chief of Naval Staff from Naval Attache
With reference to my telegram No. 199. Seventh Progress Report.

(1) Final report envisages exchange of Military Missions with the United States when the United States enter the war to collaborate continuously in the formulation of the plan governing the conduct of the war and to ensure co-ordination of administrative action and command between the military services.

(2) Report proposes that the Dominions be represented on the British Military Mission in Washington by their Service Attaches.

(3) Until the United States enter the war it is intended to set up a nucleus organisation of Military Missions in London and Washington in order that broad policies and plans that have been agreed to may be considered in detail and that the change over from peace to war be effected rapidly and smoothly.

(4) Admiral Danckwerts will represent the United Kingdom Chief of Naval Staff in the nucleus organisation.

(5) Final report includes a recommendation that a conference of military commanders in the Far East should be convened without delay to prepare plans for the conduct of military operations in the Far East in accordance with the provisions of that report.

(6) Probable that the United Kingdom Chiefs of Staff shortly will propose that a conference, vide paragraph (5), be held as soon as they have seen the final report and can telegraph the summary to the Far East.

(7) Probable that the final report will be signed on Friday, 28 March.

(8) With reference to your telegram No. 419, in view of fact that Shedden now not leaving US until early May intend to forward report by safe hand of Lieutenant Colonel Alan Milner expected to leave Los Angeles Monday 31st March in Auckland Saturday 5th April. Request special arrangements

be made in Auckland for safe hand transit to Chief of Naval Staff New Zealand.

Eighth Progress Report
From: Australian Legation
To: Department of External Affairs
Cablegram No. 250   Sent: 2 April 1941
                 Received: 3 April 1941
Chief of Naval Staff from Naval Attache
Reference my telegram 199, paragraph 2, and Acting Prime Minister's telegram No. 16, paragraph 17. Final report envisages in some circumstances Pacific Fleet (with main base at Hawaii) operating in Caroline Islands area. Navy Department's War Plans Division are investigating the problem of advanced bases to the south and would appreciate Commonwealth Government's intentions regarding Rabaul e.g. garrison and fixed defences.

Ninth Progress Report
From: Australian Legation
To: External Affairs
Cablegram No. 260   Sent: 5 April 1941
                 Received: 6 April 1941
For Chief of Naval Staff from Naval Attache
(1)   (See note 5 — Progress Report 6)
(2)   United States representatives adhered to the last to views expressed in paragraphs 4 and 6 of my fifth progress report, my telegram No. 159.
(3)   Understand that Singapore conference is being held on April 18th and that Australia and New Zealand will be informed officially shortly.
(4)   Conference will be presided over by Commander in Chief Far East with representatives of Dutch, New Zealand and Australian Governments and Commander-in-Chief, China and East Indies present in addition to United States representative.
(5)   Commander-in-Chief Far East presumably will be in possession of all relevant matters emanating from Washington conversations and I understand that United States representatives at Singapore will be in possession of final report.

(6) Final report proposes that Singapore conference should 'Prepare plan for conducting of military operations in Far East in accordance with provisions of this report'.

(7) My telegram No. 239. Clipper departure delayed. Milner now leaves Los Angeles 6th April. It is therefore just possible that Australia and New Zealand representatives to Singapore conference will be in possession of final report before departure. United Kingdom Chiefs of Staff have been informed of this possibility.

(8) Harries has arrived at Washington and will assume duty as Naval Attache Sunday April 6th. Burrell will leave for United Kingdom immediately by ship on that date.

Casey

Appendix II
Letter from Author to Parliamentary Sub-committee on Defence Matters

From Vice-Admiral Sir Henry Burrell RAN (Rtd)

49 National Circuit
Forrest ACT 2603
24-5-82

The Secretary
Sub-Committee on Defence Matters
Joint Committee on Foreign Affairs
    and Defence
Parliament House
Canberra ACT
Dear Sir,

I understand your Sub-Committee is enquiring into matters concerned with the intended purchase of HMS Invincible and has invited expressions of interest. I desire to express interest in

(a)   the relevance of an aircraft carrier in Australia's current and perceived environment

(b)   the role of an aircraft carrier in the defence structure of Australia.

2.   My credentials are that I served in the RAN from 1918 to 1962.

I —   was Deputy Chief of Naval Staff when the Government approved the introduction of a 2 carrier/2 air field Fleet Air Arm (FAA) in 1948;

—   Commanded HMAS Vengeance 1953-54 (Straightdeck carrier on loan);

—   Commanded HMA Fleet in 1955-56, flying my flag in HMAS Sydney and for a few weeks in HMAS Melbourne;

—   Commanded the Fleet in 1958 with Melbourne as flagship and was Chief of Naval Staff from February 1959 to February 1962, when the future of the Fleet Air Arm was last in doubt.

3. My references to 'Background Information' refer to 'Background Information to the decision to purchase a new aircraft carrier for the Royal Australian Navy' issued by the Directorate of Public Relations, Department of Defence, which no doubt is available to your Committee.

4. Reference (a).

Except to observe that recent events in this hemisphere underline the rapid development of unexpected confrontation situations between nations, I will not deal with possible warlike situations, since selected scenarios have been examined at length elsewhere. However it is generally accepted that the importance of the Indian Ocean to Australia has increased greatly. We now have two oceans in which events could occur, perhaps simultaneously.

5. Australia has the great advantage of being an island and we must take advantage of that. To neglect the Navy would be bad strategy. The 'policeman' analogy holds good. A policeman on the beat or in the patrol car makes people slow down and think twice before committing themselves to action.

6. The possession of a carrier task force gives the Government an opportunity to show Australia's interest in a particular area. I agree with the final sentence of the penultimate paragraph in 'Background Information' page 13 where it refers to the 'potential to deter opponents by demonstrating a formidable combat capability'.

7. I would like to draw the Sub-Committee's attention to the value of a warship 'in being', that is to say — in the hands of the user. In this day and age, there is no credible way in which a major war vessel can be obtained rapidly when a sudden need arises.

8. Reference (b).

Reference 'Background Information' pages 31–34, I think, need elaborating to show the chequered career of the Fleet Air Arm (FAA) viz:–

1947   The Labor Government approved of 2 carrier/ 2 airfield FAA — the carriers being 'straight deck'.

February 1949	Vengeance commissioned to cover the time required for Melbourne to complete her construction with angled deck, mirrored landing sight and steam catapult and, I assumed, for Sydney to be modernized similarly.
1954	The Liberal-Country Party Government halved the size of the FAA — to one carrier (Melbourne) and one Air Station (HMAS Albatross), presumably on account of cost. This was a big let down for FAA, recruited from so many sources (6000 personnel).
April 1955	Sydney became fleet training ship and paid off in 1958.
Late 1955	Vengeance returned to UK (subsequently sold to Brazil, was converted to angle deck and is still in commission).
Oct 1955	Melbourne commissioned.
Oct 1959	Government decided FAA should cease in 1962 when its aircraft (Sea Venoms and Gannets) would be due for replacement.
1960	Fortunately Wessex 31A helicopters proved their value in anti-submarine work. Government agreed to purchase 27 and retain Melbourne as an A/S carrier.
1962	Sea Venoms and Gannets were still in good shape so Government decided to retain them in operation.
1965	Government approval was given to the purchase of Sea Hawks and Tracker Aircraft thus bringing the FAA back to life (half life).
1972	The Wessex 31 series helicopters were replaced by the more modern Wessex Sea King MK 50.
Mid 1982	Melbourne to be paid off after an invaluable and memorable career. Her presence added prestige and credibility to Australia's position in S.E. Asia and Pacific areas during her 27 years service.

So Melbourne continued to be the nucleus of our Fleet until age caught up with her.

9.   Invincible to me seems a readymade answer to Melbourne's replacement with one exception — the lack of fixed wing aircraft, i.e. the absence of the fighter

element (the Harrier jump-jet). They are required to deal with enemy bomber and reconnaissance aircraft; beyond the range of anti-aircraft-missiles and ships' radar. If the enemy carries a Harpoon type (ship-to-ship) missile of considerable range, her aircraft on reconnaissance must be shot down before it can give details of our forces (position, course and speed). I realize the purchase of Harrier (or similar) jump-jets in the desired numbers is too expensive at this stage. In the control of operations, the sophistication of modern ships and weaponry requires a command ship to control the computerised intelligence and operations of all ships and aircraft in the task force. 'Background Information' on the bottom of page 7 and top of page 8 gives details of many Data Systems, plots and displays in the command position and the complicated communications room required to operate a modern task force. These require a sizeable ship to carry and operate. Invincible is so fitted.

10.   My recommendation therefore would be to buy four or five Harriers and train pilots and ground staff in their operation, so that, if an emergency situation looks like developing, additional Harriers could be purchased. In that way the necessary skills would be at hand and our defence forces would be keeping abreast of technical developments.

11.   My view is that the Navy's commitments have increased by the added naval interest in the Indian Ocean. It would be logical therefore for the RAN to possess two carriers with A/S and fighter/reconnaissance capabilities by the end of this decade. This of course would increase the Defence Budget but we have a valuable country to defend. There is also the mathematical absurdity which, in this case turns out to be true, that two carriers are greater than twice one. With one refitting, there will always be one on duty.

12.   I am not fully aware of the cases made by the opponents to the purchase of Invincible. I can find no fault with 'Background Information' — Common Controversial Points pages 16, 17 and 18.

13.   I can find fault with any statement that the RAAF can protect our sea communications solely by shore

based aircraft. Picture an important convoy of tankers, troopships and important container ships passing through waters where there was risk of submarine and air attack. This would be escorted by a carrier, (with anti-submarine helicopters and fighters) and the unit screened by destroyers and frigates (with their A/S equipment — including Ikara — and surface to air guided missiles). In these times with Harpoon, (surface to surface missiles of relatively long range), data (position, course and speed of our convoy) is an obvious prerequisite to the firing of such a weapon. Just loosing one off into the blue would be an absurdity. The enemy would have to locate our convoy by aircraft or submarine. Our job would be to deal with the submarine with our A/S resources (and that includes long range RAAF Orions) and the reconnaissance aircraft (and bombers) by jump-jet aircraft — having first been detected by ship-borne radar.

14. How would the RAAF deal with this snooper or a bombing attack? Firstly, once alerted, the time taken for interceptors to arrive, in most cases, would be far too late. Secondly, to maintain a combat air patrol over the convoy would require hundreds of fighters from many airfields — just impracticable. Once the convoy or task force moves out an appreciable distance from the mainland, provision of any combat air patrol from the shore becomes impossible.

15. I attended Courses and post-exercise discussions at the Joint RAN/RAAF A/S School at Albatross. The possibility that RAAF could take over the carrier role was never raised in my presence when in command of Vengeance and of our Fleet. At Defence Committee and Chiefs of Staff meetings it was not stated openly either.

16. I have not stressed the personnel side or the special skills currently existing in the FAA. A highly specialized service, such as this, requires continuity to maintain this level of skill, to be fair to those who joined it and to attract good men to it.

17. I can only congratulate the Government on deciding to purchase Invincible and repeat my recommendations that

— as soon as practicable, four or five Harrier

jump-jets be purchased for training purposes
(pilots, ground and ship's crew)
— before the end of the decade, a second carrier
be purchased.

18.   It is my view that the acquisition of Invincible to replace Melbourne is essential for the defence of our country. As an A/S helicopter carrier, she can assist greatly in dealing with the submarine menace and she has the potential to increase her fighting qualities in later years if and when the situation demands and finance permits.

Notes

1.   At Wentworth Falls at that time the Church of England rector was the Reverend R. C. Robinson who had christened me and whose son was to be captain of HMAS *Voyager* when she was sunk attempting to supply Australian troops in Timor in 1942.

2.   F. B. Eldridge, *A History of the Royal Australian Naval College* (Melbourne, 1949), p. 101.

3.   A complicated operation which involves inserting a swivel between two anchors and their chain cables laid 180 degrees apart. This restricts the area covered by a ship swinging through 360 degrees and is useful in congested harbours.

4.   Admiral of the Fleet Viscount Cunningham of Hyndhope, *A Sailor's Odyssey* (London, 1951), p. 174.

5.   MP 1049/5, item 2026/3/495, Australian Archives.

6.   Cablegram No. 14, R. G. Menzies to R. G. Casey, copy in author's possession.

7.   Cablegram No. 17, *ibid*.

8.   Cablegram No. 379, 15 November 1940, copy in author's possession.

9.   Cablegram No. 385, 19 November 1940, *ibid*.

10.   Cablegram No. 390, 23 November 1940, copy in author's possession.

11.   Cablegram No. 395, 26 November 1940, copy in author's possession.

12.   Cablegram No. 399, 27 November 1940, copy in author's possession.

13.   Cablegram No. 407, 2 December 1940, copy in author's possession.

14.   Cablegram No. 76, 31 January 1941, copy in author's possession.

15.   Cablegram No. 92, 6 February 1941, copy in author's possession.

16.   Herbert Feis, *The Road to Pearl Harbor* (Princeton, 1950), pp. 168–9.

17.   Sir Alan Watt, *Australian Diplomat* (Sydney, 1972), p. 35.

18.   Vice-Admiral B. B. Schofield, *Navigation and Direction: The story of HMS Dryad* (Havant, 1977), pp. 66–7.

19.   My officers on commissioning were: First Lieutenant J. H. Dowson, RAN; Engineer Officer Lieutenant-Commander (E) N. McGuire, RAN; Watchkeeper and Navigating Officer Lieutenant W. G. Wright, RAN; Medical Officer Surgeon Lieutenant P. Simons, RANR; Watchkeepers Sub-lieutenants N. E. McDonald, RAN, and R. T. Guyett, RANR; and Sub-lieutenant R. C. Whitehead, RANVR; Torpedo Officer and Watchkeeper Mr J. C. Mitchell (Gunner T), RN; and Gunner and Watchkeeper Mr G. Glossop (Gunner D F and I) RN.

20.   A boom consists of nets and a gate suspended by drums giving anti-submarine protection to harbours.

21.   Victor Kravchenko, *I Chose Freedom* (London, 1948), p. 451.

22.   S. W. Roskill, *The War at Sea*, Volume II (London, 1956), p. 25.

23.   D. Macintyre, *Fighting Admiral* (London, 1961), p. 192.

24.   I have since come by a vivid story of the day's events by *Dorsetshire*'s canteen manager which includes: 'about mid-morning we had word from a rating passing through the sick bay, that a Jap scout plane had been sighted'. I find this disturbing.

25.   Roskill, *op. cit.*, p. 31.

26.   Roskill, *op. cit.*, p. 71.

27.   Ehrman, John, *Grand Strategy*, Volume V (London, 1956), pp. 425–6. See also Horner, D. M., *High Command* (Sydney, 1982), Chapter 13.

28.   Ehrman, *op. cit.*, Vol. VI, p. 220.

29.   Ehrman, *op. cit.*, Vol. V, p. 498.

30.   *Ibid*, p. 501.

31.   Horner, *op. cit.*, p. 330.

32.   Roskill, *op. cit.*, Vol. III, Part II, p. 430.

33.   Gill, H. G., *The Royal Australian Navy 1942–1945*,

p. 366, quoting from Roskill, *op. cit.*, Vol. III, Part II, p. 333.

34.   Gill, *op. cit.*, pp. 681–2.

35.   *Bataan*, Letter of Proceedings, 1 October 1946.

36.   'Hand to make and mend clothes' was still piped in ships to indicate a half holiday. In the 'good old days' sailors were their own tailors and 'sew-sew' men.

37.   *Navy News*, Vol. 17, No. 8, 26 April 1974, p. 7.

38.   Gray, T. I. G., *The Imperial Defence College and the Royal College of Defence Studies 1927–1977* (London, 1977), p. 3.

39.   *Ibid*, p. 5.

40.   *Ibid*, p. 18.

41.   *Ibid*, p. 15.

42.   I have the outcome of my proposals to the Naval Board, but the Australian Archives have been unable to produce my submissions and so in that regard I must rely on memory. See 'Commonwealth Navy Order 1022/56, 22 October 1956 — The New Officer Structure'.

43.   See Naval Board Minutes, Australian Archives.

44.   Article 1831 prohibits gifts.

45.   Mr Athol Townley was Minister for Defence and Mr Edwin Hicks was the Secretary of the Department, with Lieutenant-General Ragnar Garret and Air Marshal Sir Frederick Scherger as CGS and CAS respectively. My Minister was Senator John Gorton and Rear-Admiral Alan McNicoll was Second Naval Member. Charles Clark, who had joined me in a seasick session off the Bay of Islands (NZ) in 1933, was now a Rear-Admiral (E) and Third Naval Member. Mr T. J. Hawkins was the Secretary. My deputy was Rear-Admiral Humphrey Becher, and my personal secretary was Captain (S) W. D. H. Graham. The Defence Committee, presided over by Ted Hicks, comprised the Chairman of the Chiefs of Staff Committee, the three Chiefs of Staff, Arthur Tange from External Affairs (as Maria wrote to Malvolio, 'let thy tongue tang arguments of state'), Jack Bunting (Prime Minister's Department) and Len Hewitt (Treasury). Eventually they all become knights of the rectangular table.

46. 'The Three-Year Defence Programme 1959/60–1961/62, Department of the Navy — Narrative Statment of Plans', Navy Office file 5245-12-7 (declassified 10 June 1982).
47. Letter, J. G. Gorton, Minister for the Navy, to Minister for Defence, 20 October 1959 (declassified 15 June 1982).

Bibliography

Bastock, John, *Australia's Ships of War* (Angus and Roberston, Sydney, 1975).

Churchill, W. S., *The Second World War*, Volume IV, *The Hinge of Fate* (Cassell, London, 1951).

Churchill, W. S., *The Second World War*, Volume V, *Triumph and Tragedy* (Cassell, London, 1952).

Cunningham, Viscount, *A Sailor's Odyssey* (Hutchinson & Co. Ltd, London, 1951).

Ehrman, John, *Grand Strategy*, Volume V (Her Majesty's Stationery Office, London, 1956).

Ehrman, John, *Grand Strategy*, Volume VI (Her Majesty's Stationery Office, London, 1956).

Eldridge, F. B., *A History of the Royal Australian Naval College* (Georgian House, Melbourne, 1949).

Feis, Herbert, *The Road to Pearl Harbor* (Princetown University Press, New Jersey, 1950).

Gill, Hermon G., *Royal Australian Navy 1939–42* (Australian War Memorial, Canberra, 1968).

Gill, Hermon G., *Royal Australian Navy 1942–45* (Australian War Memorial, Canberra, 1957).

Hansard, Australian Government Publishing Service.

Horner, D. M., *High Command* (Australian War Memorial, Canberra; George Allen and Unwin, Sydney, 1982).

Kravchenko, Victor, *I Chose Freedom* (Robert Hale, London, 1947).

Link, L. J. and Payne, M. A., *N Class* (The Naval Historical Society of Australia, Sydney, 1972).

Long, Gavin, *The Final Campaigns* (Australian War Memorial, Canberra, 1963).

McGuire, F. M., *The Price of Admiralty* (Oxford University Press, 1944).

McIntyre, D., *Fighting Admiral* (Evans, London, 1961).

Morison, S. E., *History of the United States Naval Operations in World War II,* Volume I: *The Battle of the Atlantic 1939–43* (1962); Volume II: *Operations in North African Waters, October 1942–June 1943* (1962); Volume III: *The Rising Sun in the Pacific, 1931–April 1942* (1962); Volume XIII: *The Liberation of the Philippines 1944–45* (1962); Volume XIV: *Victory in the Pacific 1945* (1961). (Little, Brown and Company, Boston.)

Navy Lists, Royal Australian Navy, 1918–1962 inclusive. (The Commonwealth of Australia, Sydney and Canberra, 1918–62.)

Payne, Alan, *HMAS Perth* (The Naval Historical Society of Australia, Sydney, 1972).

Roskill, Captain S. W., *The War at Sea,* Volume I (H.M. Stationery Office, London, 1954).

Roskill, Captain S. W., *The War at Sea*, Volume II (H.M. Stationery Office, London, 1956).

Roskill, Captain S. W., *The War at Sea*, Volume III, Part I (H.M. Stationery Office, London, 1960).

Roskill, Captain S. W., *The War at Sea*, Volume III, Part II (H.M. Stationery Office, London, 1961).

Thomas, Hugh, *The Spanish Civil War* (Eyre & Spottiswoode, London, 1961).

Watt, Alan, *Australian Diplomat* (Angus & Robertson, in association with the Australian Institute of International Affairs, Sydney, 1972).

Index

Adelaide, HMAS, 84–6
Allison, Sir John, 229
Allison Committee, 229
Anstice, Capt. F. W., RN, 184
Armstrong, Cdre James, 183, 197
Australia, HMAS, 11, 33, 37, 38, 51, 54, 57, 59, 60, 73–4, 75, 77, 80, 81, 186; under Burrell's command, 188–9

Backhouse, Capt. Roger, RN, 18
Baldwin, Capt. C. C., 157
Bastyan, Brig. E. M., 191
Bataan, HMAS, 212, 214; under Burrell's command, 163–81
Beatty, Capt. S. H., VC, 211
Becher, Capt. Humphrey, 230, 246, 247
Bellairs' Mission, 102–6, 107–8
Berryman, Lt.-Gen., 170
Bierwirth, Maj.-Gen. Rudolf, 196, 198, 199
Blamey, Gen. Sir Thomas, 170
Bostock, Air Vice-Marshal, 170
Boucher, Cdre M. W. S., RN, 70
Brisbane, HMAS, 55–8
Brownell, Air Cdre, 170
Bruce, S. M., 115
Buchanan, Cdr A. E., 91
Buchanan, Capt. A. J., 192

Buchanan, Capt. H. J., 152, 183, 188
Burke, Adm. Arleigh, USN, 256
Burnett, Capt., 86, 123
Burrell, Ada Theresa (Terry) (wife), 157, 178, 184–5, 187, 190, 194, 195, 197, 201, 220, 234, 237, 269, 281–2
Burrell, Fayne (daughter), 164
Burrell, Sir Henry
  early years, 1–4
  cadet-midshipman, Jervis Bay, 4–11
  training and service with Royal Navy, 15–24
  HMS *Caledon*, 15–18
  HMS *Malaya*, 18–20
  passes seamanship exam, 20
  at RNC Greenwich and HMS *Excellent*, 21
  decision to become navigating officer, 22
  on HMAS *Melbourne*, 25, 26
  on HMAS *Tasmania*, 26–31
  on HMAS *Canberra*, 32–7
  circumnavigation of Australia, 38–9
  attached to Royal Navy, 41–6
  navigation training, Portsmouth, 41–2

313

to India, HMS *Hindustan*,
42–3
minesweeping, HMS
Pangbourne, 44–5,
46–50, 51
royal levee, 46
lieutenant/navigator, HMAS
Tattoo, 51–2
flotilla navigator, HMAS
Stuart, 52, 53, 54–5
promoted lieutenant-
commander, 54
on HMAS *Brisbane* (to UK),
55–8
further navigation training
(UK), 55, 58
attached to Royal Navy,
60–8
HMS *Coventry*, 58, 60–1
HMS *Devonshire*, 61, 62–5
Staff Course 1938,
Greenwich, 65–8
Director Operations and
Planning, Naval Board,
70–91
troop movements to ME,
76–9
German raiders, 87–91
in Washington, 92–110
with R. G. Casey, 92–7
Naval Attaché, 97–102
Bellairs' Mission, 102–8
first command, HMS
Norman, 111–50
commissioning, 111–17,
122
to Archangel, 118–21
escort duty, 124–32
Operation 'Vigorous',
136–41
rejoins Eastern Fleet,
142–6

U-boat campaign (Sth
Africa), 147–8
refitting and recuperation,
149–50
Director of Plans (Melb.),
154–63
Bataan command, 163–81
joins US 7th Fleet, 168
and Japanese surrender,
170
POW transport, 171–3
Captain 10th Destroyer
Flotilla, 178
with Occupation Force,
179
Korean patrol, 179–81
Deputy Chief of Naval Staff,
182–8
and Fleet Air Arm, 183–5
Joint Planning
Committee, 186
and Antarctic research
voyages, 186
ADC to Queen, 187
Australia command, 188–9
at Imperial Defence College,
189–95
Assistant Defence
Representative, London,
196–200, 201
Vengeance command, 200–15
refitting and training
exercise, 202–9
Royal Visit (1954),
213–14
FOCAF (HMAS *Sydney*),
217–22
New Zealand visit, 219–21
appointed to Navy Office,
223
Second Naval Member,
226–9

recommends review of
service conditions,
228–9
FOCAF (HMAS *Melbourne*),
229–36
SEATO exercise 'Ocean
Link', 231–3
Chief of Naval Staff, 234,
237–81
Three-Year Programme,
241–67
anti-submarine weapon
research, 245–8
Fleet Air Arm decision,
249–50
acquires Illogan Park,
251–2
surface-to-air missile issue,
253–4
US visit, 256–8
programme
recommendations,
264–5
'Charles F. Adams
project', 263, 266, 268,
270–1
(2nd) Three-Year
Programme, 273
review of work as CNS,
272, 274, 275–80
retirement, 281
Burrell family, 189, 190, 201,
205, 235
Burrell, Lynne (daughter), 187,
188
Burrell, Stuart (son), 187
Burrell, Thomas (grandfather),
1, 2
Burrell, Thomas Henry (father),
1, 2–3, 10, 40

Caledon, HMS, 15, 16, 17, 18, 47

Campbell, Lt.-Cdr A. F., 58–9
Canberra, HMAS, 33–6, 38, 39,
51, 80, 90, 91, 144
Carrington, Lord, 253
Casey, R. G., 92–3, 94–8, 101,
109, 141
Chaney, Frederick, 268
'Charles F. Adams' (CFA)
Project, 263, 266, 268,
270–1, 277–8
Churchill, Winston Spencer,
157, 160, 192
Clark, Cdr M. J., 173, 178
Collins, Cdre John A., 58,
70–1, 74, 75, 156, 163, 167,
169, 170, 173, 174, 177, 187,
217
Colvin, Admiral Sir Ragnar,
26, 70, 107
convoy operations, 76–91 *passim*
Cook, A/Lt.-Cdr W. F., 178
Coptic, SS, 84–6
Coventry, HMS, 58, 60
Craft, Cdr R. G., 226
Cutler, Sir Roden, VC, 205,
276

Dalglish, Rear-Adm. R.C., 51,
53
Daniel, Adm. Sir Charles, RN,
162, 191, 195
Daniel, T. F., 226
De L'Isle, Viscount, 270, 272–3
*Detailed Overall Administrative
Plan* (DOAP), 162, 166
Devonshire, HMS, 61–4
Dowling, Sir Roy R., 28, 170,
217, 229, 234, 235, 237, 267,
269
Downes, Cdr(Air), A., RN,
202
Dowson, Capt. J. H., 252, 256

Doyle, Eng. Rear-Adm., 183
Dryad, HMS, 22, 58
Duckworth, Cdr R. C. N.,
    RN, 162

Eddy, Cdr V. C., 73
Ehrman, John, 159
Excellent, HMS, 21, 41

Farncomb, Rear-Adm., 91,
    156, 163, 177, 187
Farquhar-Smith, Capt. Charles,
    55
Ferrall, Rear-Adm., USN, 259
Fleet Air Arm, 183–5, 205–11,
    215, 249–50, 252, 253, 270
Flynn, J. L., 226
Foley, Capt. (S.) Bernard, 227
Ford, Rear-Adm. W. T. R., 53
Fraser, Adm. Sir Bruce, 162
Fyfe, Wing-Cdr Ted, 196, 197,
    198

Gatacre, Rear-Adm. Galfrey,
    65, 111, 178, 188, 235, 256,
    268
German, Barry, 102, 103
German raiders, 87–91
Gorton, John, 238, 239, 247,
    248, 265, 271, 280
Gullett, Jo (H.B.), 251

Hamilton, Adm. Sir Louis, 122,
    183, 184
Hancock, Val, 267
Harries, Capt. David D., 6, 29,
    110, 179, 192
Harrington, Adm., 273, 275
Harwood, A/Adm. Sir Harry,
    76, 137
Hastings, HMS, 55–7
Hewitt, Len, 247

Hicks, E. W., 235
Hindustan, HMS, 42–3
Holden, William, 231
Hopwood, Adm. Herbert G.,
    USN, 259
Howden, Lt. Harry, 26, 27, 30
Hughes, W. M., 89
Hutcheson, Eng. Capt. G. I. D.,
    167
Hyde, Rear-Adm. Sir G.
    Francis, 14, 25–6, 37

Ikara anti-submarine project,
    246–8, 278–80
Imperial Defence College,
    191–3

James, Adm. Sir William, 116

Kendall, Senator, 238
Kenny, W. J., 227
King, Adm., USN, 157, 161
Knight, Cdr A. V., 73
Knox, Lt.-Cdr G. F. E., 178
Komet, 88, 89
Korean patrol, 179–81

Labuan, 186–7
Lamb, Adm. Sir Charles, RN,
    261
Lilley, Capt. A. G., 52

MacArthur, General Douglas,
    155, 156, 163, 167
McBride, Sir Philip, 215
McIntosh, Cdr Alan, 223
McKinnon, Capt. N. A., 252
McNeil, Eng. Rear-Adm., 83
McNicoll, Adm. A. R. W., 8,
    275
Macandie, G. L., 70
Malaya, HMS, 18–20

'Malaya Force', 78
Martin, Cdr W. H., 91
Massey, Capt. G. L., 31
Melbourne, HMAS, 25, 26, 184, 200, 202, 215, 222, 244, 245, 249, 262, 264; under Burrell's command, 230–3
Menzies, R. G., 234, 250
'Middle Strategy' (SEA), 157–8, 160–1
Miller, Cdr-Capt. J., USN, 258
Miller, Lt.-Cdr John, 51
Miles, Capt. G. J. A., 47
Mountbatten of Burma, Adm. The Earl, 157, 160, 204, 222, 252, 261
Muirhead-Gould, Capt., DSC, 61-2

Nankervis, A. R., 70, 183
Nelles, Lt. Cdr., 17, 18
Nimitz, Adm. Chester, USN, 155, 156, 163
Non-Intervention Committee (1936), 64
Norman, HMAS, 98; under Burrell's command, 111–32, 135–52
North, Cdr Dudley, 10, 16

officer structure, reorganisation (1956), 223–6
Oldham, Cdre George, 71, 73, 86, 189, 217, 230
Oliver, Maj.-Gen. W. P., 191
Oom, Midshipman Karl, 15
Orion, 83, 88, 89

Pangbourne, HMS, 44–51
Parker, Capt. 'Charlie', 31–2
Percival, Gen., 171
Pinguin, 87, 90

Powell, Capt. James, 44, 45, 47
Price, Cdr C. R., 73
prisoners of war, 171–3

Queen Mary, 77, 78

Rawlings, Vice-Adm. Sir Bernard, 168
Richmond, Adm. Sir Herbert, RN, 191–2
Rivett-Carnac, Capt. J. W., DSC, 58
Robinson, A/Cdr B. J. J. P., RN, 184
Rosenthal, Cdr, 139–40
Rowell, Lt.-Gen. Sir Stanley, 198
Royal Australian Naval College (Jervis Bay), 6–11
Royal College of Defence Studies, 195–6

Scherger, Air Marshal Sir Frederick, 247, 264, 267, 269, 275
Sea Slug missile, 253
Selkirk, Lord, 235
Sendai operation, 172–3
Shedden, Sir Frederick, 186, 197, 198
Sherbrooke, Capt. Robert St Vincent, 67–8
Sherlock, Neil, 5, 15
Shinn, Rear-Adm., USN, 259
Showers, Capt., 163
Singapore Naval Conference, 86, 107
Slessor, Marshal of the RAF Sir John, 192, 193
Slim, FM Sir William, 192, 193, 217
Smith, Adm. Sir Victor, 184
Spencer, Rodney, 46, 47, 51

Spurgeon, Cdr A. H., 81
Stewart, Lt. D. H., RANVR, 172
Stewart, Capt. R. R., RN, 74
Stuart, HMAS, 52–5
submarine squadron, established (1969–70), 276
Sydney, HMAS (cruiser), 12–13, 25, 28, 31
Sydney, HMAS (aircraft carrier), 55, 58, 59, 75, 81, 82, 89, 122–3, 184, 189, 202, 210, 211, 271, 276; Burrell's flagship, 218–22

Tapp, Cdr W. K., 226
Tartar missile, 254
Tattoo, HMAS, 51
Townley, Athol, 248
troopships, 76–7, 78, 79, 83, 90

Turner, A/Cdr A. F. L., RN, 184
Urquhart, Rear-Adm. (E.) K., 252, 254

Vengeance, HMAS, 200, 219; under Burrell's command, 201–15
Vernon, HMS, 23
Vian, Rear-Adm., 137, 139, 140, 141

Wainright, Gen. J., 171
Walton, Cdr J. K., 178
Washington Naval Treaty (1921), 10, 11, 14, 33
Watt, Alan, 93–4, 101, 103
Wells, Capt. D. H., 252, 265
Winchester, HMS, 41–2
Wright, Adm. Jerauld, USN, 257